WHAT TEST-TAKERS ARE SAYING ABOUT LEARNINGEXPRESS PREPARATION GUIDES

"The information from the last two study guides I ordered from your company was invaluable. . . . Better than the $200 6-week study courses being offered. . . . After studying from dozens of books I would choose yours over any of the other companies."
S. Frosch

"Excellent . . . It was like having the test in advance!"
J. Kennedy

"Without this book, I wouldn't have understood the test."
R. Diaz

"Told me everything that was going to be on the test [and] gave me a good understanding of the whole process, too."
J. Molinari

"The best test-prep book I've used!"
H. Hernandez

"I felt 100% prepared when I took the Suffolk County exam this past June. I scored a 96 on it. I had taken it previously in 1992 and only scored an 82. Your guide helped me add 14 points to my score!"
R. Morrell

CONTENTS

LIST OF CONTRIBUTORS

The following individuals contributed to the content of this book.

Susan Camardo is a business and careers writer and communications consultant based in New York City.

Elizabeth Chesla is an adult educator and curriculum developer in New York City, who has also taught reading and writing.

Jan Gallagher, Ph.D., is a test-development specialist, editor, and teacher living in Jersey City, New Jersey.

Judith F. Olson, M.A., is chairperson of the language arts department at Valley High School in West Des Moines, Iowa, where she also conducts test preparation workshops.

Judith Robinovitz is an independent educational consultant and director of Score At the Top, a comprehensive test preparation program in Vero Beach, Florida.

Shirley Tarbell is a test development specialist and writer living in Iowa City, Iowa.

The following LearningExpress staff members also contributed to the writing and researching of this book: **Jean Eckhoff, Edward Grossman, Meghan Johnson,** and **Kisha Miller.**

C·H·A·P·T·E·R 1

WORKING FOR THE U.S. POSTAL SERVICE

CHAPTER SUMMARY

Congratulations on taking the first step toward a career with the United States Postal Service (USPS). This chapter introduces you to your career options at the Postal Service and to the benefits of working for the USPS. You'll also learn about its history, its organization, and the many services it provides.

erhaps you'd like to greet customers at the window. Maybe you'd rather work behind the scenes, sorting some of the millions of pieces of mail delivered each day. Or perhaps you'd like to be a carrier, delivering mail door to door, customer by customer. Whatever your interest, you should know that a job with the United States Postal Service (USPS) has a lot to offer, including competitive salaries, job security, government benefits, and upward mobility. That's why every year hundreds of thousands of people seek employment with the USPS. Since you're thinking of joining these ranks, let's take a closer look at what working for the USPS could mean for you.

WHY WORK FOR THE USPS?

The USPS is an indispensable part of our society. Other industries may come and go, but mail service is as essential to the functioning of our society as fuel is to a car. Without organized mail service, government and business would not be able to run. Mail service is the national circulation system that keeps communication moving. You may even want to think of mail service as the "lifeblood" of our society.

Mail service is so important, in fact, that it was one of the very first organizations formed by the Continental Congress when America first sought independence from England. Every year since, as our country's population has grown and our technology has advanced, the USPS has expanded to meet the growing demands of the businesses and people of this country.

Salaries and benefits

The USPS has dozens of entry-level jobs—and between expansions, promotions, and retirements, tens of thousands of job vacancies open up each year. As a career employee, you'll enjoy regular raises and the opportunity to bid for some of the over 2,000 job titles within the USPS. You'll also enjoy a competitive salary, even at the entry level. In fact, the average annual salary of a USPS employee is over $30,000, and this figure increases to $45,000 per year when benefits and overtime are included. (For more detailed salary information, see page 15.)

Because the USPS is a government agency, its benefits package is outstanding. Career employees receive:

- 10 paid holidays per year
- 13 paid sick days per year
- 13–26 paid vacation days per year
- Life insurance
- Health insurance
- Government pension

In addition, career employees are backed by strong, successful unions, including the National Association of Letter Carriers (NALC), the National Postal Mail Handlers Union (NPMHU), the American Postal Workers Union (APWU), and the National Rural Letter Carriers Association (NRLCA), which negotiate for regular salary increases and cost of living adjustments as well as increasingly better working conditions for USPS employees.

Job security and steady hiring

In these times of downsizing and layoffs, two facts are important to note. First, the USPS has never had a layoff. Second, while automation has made it possible for fewer people to do more work, hiring by the USPS remains strong. In 1994, for example, the USPS hired 37,221 employees and in 1995 it hired an additional 24,440. A recent report in the *Federal Job Digest* shows that the USPS continues to hire approximately 2,000 career employees *each month*—and this figure does not include the thousands people hired each year for casual or temporary work.

Similarly, while many businesses are seeing decreased profits, the USPS had a record year in 1995, earning over $1.8 billion in net income and annual revenues of $54 billion. And the USPS has done so well that it hasn't used a penny in taxpayer's money since 1982. The USPS ranks #33 on the Fortune Global 500 list and it's the United States' 12th largest business.

GOOD PROSPECTS
In 1995, the USPS:
- earned revenues of $54 billion
- earned a net income of $1.8 billion
- handled 180.7 billion pieces of mail
- handled 40% of the world's mail volume
- employed a total of 874,972 employees in 39,149 offices, stations and branches
- hired 24,440 people

Employee programs

The USPS offers its employees support in many ways. One of them is the Postal Employee's Relief Fund (PERF), an emergency relief fund which offers monetary relief to employees who have experienced significant losses of uninsured property because of a major natural disaster. To date, over $3 million in PERF funds has been given to USPS employees in need.

The USPS also has a Quality of Work Life (QWL) program co-sponsored with the NPMHU. The QWL program aims to improve the quality of USPS work and of USPS working conditions by tackling issues such as automation and labor/management relations. There is also an Employee Assistance Program (EAP), which offers USPS employees and their families access to over 15,000 experienced counselors throughout the U.S. The EAP also provides a hotline for employees to call with questions and concerns about Equal Employment Opportunity (EEO), sexual harassment, and potential violence as well as any other job-related issues.

The environment and safety

The USPS is actively involved in environmental protection measures, particularly recycling. It uses a large portion of recycled products and many of its own products are made out of recycled materials. The USPS also experiments with alternative fuel vehicles. In fact, over 6,500 USPS vehicles now operate on compressed natural gas. In addition, in 1995 and 1996, the USPS received 14 "Closing the Circle" awards from the White House for its environmental achievements in waste prevention and management.

The USPS is also concerned about employee safety. A new program called STOP—Safety Training Observation Program—has been put into place to train managers and supervisors in safety measures and effective communication with employees. Furthermore, the USPS has increased inspections at its locations and significantly reduced employee accidents (including dog bites and driving accidents) in recent years. The USPS has also instituted measures to prevent injuries in the workplace from repetitive motion—an important concern for the large percentage of USPS employees who do physically repetitive work. And USPS facilities are smoke-free environments.

If you're concerned about workplace violence at the USPS, the USPS has good news. Despite fears that the post office is a dangerous place to work, the USPS has an occupational fatality rate that, according to the Center for Disease Control, is *half* the rate of *all other workers* combined. In other words, it's one of the safest places to work. Still, the USPS would rather err on the side of safety, so it has instituted a Workplace Violence Awareness program to help people recognize warning signs of violent behavior to prevent future violence.

JUST THE FACTS
According to the USPS Annual Report, dog bites to USPS employees on the job have dropped from 7,003 in 1983 to only 2,851 in 1995. The thanks for this jaw-dropping reduction go to the USPS's campaign to teach pet owners ways to manage aggressive pets.

Community service

The USPS and its employees are active in community service. Each May, for example, the NALC holds an annual food drive. Last year, the NALC collected a record 44.4 million pounds of food. Since 1985, the USPS has also participated in ADVO, Inc.'s missing children campaign by circulating "Have You Seen Me" cards with pictures of missing children through the mail. Since the start of this program, 75 of those children—one out of every seven—have been found. The USPS also sponsors a "Books for Kids" book drive and the "Wee Deliver in School Postal Services" program, which teaches children about the postal system while helping them practice their reading and writing skills.

SHEER NUMBERS

We've said the USPS is a big business, but just how big is it? The USPS currently employs over 800,000 workers and, since the end of its restructuring earlier this decade, it has hired an average of about 30,000 employees each year. It's one of the largest employers in the nation—bigger than Ford, Chrysler, and General Motors *combined*. In fact, almost 1 in every 170 people in the domestic workforce work for the USPS.

> **JUST THE FACTS**
> **California is the biggest USPS employer with more USPS employees than the third and fourth largest states combined!**
>
> | California | 88,000 | Texas | 45,000 |
> |-----------|--------|---------|--------|
> | New York | 64,000 | Florida | 40,000 |

> **JUST THE FACTS**
> **Did you know . . . the USPS delivers more mail in one day than Federal Express does in a whole year.**

The USPS has over 39,000 facilities nationwide which handle an average of 580 million pieces of mail per day. Approximately 336,000 letter carriers and a fleet of over 200,000 vehicles distribute this mail across the nation. In fact, forty percent of the world's mail volume is handled by the USPS, making it the world's largest mail delivery system (Japan, the second largest, handles only 8% of the world's mail volume).

Diversity of opportunity

There are approximately 2,000 different job categories at the USPS. Most employees—in fact, well over 50%—work in one of the following entry-level positions:

- Clerk
- Carrier, City and Rural
- Mail Handler
- Mark-Up Clerk
- Mail Processor
- Flat-Sorting Machine Operator
- Distribution Clerk

Because most career employees start off in one of these seven positions, we'll discuss each in detail later in this chapter.

The USPS also employs thousands of others in technical or maintenance positions (such as mechanics, technicians), professional positions (such as engineers, computer specialists, accountants), and management positions (such as branch managers, customer service supervisors), and even health care (nurses and psychologists) and security (police officers and security guards). There is a tremendous diversity of opportunity within the USPS. (See the end of this chapter for a sampling of USPS job titles.)

WHAT IT TAKES TO WORK FOR THE USPS

Now that you know a little about the benefits of working for the USPS, you need to know what it takes to become an employee. The next section will summarize the hiring process, which is discussed in detail in Chapter 2.

Getting in the door

Most employees begin their tenure with the USPS in one of the seven entry-level positions we'll discuss. To be hired, applicants for these positions must first meet certain minimum requirements and pass an exam. Applicants for each of these seven positions must meet the same requirements and take the same examination—the 470 Battery Test. (To find out about casual or temporary employment with the USPS, which has a different set of requirements, see the section entitled Working for the USPS on page 12 of this chapter.)

Minimum requirements

Before you attempt to register for the 470 Battery Test, make sure you meet the following minimum requirements:

- You must be 18 years of age or older, or 16 if you're already a high school graduate;
- If you are a male, you must be registered with the U.S. Selective Service;
- You must be a U.S. citizen or a legal resident alien;

- You must be able to lift 70 pounds; and
- You must have 20/40 vision in one eye and 20/100 in the other (glasses are permitted).

If you meet these requirements, you can apply to the USPS when a postal district offers an "application period." These periods are usually announced in local papers and at employment offices. During this application period, you may go to any local Post Office and fill out an application card (you can fill it out on the spot or mail it back in). The USPS will then notify you of the examination date, time and place. Along with this information you'll receive an "admission ticket" for the test, sample exam questions, and a sample answer sheet.

> **JUST THE FACTS**
> **In 1995, the USPS had:**
> **28,392 Post Offices**
> **9,131 Stations and Branches**
> **1,626 Community Post Offices**
> **54,442 Rural Delivery Routes**

The exam

Now you'll need to pass an exam. All candidates for these seven entry-level positions must take the 470 Battery Test (Rural Carriers take the 460 Battery test, which is essentially the same as the 470 Battery but is classified differently). The 470 Battery is a national USPS exam which evaluates your skills in four areas:

- Address Checking
- Memory for Addresses
- Number Series
- Following Oral Directions

Chapters 6–12 describe the 470 Battery Test in detail and provide sample test questions from the USPS, practice exams, and instructional material to help you prepare for the exam.

Stiff competition

If you pass the test, you will be placed on an eligibility list (a list of people eligible for hire). You need a score of 70 to pass, but because there is so much competition, a 70 isn't likely to land you a job. Plan on preparing carefully so you can achieve a high score, because the competition is tough. In fact, in 1994 alone, 1.4 million people took postal exams; in 1995, over 750,000. That means that on average less than 2% of test-takers actually got hired.

This number may seem discouraging, but remember you've already increased your chances of getting hired by deciding to research and prepare for the exam. And the more prepared you are, the better your chances of getting hired. Also, keep in mind that approximately 50% of test takers fail the exam in the first place, so the percentage of those people who pass the test and get hired is significantly higher.

> **JUST THE FACTS**
> **Explore the USPS on the Internet at http://www.usps.gov.**

Aim high

The higher your score on the exam, the higher you'll be placed on the eligibility list and therefore the more likely it is that you'll be offered a job (candidates are selected from the top of the list). In fact, most people who are hired score between 90–100%. It's important, therefore, to score as high as possible on the exam. Experts also suggest that you test for several different positions if your area is looking to hire in more than one job category. Applying for more than one position (even though they all require the same exam) increases your chances of getting hired.

Once you're selected from the eligibility list, you must go through a screening process before you can be offered a job. This process includes the following:

- Background Investigation
- Personal Interview
- Drug Test

If you successfully complete this screening process, and pass any required physical agility tests, you should receive a conditional offer of employment, pending a clean bill of health (a complete overview of the screening and selection process is given in Chapter 2 of this book).

The USPS is an Affirmative Action employer and for most positions offers on-the-job training.

A BRIEF HISTORY OF THE USPS

Since you're considering a future with the USPS, you might be interested in its history. We'll take a look at that next.

> **JUST THE FACTS**
> **Did you know . . . Benjamin Franklin was America's first Postmaster General.**

An inauspicious beginning

The USPS has a long and fascinating history which began, of all places, in a bar. Yes, that's right—the very first "post office" in the colonies was none other than Richard Fairbanks' Tavern in Boston. In 1639, this tavern became the first official repository for overseas mail. This may sound odd to us today, but at the time it wasn't an unusual practice; this is how mail was generally distributed in England and other parts of Europe. It wasn't until almost 50 years later (1683) that the first official post office was established in Pennsylvania by William Penn. In the south, on the other hand, most mail was delivered not by post offices or taverns but by messengers (often slaves) who ran mail between the plantations.

Postal service in the colonies was centralized in 1691, but service was lackluster until Benjamin Franklin was appointed Joint Postmaster General for the Crown in 1737. He reorganized the system and improved postal routes, thereby dramatically improving mail service. Under Franklin's tenure, the colonial mail system had its first profitable year ever. As the Revolutionary War neared, however, Franklin was fired for his support of the rebellious colonies. But by the time he was dismissed, he had established 30 post offices in the Northeast.

Mail service in the colonies

When the colonies started to break away from England, the Continental Congress—first organized in May 1775—met to address the needs of the new nation they were forming. One of their primary concerns was the mail, and on July 26, 1775, Benjamin Franklin became the first Postmaster General of the new Post Office Department (POD). In just over a year, Franklin devised the Post Office Department system that remains the core of our country's mail service today.

JUST THE FACTS
Title 39 of the US Code, the Postal Service Mission Statement:

The Postal Service shall have as its basic function the obligation to provide postal services to bind the Nation together through the personal, educational, literary, and business correspondence of the people. It shall provide prompt, reliable, and efficient services to patrons in all areas and shall render postal services to all communities.

MAIL DELIVERY IN THE UNITED STATES

Today we have many options for sending and receiving mail, which is delivered by truck, train, plane, and hand. But there weren't always so many choices, and some of the ways mail is delivered—means of transportation we now take for granted—have the POD and the USPS to thank for their advancement.

A large percentage of today's mail still moves by foot, but this is just one of many means through which mail has been delivered. Mail has traveled by horse, by stagecoach, by steamboat, by railroad, by automobile, and by airplane as well as by balloon, helicopter and even, on one occasion, by missile.

The Pony Express

Perhaps the best known means of early mail delivery is the Pony Express. While the West was first being settled and during the years of the Gold Rush (which began in 1849), mail to the West Coast had to travel by boat to Panama, cross Panama by train, and then move by boat up to California. Mail rarely reached its destination in less than a month. In fact, it often took months for mail to reach the West Coast.

There had to be a better way, and entrepreneur William Russell thought he had the answer. So, in 1860 he published an ad that ran:

"Wanted: Young, skinny, wiry fellows not over 18. Must be expert riders willing to risk death daily. Orphans preferred."

Thus began the Pony Express, a system of horses and riders that delivered mail across the continent in less than two weeks. Though short-lived in reality (the Pony Express went out of business in late 1861 when the transcontinental telegraph line was completed), the Pony Express lives on in legend.

Rail and rural delivery

Meanwhile, mail was being increasingly delivered by rail, and much of it was actually sorted right on the trains. These trains became known as "post offices on wheels." For almost a century, from 1860–1950, railways were the main way of transporting mail.

> **JUST THE FACTS**
> **For years the POD was plagued by armed bandits who robbed trains and stagecoaches carrying U.S. mail. Postal inspectors worked hard to solve these crimes, and the last stagecoach robbery was solved in 1916.**

Through mail delivery, the POD helped make major advances and improvements in transportation, aviation, and business in America. For example, unlike city residents, farmers and other rural residents used to have to travel—sometimes a whole day—to pick up their mail at their "local" post office. When they finally began to receive free rural delivery in 1896, roads and bridges, which were often crude and dangerous, had to be improved so that mail could be delivered properly. Free rural delivery was therefore central to rural development and to relieving the isolation of farmers.

Parcel post (package delivery), which became available in 1913, had a tremendous impact on the economy and led to the development and explosion of mail-order houses. The first of these was the famous Montgomery Ward, whose catalogs were considered "bibles" by the rurally isolated farmers. Sears, Roebuck and Company was also a famous mail order house which tripled its revenues with just five years of parcel post service.

Aviation advancements

But it's in aviation that the POD may have had the most profound effect. Sensing not only the feasibility but the practicality of mail transportation by air, the POD encouraged experimental flights for mail delivery. The first was in 1911, between Garden City and Mineola, New York. Then the POD enlisted the Army Signal Corps, whose students got to practice their flying while delivering the mail. Soon regular flights were delivering mail between New York and Washington.

But early planes were primitive, and safety measures and features were nearly non-existent. Landing fields, towers, searchlights, lighted instrument panels, navigational lights, and other safety features and measures we now take for granted were implemented largely at the impetus of the POD, which was concerned for the safety of its pilots and the efficiency of its delivery program. In fact, the POD contributed so much to the development of aviation safety that in 1922, 1923, and 1926, the POD received awards for its contributions to aeronautics.

EVOLUTION OF EFFICIENCY

Because the transportation of mail was becoming more efficient, mail sorting and processing had to improve as well. We'll now look at how the POD met this challenge to make the USPS what it is today.

ZIP Codes

Because of the dramatic increase in mail and evolution of transportation in the first half of the 20th century, the POD had to develop a more efficient way of sorting and delivering mail. The solution? ZIP (Zoning Improvement Plan) Codes, which went into effect in 1963. This five-digit system allows sorters to pinpoint the location of addressees. The first digit in the ZIP Code, for example, indicates one of nine zones across the U.S. (0 in the Northeast, 9 in the far West). The second and third digits identify increasingly specific regions within that zone and the last two numbers indicate the local post office.

Reorganization

Though the ZIP Code was designed to help make the POD more efficient, the 1960s were a turbulent and troubled era for the POD. Mail volume was increasing but efficiency was not, despite the new ZIP Code. There was also labor trouble, and in 1966 the Chicago Post Office was so backlogged with mail that it was unable to function. An ensuing labor strike across the nation led to a much-needed Postal Reorganization Act, which went into effect in August of 1970. This reorganization officially separated the POD from the Congress, and the POD became the new United States Postal Service (USPS), an independent part of the executive branch of the Government. This Act gave the USPS the structure it has today and instituted regulations for employees, labor management, transportation, finances and rates.

Mechanization

Later that decade, the USPS began an important era of mechanization by introducing the optical character reader (OCR). The first OCRs read the address on a letter one line at a time and printed a corresponding barcode on the envelope. Then a barcode sorter (BCS) read the barcode and sorted the envelope accordingly. These machines automated much of the sorting process and increased sorting time dramatically.

To further maximize efficiency, the USPS expanded the ZIP Code to ZIP+4. These additional four numbers further narrow down the addressee's delivery sector, making sorting and delivery more accurate and efficient.

Today, the single-line OCRs of the late seventies have been replaced by fast multiple-line OCRs (MLOCRs) which can read an entire address and apply the appropriate barcode in milliseconds. Handwritten or difficult to read mail is sorted out and handled by remote barcoding systems (RBCSs), which send an image of the envelope to an operator at another site. The operator reads the address, inputs the correct information, and sends it back to the RBCS, which then applies an appropriate barcode.

Because 70% of USPS mail is letter mail, barcoding technology has dramatically increased its speed and efficiency. Barcoding machines can read and sort 30,000 letters per hour, thus sorting mail 10 times faster and 5 times cheaper than sorting by hand. The USPS is working to automate all offices with barcoding equipment by 1998 so that 90% of all letter mail will be barcoded. This should save the USPS nearly $20 billion a year. Barcoding and other automation technologies have also transformed many jobs at the USPS, replacing manual labor with automated tasks.

IMPROVED CUSTOMER SERVICE THROUGH AUTOMATION

Because of increasing competition not only from other mail carriers but also from technologies like fax machines and e-mail, the USPS has been using modern technology to develop products and services that meet customer needs for convenience, flexibility and profitability.

Credit/debit service

One of the most anticipated of these services is credit/debit card service at post offices. Over 6,000 Post Offices now accept ATM cards for all products and services (except passport application fees) and American Express, Discover, and Mastercard credit cards for all window retail purchases (except money orders and C.O.D.). In addition to providing convenience to customers, this saves the USPS thousands of dollars in banking fees. Over 50,000 card processing terminals at 33,000 locations are expected to be in place by 1997. In addition, over 10,000 vending machines with 24 hour access to stamps are in Post Office sites around the country.

Other services

Other services being tested include:

- "Pack and Send" services, where customers can bring items they wish to send and have them packaged by the USPS for a fee.
- **Computer Kiosks**, currently in Baltimore and other test sites, which allow customers to access government information and services, including job vacancy information and on-line job screening for government positions. These kiosks should become available in libraries, post offices and malls.
- **Post Office Express Units**, special service locations that are open 7 days a week into the evenings. These units, designed to make post office products and services more accessible and available, are full service and located in high-volume areas like large food, drug, or discount chain stores. The USPS

plans to continue expanding these units into locations such as malls and airports as well as sporting events and conventions.

- The **Business Travelers Program** makes it easy for busy executives staying at a major national hotel chain to use Express Mail, Priority Mail, and Express Mail International services right from their hotel lobbies.
- **Voting through Mail** has drastically increased voter "turnout" in San Juan, New Mexico, where citizens vote for all bond issues and constitutional issues by mail. Voter participation has increased from 8% to 42%.
- **FASTNET**, a service piloted in Orlando, FL, provides overnight delivery for local parcel post mail. This service is now available in 13 different areas.
- **Decorative Packages** centers, tested successfully in the Southeast, offer special tamper-resistant, self-locking decorative boxes for packing and shipping. Boxes come in three different sizes and designs.

In addition, technology like the OPEX Magnetic Detection Sorter helps the USPS recover, identify, and return undeliverable or damaged mail.

JUST THE FACTS
Customer Service Objectives of the USPS *CustomerPerfect!* program:
1. Deliver All Mail Right
2. Be Easy to Use
3. Provide Effective Customer Contact
4. Inform and Communicate
5. Offer Value for the Price

USPS SERVICES AND STRUCTURE

Now that you know the history of the USPS, let's take a brief look at where it is today. First we'll look at some current USPS services, then we'll get an overview of its organizational structure so as to give you a better idea of where the employee fits into the big picture.

SERVICES

The USPS currently offers a wide range of services to businesses and private customers. There are three classes of mail—first class, periodicals (formerly second class), and standard (formerly third and fourth class). First class mail is generally delivered within two to three business days. For urgent mail, the USPS offers Express Mail (guaranteed next day delivery) and Priority Mail (usually reaches the addressee within two to three days). A new service, Global Priority Mail, sends packages from high-volume customers to Japan within four days.

The USPS also offers dozens of other mailing services. Several of these services provide you with proof that your mail was sent and/or received. If you're sending a valuable package, you can send it Registered Mail, which means your package will be carefully guarded until it reaches its destination. You can also have valuable packages insured. Special Handling for packages that require special care (like live animals) and Special Delivery services are also available. And if you don't want mail sent to your home or office, the USPS will rent you a post office box and deliver all of your mail there for you to pick up at your convenience.

JUST THE FACTS
Mail Forwarding
One of the most important services provided by the USPS is mail forwarding. According to the USPS, 17% of Americans move each year, and this service allows customers to continue receiving mail from senders who don't have the new address. After filling out a change of address form and submitting it to the local post office, customers' first-class mail will be forwarded free of charge for one year through the CFS—Computerized Forwarding System. Second-class mail (magazines, newspapers) will be forwarded for 60 days.

In addition, the USPS offers special services for customers and consumers. If a package has been lost, you can have it traced; if your insured, registered, C.O.D. (collection on delivery) or Express mail has been damaged or lost, you can file a claim to recover your losses. If you suspect mail fraud, you can call the U.S. Postal Inspection unit, the law enforcement division of the USPS, which will investigate your complaint. You may also purchase money orders (up to $700) at post offices and pay for most purchases with personal checks (with a photo ID). And the Postal Answer Line can give you 24-hour automated information, such as package mailing costs.

ORGANIZATIONAL STRUCTURE

Just as it's important to know what services the USPS offers, it's important to know how the USPS is organized. A sense of the USPS structure will help you understand how it provides all of its services to its customers and how you would fit into the larger organization.

Board of Governors

The USPS is governed by a Board of Governors, which is equivalent to the Board of Directors of a corporation. Nine governors are appointed by the President with the approval of Congress. Their nine-year terms are staggered, so one governor's term expires each year, and no more than five of these nine can be members of the same political party. These Governors then select a Postmaster General, and together they select a Deputy Postmaster General. These 11 members form the governing board of the USPS, which directs the finances, policies, planning, and practices of the USPS.

Territory divisions

The USPS has divided the United States into 10 Postal Service areas. Each area has a manager of Customer Services and a Processing and Distribution manager. These 10 areas are further divided into 85 local Customer Service districts. There are also 350 processing and distribution plants within these areas, and each area has a marketing and sales office.

To manage all this, the USPS opened a National Operations Center (NOC) in the fall of 1994. There the USPS monitors the "big picture" of mail processing by managing mailing activity, making sure the USPS network functions effectively, and redirecting USPS resources in emergency situations. Smaller versions of the NOC have opened in each of the 10 areas.

National Operations Center

↓

10 Postal Service Areas

Customer Services Manager

Processing and Distribution Manager

Regional Operations Center

↓

85 Customer Service Districts

↓

350 Processing and Distribution Plants

Special divisions

The USPS has several special divisions. One of the newest is the International Business Unit, designed to address increasing competition in international mail delivery services. It is using technology to increase efficiency in international business mail with services like Electronic Data Interchange (EDI). EDI helps the USPS send and track international mail.

Other special divisions include Postal Inspection, Human Resources, Corporate Relations, Labor Relations, Marketing, and Finance. Postal Inspection is perhaps the most interesting of these divisions. This division is responsible for "policing" the mail—that is, inspectors investigate cases of mail fraud and mail theft as well as any other violations of postal laws. Recently, the Postal Inspection unit of the USPS completed one of its most successful investigations and brought down an extensive child pornography distribution ring. Though Postal Inspection isn't usually a high-profile branch of law enforcement, Inspectors play a very important role in maintaining the quality of USPS services.

WORKING FOR THE USPS

You're probably most interested in how USPS jobs are organized. We'll look at that next.

EMPLOYEE CATEGORIES

USPS employees generally fall into three categories:

- *Career Bargaining Employees*, who are entitled to all benefits and who are represented by unions. They may be full-time or part-time regular employees.
- *Career Non-Bargaining Employees*, who also receive benefits (scaled to their hours) but are not

represented by unions. They are part-time flexible employees.

- *The Supplemental Work Force*, which is composed of casual or temporary employees who do not receive benefits and are not represented by unions. This category also includes transitional employees.

Let's look at each of these categories in more detail.

Career Bargaining

Full-time—There are about 657,000 full-time employees within the USPS. These employees work at least 40 hours a week (8 hours a day, Monday through Friday) and have full benefits. Their overtime rate is 1-1/2 times their hourly equivalent. Employees who work the night shift receive a higher wage.

Part-time regular—There are about 8,000 part-time regular employees, half of whom are clerks. Part-time regular employees work on a fixed schedule of less than 40 hours per week. They are career employees who earn hourly wages which increase according to a set schedule.

Career Non-Bargaining

Part-time flexible—There are about 86,000 of these career employees. Though they can be called in at any time and their schedule can be changed without their consent, they are guaranteed at least 4 hours of work a day (20 hours a week) and do receive benefits scaled to their hours. And, after a certain number of years (the exact number varies from office to office), part-time flexibles are automatically moved into full-time regular status. In the meantime, they often move around within their offices to meet particular needs and therefore can gain experience in several positions. Though these employees are called "part-time," many work more than 40 hours a week. But they are not covered

by any bargaining unit agreement and are paid hourly like part-time regulars.

Supplemental

Part-time casuals/temporaries—These employees are generally hired to meet the cyclical demands of the industry. Employees are limited to two 89-day appointments in a given year but may be offered an extra 21 days of employment with the USPS to meet delivery demands for a total of 199 days of employment each year. Most casual/temporary employees do manual clerk or mail handling work. These are not career employees and are not eligible for benefits. They are hired year round, but particularly around Christmas and other busy times of year. (In 1995, 45,000 casual workers were hired nationwide to meet the mailing demands of the Christmas season.) Many will work July through December and then January through June for a full year of employment, but then they must wait a full year until they can work for the USPS again. Part-time casual/temporary employees do not need to take an entrance test (the 470 Battery Exam). Interested candidates can simply apply at their local post office. Pay for part-time casual/temporary employees generally falls between minimum wage and $8 an hour.

Transitional employees—Because the USPS is becoming more and more mechanized, there has been a decrease in the number of some full-time positions available. The USPS has formed an agreement with its employee unions that while going through transitions resulting from automation (e.g., when employees need to be retrained, new positions are established and/or old ones eliminated or revised), it will hire transitional employees for a limit of two years. These temporary employees are technically part-time flexible employees, but they usually work a full 40 hours a week. These employees are at the lowest step of the part-time flexible schedule, so they're really more like casual employees. This class of employee began in 1992 with 9,732 transitional employees; last year there were 31,548.

A note about Rural Carriers: Because of the unique nature of their job, Rural Carriers are a separate category. About half of the USPS Rural Carriers are Rural Carrier Associates, part-time non-career employees who cover routes for regular Rural Carriers on their days off. The career position of Rural Carrier is filled exclusively from the ranks of the Rural Carrier Associates. You can think of the Rural Carrier Associate position as a training ground for the Rural Carrier Position (for more information, see the section on Rural Carriers and Rural Carrier Associates at the end of Chapter 2).

ENTRY-LEVEL JOB DESCRIPTIONS

Now let's take a look at the specific entry-level jobs you're likely to apply for. (These are all jobs that require the 470 Battery Test.) We'll briefly discuss each position and then look at pay scales, raises, and promotions within the USPS. Then we'll discuss each position in detail.

Window Clerk: Window Clerks are the people who serve you at the post office. They have a variety of duties, including selling stamps, weighing packages, preparing money orders, and answering your questions about USPS policies and services.

Mail Carrier, City: City Carriers deliver mail to city businesses and residents. They usually have a set route on which they deliver and collect mail, by foot or vehicle depending upon their area. They spend much of their time alone and unsupervised.

Mail Carrier, Rural: Rural Carriers, like City Carriers, deliver and collect mail but to rural businesses and residents along a set route. They have a wider variety of duties than City Carriers because they often have more direct contact with customers and provide services that city residents generally get only in local post offices.

Mail Handler: Mail Handlers load and unload mail from trucks and bins and help in the initial sorting phases. They also cancel stamps.

Mail Processor: Mail Processors run equipment that processes mail. They also do some loading and sorting of mail in the initial stages of distribution.

Distribution Clerk: Distribution Clerks begin the process of distributing mail. They sort mail by destination location.

Flat Sorting Machine Operator: Flat Sorting Machine Operators read ZIP codes to sort mail in the next phase of distribution. They also do some loading and unloading and need good hand-eye coordination.

Mark-Up Clerk: Mark-Up Clerks work with mail that's undeliverable to correct addresses, reroute, and/or return mail to sender.

GRADES AND PAY SCALES

The bulk of USPS positions are classified into a certain category and grade. For example, most clerks (distribution, window, etc.) are in the PS (Postal Service) category. Within this category, each clerk position falls into a certain grade, usually from 1–10, based upon the level of skill and training required for each position. This is one reason why there are so many different job titles with the USPS.

The grade for each position determines the salary. For example, an entry-level Window Clerk, who has to deal with the public and have a general knowledge of

USPS services and policies, will start at PS Grade 5. Entry-level Mail Processors, on the other hand, do not deal with the public and start at PS Grade 4. They may, of course, move into higher grades as they gain experience. For a detailed list of salaries, see USPS rate schedules starting on page 22.

RAISES

USPS employees are awarded raises which include a COLA (cost-of-living adjustment), on a regular basis. The salary schedule for most positions is broken down into 15 steps, labeled A-O (some positions have an AA step). Generally, the first step, from starting salary A (or AA) to salary B, takes place after 96 weeks. The second and third steps (raises) take place after 88 weeks; the fourth through ninth steps, after 44 weeks; the tenth and

eleventh, after 34 weeks; the thirteenth and fourteenth, after 26 weeks; and the last step takes place after 24 weeks. So, the longer you are with the USPS, the quicker your raises come around. In fact, after just five years, your raises will come less than one year apart.

And how high are those raises? If you're a Distribution Clerk, PS Grade 5, for example, your Step A salary is $25,647. Your Step B salary is $28,497, an increase of $2,850 or 11%. And your Step C salary is $30,785, an additional increase of $2,288 or 8%. Admittedly, the closer the raises are in time, the less the increase. For example, in the final steps for PS Grade 5, from Step M to N and N to O, the salary increase is only $284 and $286, respectively. But the overall increase from Step A ($25,647) to Step O ($36,135) is an impressive $10,488, or 40%, over about 12 years. If you move

USPS RAISE SCHEDULE: AT A GLANCE	
From Step–Step for PS, MH, and CC Grades	**Number of Weeks, Grades 1–7**
A–B	96
B–C	88*
C–D	44
D–E	44
E–F	44
F–G	44
G–H	44
H–I	44
I–J	44
J–K	34
K–L	34
L–M	26
M–N	26
N–O	24

*For Grades 1–3, this step takes place in 88 weeks, in Grades 4–7, 96 weeks.

up in grade (for example, from PS Grade 5 to PS Grade 6) during those years, however, you can expect your income to increase by an additional 5–6%.

HIRING FROM WITHIN

Because the benefits of working for the USPS are so desirable, many people accept part-time positions and wait for a full-time opportunity. Thus, most full-time vacancies at the USPS are filled from within by part-time employees, making it difficult to get a full-time job from the start with the USPS. Logically, when full-time positions open up, preference is usually given to part-time employees who are already familiar with the work rather than to someone who has simply done well on the Battery Exam. The good news, as we've already noted, is that even "part-time" employees (part-time flexible) often work full-time hours and receive benefits. So while you're waiting to move into a full-time career bargaining status, you still have a highly desirable position. Your wages will be hourly rather than salaried and your duties may be diverse, but your foot will be in the door and you do get benefits. And if you do good work, you'll have an advantage when you bid for a full-time slot or another position.

Bidding for jobs

Competition for open positions can be heavy, so the USPS has instituted a job bidding process. When a vacancy occurs, employees submit written requests—"bids"—for that position. Assuming all candidates meet the qualifications for that position, the candidate with the highest seniority (measured in years of service with the USPS) is given the position. However, if you want to move into a supervisory position, you will need to do more than just bid—you'll need to take an exam and possibly get further training and, of course, you must be able to lead and manage people and resources.

Job "Detours"

Sometimes the exams for the positions you're interested in may not be offered for some time—even two or three years. Should you wait? Well, you might be in a better position if you can attain a position other than the one you desire and then move into the position you prefer. Once you have been employed by the USPS for at least a year, you're eligible to take the entrance exam for any position. You simply need to request that exam when a position is vacant. So, if you have been hired as a Mail Handler but want to become a Carrier, you don't need to retake the 470 Battery Test; you simply have to take the secondary tests for that specific position (Carriers, for example, have to pass a driving test). If you have been a good employee—on time, reliable, a fast learner—chances are good that your supervisor will be glad to give you the test for a position you are qualified to fill.

USPS JOB DESCRIPTIONS

Because each of the positions we've been discussing require the 470 Battery Exam, because a majority of USPS employees start off in one of these positions, and because it's important for you to know as much as possible about the position you're likely to apply for, we'll now focus on exactly what people in each of these positions do.

The following job descriptions and duties are based on the actual job descriptions provided by the USPS. We've also included information about working conditions, salaries, and promotions.

Title: Window Clerk

<u>Description:</u>

Window Clerks perform a variety of services at the public windows of post offices or post office branches or stations. They are expected to maintain pleasant and effective public relations with customers, so they must have a general familiarity with postal laws, regulations, and common procedures.

Duties:

The duties of a Window Clerk include:

- Selling stamps, post cards, and other products to customers;
- Accepting and delivering insured, parcel post, C.O.D. and registered mail;
- Checking and setting stamp vending machines, postage meters and permit meters;
- Handling customer claims and complaints;
- Issuing and cashing money orders;
- Handling post office box rentals and payments; and
- Answering customer questions about services and regulations.

Window Clerks may also be asked to make emergency carrier relays, assist in census matters, and separate and distribute mail.

Conditions:

Because of their constant contact with the public, Window Clerks need to be "people persons." While work with the public is often one of the joys of being a Window Clerk, they also need to maintain a level of friendliness and patience even when dealing with rude or irate customers. Window Clerks generally have little physically strenuous activity but may be pressured by long lines or busy hours. Window Clerks have good working hours—no nights—and the job has enough variety to prevent boredom from repetition.

Pay Scale:

PS-05: Step A, $25,647; Step O, $36,135.

Promotions:

Window Clerks are often promoted to a higher grade or to a supervisory position.

Title: Carrier, City

Description:

City Carriers deliver and collect mail on foot or by vehicle—whatever the weather—in a fixed area within a city. Like Window Clerks, they are expected to maintain pleasant and effective public relations with customers on their routes, so they need to be familiar with postal laws, regulations, and common procedures as well as with the geography of the city.

Duties:

The primary duty of a City Carrier is sequencing and delivering all classes of mail along a fixed delivery route, by foot or vehicle, according to a regular schedule. City Carriers also prepare and separate mail to be carried by truck to relay boxes along their route for later delivery. They also pick up any additional mail from relay boxes, including mail that requires signature for collection of charges; accept letters from and answer questions of customers; and perform initial sorting of mail to be forwarded.

Conditions:

The USPS generally provides vehicles for City Carriers who need them, but many Carriers cover their whole territory by foot. Because of the territory, City Carriers' tasks are often very specialized; they may, for example, deliver parcel post only. Carriers generally start very early in the morning (sometimes as early as 4 am), but they also finish early. They spend a great deal of time outside, which is wonderful in good weather but can be treacherous in storms and winter. Generally, Carriers walk a good deal and work with little supervision as they cover their routes alone. This allows for a good deal of freedom, but on the other hand Carriers won't have someone to turn to if they get into a difficult situation.

Pay Scale:

CC-05: Step A, $25,647; Step O, $36,135.

Promotions:

Carriers are often promoted to Carrier Technicians, who are very experienced carriers and often cover for a number of other carriers. They can also move up in grade and into supervisory positions.

Title: Carrier, Rural

Description:

Rural Carriers deliver and collect mail by vehicle on a fixed rural route, in all weather conditions. They must maintain pleasant and effective public relations with customers on their routes. This requires a general familiarity with postal laws, regulations, and common procedures as well as the geography of the area.

Duties:

The primary duty of Rural Carriers is to sequence and deliver all classes of mail along a fixed delivery route by vehicle according to a regular schedule. They also pick up any additional mail from customers, answer customer questions, and perform initial sorting of mail to be forwarded.

Conditions:

Same as City Carrier, except that Rural Carriers generally have to provide their own vehicles and usually do a wider range of tasks, so they often combine the duties of a City Carrier and a Window Clerk. A Rural Carrier's job is also more affected by weather, which may shut down delivery routes, and it often involves more direct customer contact.

Pay Scale:

Rural Carriers are paid one of two ways: by the number of hours they work or by the length of their route. Nearly all are paid by the hour. Some work as little as 12 hours a week, but many work over 40. Going by the standard number of hours in a work year, Rural Carriers earn between $24,024 and $34,242 per year.

Promotions:

Rural Carriers can also be promoted to Carrier Technicians, increase in grade or move into supervisory positions.

Title: Mail Handler

Description:

Mail Handlers load, unload, and move bulk mail. They also perform other duties incidental to the movement and processing of mail.

Duties:

Mail Handlers unload mail from trucks and, after separating the mail sacks and facing the letter mail, carry mail to distribution centers for processing. They also load processed mail into sacks and onto trucks. In addition, Mail Handlers cancel parcel post postage and occasionally operate fork lifts, rewrap damaged packages, clean or sweep work and rest areas, and may even act as guards for registered mail and/or watchmen for the post office.

Conditions:

Mail Handlers have one of the most physically strenuous positions with the USPS, even in offices that are highly automated. Mail Handlers do a great deal of lifting, pulling, and grabbing. In addition, they are on their feet most of the day and many of the tasks they perform are repetitive. Mail Handlers often work on nights and weekends, for these are the hours when most mail is sorted.

Pay Scale:

MH-04: Step A, $21,286; Step O, $33,869.

Promotions:

Mail Handlers are often promoted to a higher grade or into positions as Clerks or Carriers.

Title: Mail Processor

Description:

Mail Processors perform a combination of tasks required for mail processing using a variety of automated equipment.

Duties:

The primary duty of Mail Processors is to operate various machines that process mail. They also handle minor machine jams, remove mail that's unprocessable, load mail onto the transport system to begin the distribution process, collect and bundle mail from bins, and perform other job-related tasks.

Conditions:

Mail Processors do a good deal of physical work, but the work is not as strenuous as in the Mail Handler position, and it is balanced by automated tasks. Mail Processors will find that their work is often a combination of several repetitive tasks and will find that, like Mail Handlers, they're most needed at night when most mail is sorted.

Pay Scale:

PS-04: Step A, $24,183; Step O, $35,267.

Promotions:

Mail Processors are often moved up in grade or promoted to Clerks, Handlers, or supervisory positions.

Title: Distribution Clerk

Description:

Distribution Clerks separate incoming and outgoing mail according to established sorting and distribution schemes.

Duties:

Distribution Clerks perform the primary and secondary distributions of incoming and outgoing mail by delivery point (for example, sorting by general delivery, rural delivery, highway contract route or city carrier route). They may also maintain mailing records, face

and cancel mail, record and bill mail requiring special service, and provide service at public windows.

Conditions:

Like Mail Handlers, Distribution Clerks often work nights and weekends, when most of the mail is sorted. They also spend a great deal of their time on their feet and may find their tasks physically demanding and repetitive.

Pay Scale:

PS-05: Step A, $25,647; Step O, $36,135.

Promotions:

Distribution Clerks are often promoted to a higher grade, such as Distribution Clerk, Machine, which requires good hand-eye coordination and an ability to maintain visual attention for sustained periods of time. They may also be promoted to supervisory positions.

Title: Flat Sorting Machine Operator

Description:

Flat Sorting Machine Operators operate an automated flat sorting machine, reading ZIP codes to direct the distribution of large or bulk mail.

Duties:

Flat Sorting Machine Operators read the ZIP Code on each piece of mail and press the proper keys on the machine to direct mail to its proper destination. They may also serve as loaders, culling non-machinable pieces of mail, or as sweepers/tyers, verifying sorted mail for accuracy and bundling mail. Flat Sorting Machine Operators may perform manual distribution as required and operate other sorting machines after proper training.

Conditions:

Loading, sweeping and tying requires Flat Sorting Machine Operators to be in good physical condition, but the job is not among the most physically strenuous. The physical labor may ease the repetitive nature of some of the automated tasks. Flat Sorting Machine

Operators should have good eyesight to avoid eye strain.

Pay Scale:

PS-05: Step A, $25,647; Step O, $36,135.

Promotions:

Flat Sorting Machine Operators often move up to a higher grade or are promoted to a supervisory position.

Title: Mark-Up Clerk, Automated

Description:

Mark-Up Clerks operate a machine that processes undeliverable mail.

Duties:

Mark-Up Clerks use a computer to enter and extract data to and from several databases to redirect mail with undeliverable addresses. They select the appropriate program for each application, affix labels to mail, prepare forms for address correction services and manually distribute processed markups for further handling.

Conditions:

Mark-Up Clerks often must perform under pressure of time, so they must be able to work quickly and efficiently. They should have some mechanical/technical aptitude, since they generally work with several pieces of equipment. Mark-Up Clerks should have good vision to avoid eye strain from focusing on envelopes and computer screens for long periods of time.

Pay Scale:

PS-04: Step A, $24,183; Step O, $35,267.

Promotions:

Mark-Up Clerks, Automated may be moved up in grade or promoted to a supervisory position. They are often promoted to Distribution Clerks or Flat-Sorting Machine Operators as well.

OTHER POSITIONS WITH THE USPS

While a majority of employees enter the USPS in one of the entry-level positions reviewed in the preceding pages, there are approximately 2,000 job titles at the USPS. Most job titles are categorized as Craft, Professional, or Management jobs; tests and requirements vary from position to position.

Craft positions

Craft Positions include all clerk and handling positions as well as technical and maintenance positions such as the following:

Auto Mechanic
Blacksmith-Welder
Custodian
Electronic Technician
Elevator Mechanic
Engineman
Fireman
General Mechanic
Machinist
Maintenance Mechanic
Mason
Painter
Plumber
Security Guard

Professional positions

Professional Positions are those that generally require professional degrees, such as the following:

Accounting Technician
Architect/Engineer
Budget Assistant
Computer Programmer
Computer System Analyst

Curriculum Development Specialist

Electronic Engineer

Industrial Engineer

Stationery Engineer

Technical Writer

Transportation Specialist

Communications Specialist

Management positions

Finally, Management Positions are generally held by those with management experience and degrees or employees who have worked their way to the top. Management positions include:

Administrative Manager

Foreman of Mail

General Foreman

Labor Relations Representative

Manager Bulk Mail

Manager-Distribution

Manager-Station/Branch

Management Analyst

Management Development Specialist

Postmaster – Branch

Safety Officer

Schemes Routing Officer

Supervisor-Accounting Services

Supervisor-Customer Service

System Liaison Specialist

Tour Superintendent

Supervisor-Data Processing Unit

Supervisor-Distribution Operations

There are also a number of clerical, secretarial, and data processing positions available with the USPS. Most of these jobs require the Administration 710 Test.

This is only a partial list of positions available at the USPS. Different positions require different exams;

if you're interested, see your local post office or employment agency for details. In the meantime, the rest of this book will help you prepare for the 470 Battery Exam.

SUMMARY

Now that you've had an overview of the USPS—how it works, how it began and evolved, how you'd benefit as an employee, how you'd be working in the various entry-level positions—it's time to talk in more detail about the hiring process, which is covered in depth in the next chapter.

Included on the following pages are USPS pay schedules showing salary increases for the entry-level positions discussed earlier in this chapter. Salary schedules are shown for PS, MH, and CC Grades 4, 5, and 6, as well as Rural Carrier annual rates.

U.S. Postal Service Pay Schedule

Step	Postal Service (PS) Schedule Full-Time Annual			Postal Service (PS) Schedule Part-Time Regular (Hourly)			Postal Service (PS) Schedule Part-Time Flexible (Hourly)		
	Grade 4	Grade 5	Grade 6	Grade 4	Grade 5	Grade 6	Grade 4	Grade 5	Grade 6
A	24,183	25,647	27,203	11.63	12.33	13.08	12.09	12.82	13.60
B	26,848	28,497	30,247	12.91	13.70	14.54	13.42	14.25	15.12
C	29,075	30,785	31,427	13.98	14.80	15.11	14.54	15.39	15.71
D	32,346	32,992	33,688	15.55	15.86	16.20	16.17	16.50	16.84
E	32,611	33,227	33,999	15.68	16.00	16.35	16.31	16.64	17.00
F	32,878	33,564	34,310	15.81	16.14	16.50	16/44	16.78	17.16
G	33,144	33,848	34,618	15.93	16.27	16.64	16.57	16.92	17.31
H	33,407	34,135	34,930	16.06	16.41	16.79	16.70	17.07	17.47
I	33,673	34,420	35,240	16.19	16.55	16.94	16.84	17.21	17.62
J	33,939	34,706	35,548	16.32	16.69	17.09	16.97	17.35	17.77
K	34,206	34,993	35,860	16.45	16.82	17.24	17.10	17.50	17.93
L	34,473	35,277	36,171	16,57	16.96	17.39	17.24	17.64	18.09
M	34,738	35,565	36,481	16.70	17.10	17.54	17.37	17.78	18.24
N	35,003	35,849	36,794	16.83	17.24	17.69	17.50	17.92	18.40
O	35,267	36,135	37,104	16.96	17.37	17.84	17.63	18.07	18.55

U.S. Postal Service Pay Schedule

Step	Mail Handler (MH) Schedule Full-Time Annual			Mail Handler (MH) Schedule Part-Time Regular (Hourly)			Mail Handler (MH) Schedule Part-Time Flexible (Hourly)		
	Grade 4	Grade 5	Grade 6	Grade 4	Grade 5	Grade 6	Grade 4	Grade 5	Grade 6
A	21,676	22,944	24,292	10.42	11.03	11.68	10.84	11.47	12.15
B	26,295	27,879	29,562	12.64	13.40	14.21	13.15	13.94	14.78
C	28,432	30,076	30,693	13.67	14.46	14.76	14.22	15.04	15.35
D	31,582	32,204	32,872	15.18	15.48	15.80	15.79	16.10	16.44
E	31,836	32,477	33,170	15.31	15.61	15.95	15.92	16.24	16.59
F	32,092	32,754	33,468	15.43	15.75	16.09	16.05	16.38	16.73
G	32,347	33,026	33,765	15.55	15.88	16.23	16.17	16.51	16.88
H	32,602	33,302	34,064	15.67	16.01	16.38	16.30	16.65	17.03
I	32,857	33,579	34,362	15.80	16.14	16.52	16.43	16.79	17.18
J	33,115	33,851	34,659	15.92	16.27	16.66	16.56	16.93	17.33
K	33,370	34,127	34,958	16.04	16.41	16.81	16.69	17.06	17.48
L	33,625	34,399	35,260	16.17	16.54	16.95	16.81	17.20	17.63
M	33,880	34,675	35,556	16.29	16.67	17.09	16.94	17.34	17.78
N	34,135	34,949	35,855	16.41	16.80	17.24	17.07	17.47	17.93
O	34,390	35,224	36,154	16.53	16.93	17.38	17.20	17.61	18.08

U.S. Postal Service Pay Schedule

Step	City Carrier (CC) Schedule Full-Time Annual		City Carrier (CC) Schedule Part-Time Regular (Hourly)		City Carrier (CC) Schedule Part-Time Flexible (Hourly)	
	Grade 5	Grade 6	Grade 5	Grade 6	Grade 5	Grade 6
A	25,647	27,203	12.33	13.08	12.82	13.60
B	28,947	30,247	13.70	14.54	14.25	15.12
C	30,785	31,427	14.80	15.11	15.39	15.71
D	32,992	33,688	15.86	16.20	16.50	16.84
E	33,277	33,999	16.00	16.35	16.64	17.00
F	33,564	34,310	16.14	16.50	16.78	17.16
G	33,848	34,618	16.27	16.64	16.92	17.31
H	34,135	34,930	16.41	16.79	17.07	17.47
I	34,420	35,240	16.55	16.94	17.21	17.62
J	34,706	35,548	16.69	17.09	17.35	17.77
K	34,993	35,860	16.82	17.24	17.50	17.93
L	35,277	36,171	16.96	17.39	17.64	18.09
M	35,565	36,481	17.10	17.54	17.78	18.24
N	35,849	36,794	17.24	17.69	17.92	18.40
O	36,135	37,104	17.37	17.84	18.07	18.55

U.S. Postal Service Pay Schedule

Rural Carrier Annual Rates
Based on Weekly Hours Worked

Step	12 hours	20 hours	30 hours	40 hours
A	7,240	12,066	18,096	24,128
B	8,052	13,422	20,135	26,840
C	8,674	14,460	21,691	28915
1	9,305	15,512	23,266	31,016
2	9,397	15,663	23,491	31,318
3	9,487	15,814	23,721	31,622
4	9,578	15,964	23,945	31,923
5	9,668	16,119	24,171	32,227
6	9,762	16,271	24,399	32,529
7	9,853	16,421	24,626	32,832
8	9,942	16,575	24,852	33,136
9	10,035	16,727	25,079	33,437
10	10,125	16,877	25,307	33,742
11	10,217	17,028	25,535	34,043
12	10,307	17,183	25,760	34,346

C·H·A·P·T·E·R

HOW POSTAL WORKERS ARE SELECTED

2

CHAPTER SUMMARY

Now that you have a good idea of what it's like to work for the USPS, you'll want to know how to go about getting a job with the Postal Service. This chapter describes in detail the USPS's hiring process, from applying to take a test to your first day on the job, and it lets you know what you'll be up against each step along the way. You'll also learn about Casual Employment, an often overlooked path to employment with the USPS.

very year, hundreds of thousands of people apply for a job with the USPS. Only a small percentage of these are ever hired. You've taken the first step in gaining a competitive advantage for yourself by purchasing this book. Now it's time to take the next step in putting yourself out in front of the pack.

At the end of this chapter we've provided you with a list of phone numbers and addresses for every postal district in the country, to help you find a job in your area. For now though, let's uncover the process by which you get a job with the USPS. If you know what to expect each step along the way, you'll be better prepared to meet the challenges you face. With such huge numbers competing for the same jobs, you'll need every advantage you can get! Be smart—be prepared.

First Things First: Tracking Down Job Openings

One of the most important things to know about when looking for a job with the USPS is how to find out where the job openings are. Most states are made up of more than one postal district, and the districts themselves consist of hundreds of individual post offices. Because the hiring process at the USPS is decentralized—in other words, individual postal districts and post offices hire based on their own needs and on their own schedule—there's no one place to locate current openings, and there's no one person to call to find out about upcoming tests. Instead, you're going to have to find out for yourself where the opportunities are. There is a resource that can help you do that, though, and you're holding it in your hands right now.

Postal Job Information Lines

The first thing to note is that most postal districts have what is known as a Postal Job Information Line. This is a number you can call to get automated information about current openings and current or upcoming tests. It's usually a simple recording, listing the current job opportunities and providing you with either a phone number or a place to go for an application and further information.

Starting on page 14 you'll find a listing of *every* postal district in the country, including Job Information Lines for the districts that have them (for postal districts without Job Information Lines, we have provided the phone number to the district personnel office). Call the Job Information Line in a district in which you are interested in working, listen to the listings, and pay close attention: *this is an official listing of where the jobs are.* The Job Information Line is a service of the USPS; take advantage of it.

Job Tip
To keep up with open exams around the country, check out the LearningExpress web site at http://www.learnx.com.

Don't Forget Your Local Post Office

While Job Information Lines list current openings, they are maintained at a district level. A district, as you'll remember, can have hundreds of individual post offices under its jurisdiction. Some smaller post offices, especially in rural areas, may keep their recruiting closer to home. Instead of asking the district office, which could be hundreds of miles away, to announce their openings, they may post openings at their own location or in local papers.

You may want to call or visit your local post office directly to see if they have any openings, especially if you live in a rural or outlying area, or if you are interested in working for a smaller post office rather than for a high-volume urban facility. To contact your local post office, check your phone book for the personnel office, and give them a call. Better yet, go down and visit it in person—most post offices post any job openings on bulletin boards in their lobbies.

State Employment Offices

Another place to keep in touch with is your state's Department of Labor employment offices. These offices provide placement services and, through their vast computer databases, are often aware of jobs that may not be listed in other sources, including openings at local postal facilities. Check the state governmental listings in your phone book under "Department of Labor, Job Placement Services" for the office nearest you.

And Keep Your Eyes Peeled!

Perhaps most important of all in identifying opportunities with the USPS is keeping your eyes peeled. Because of the large number of applicants for postal jobs, when a district offers applications for an upcoming test, it doesn't have to offer them for long before it has more than enough applicants to take the test. A real-life example helps drive this point home.

On Friday, June 7, 1996, a local New York City newspaper announced that the USPS would be accepting applications for several entry-level positions (all tested by the 470 Battery Examination, covered in Chapters 7–12 of this book) in three counties bordering New York City. The article stated that applications would be accepted from Monday, June 10 through Friday, June 14; in other words, *the following week only.* The announcement came only three days before applications were to be accepted, and applications were going to be accepted for just five days! If you happened not to read that paper, or were out of town, or just missed the article, you would have been out of luck. Those who took and passed that exam will be eligible for employment with the USPS for at least the next two years; it is unlikely that those counties will test again anytime soon.

The point is, Stay on the ball, keep your eyes peeled, pay attention! You may have just a couple of days' notice for an application period, and there may not be another one in the same area for a couple of years.

APPLYING TO BECOME A POSTAL WORKER

To be eligible for employment with the USPS, you must meet certain minimum requirements:

- You must be 18 years of age or older, or 16 if you're already a high school graduate
- If you are a male, you must be registered with the U.S. Selective Service
- You must be a U.S. citizen or a legal resident alien
- You must be able to lift 70 pounds
- You must have 20/40 vision in one eye and 20/100 in the other (glasses are permitted)
- If you are applying for a job that requires driving, you must have a valid driver's license and a safe driving record

If you meet all of the above requirements you may apply for a position with the United States Postal Service.

THE HIRING PROCESS

The United States Postal Service divides its hiring process into four parts, and further divides the fourth part into three separate stages, as follows:

1. Recruitment

2. Examination

3. Register

4. Suitability & Selection
   a. Suitability
   b. Selection
   c. Appointment

We'll go through each one of these steps in detail to let you know what you'll face, and what will be expected of you, at each step along the way.

STEP ONE: RECRUITMENT

As you read in Chapter 1, the USPS employs well over 800,00 workers. Maintaining a workforce of that size—filling new positions and positions that are open due to promotion or retirement, and covering positions when people are sick or on vacation—requires a significant recruitment effort to make sure there are enough qualified people to keep the mail moving. Keep in mind that operating the Postal Service doesn't just happen weekdays from 9–5. The USPS moves an average of 495 million pieces of mail every day, much of the work being done overnight.

To recruit the most qualified applicants, nearly every postal district, as discussed earlier, maintains a Job Information Line that gives out current exams and job openings. Openings are also listed at local post offices and announced in local newspapers. These are all meant to get the word out to the public—that's you—when a post office has openings or plans to "open" a test.

While the USPS makes recruitment a high priority, you need to tune in to the right resources (the Job Information Lines, local employment offices) or you'll miss out on the opportunities recruitment brings your way.

When you find out about an upcoming examination, that's the time to move on to Step Two: Examinations, detailed below.

Note that certain positions, including Casual Employment, do not require an examination. Casual employment, an important path into the USPS, is discussed at the end of this chapter, in the section entitled "Other Postal Service Opportunities."

STEP TWO: EXAMINATION

To determine whether those who are interested in working for the Postal Service are in fact qualified, the USPS has put in place an extensive screening process, the first part of which is a qualifying examination. In the case of those entry-level jobs that require the 470 Battery Examination, the following procedures apply.

The Application Card

When a local Postal District or post office decides that there are, or soon will be, enough openings to merit offering an examination, they announce what is known as an "application period." The application period is the period of time in which applications for an exam will be accepted, and it often lasts just a few days.

During the application period you need to go to the post office that is offering the examination and fill out an application card. If an entire city, county, or postal district is offering an examination, you may be able to get your application card at any post office within that city, county, or district; alternatively, you may be required to get an application card at one specific application center. The Postal Job Information Line for the region that is holding the application period will probably let you know where to pick up an application. If not, call the post office that is offering the examination and ask them directly. It is worth a few minutes on the phone to find out this information, rather than going down to a local post office only to find out that you have to go somewhere else to get your application card.

Once you get your application card, otherwise known as PS Form 2479, fill it out *completely*. As you can see from the copy of the application card reproduced here, you will need to fill in your name, address, birthdate, social security number, the title of the exam you're applying for (Test 470), and the name of the post office you're applying to. (Note: *Do not separate the cards along the perforation,* we have separated the card here

APPLICATION CARD

Name (Last, First, Middle Initials)

Address (House/Apt. No. & Street)

City, State, ZIP Code

Birthdate (Month, Date, Year)

Do Not Write In This Space

Telephone Number | Today's Date

Title of Examination

Post Office Applied For

PS Form 2479-A, April 1987

Title of Examination | Social Security No.

Date of Birth | Today's Date | Post Office Applied For

If you have performed active duty in the Armed Forces of the United States and were separated under honorable conditions indicate periods of service

From (Mo., Day, Yr.) _____ to (Mo., Day, Yr.) _____

DO YOU CLAIM VETERAN PREFERENCE? ☐ NO ☐ YES IF YES, BASED ON
☐ (1) Active duty in the Armed Forces of the U.S. during World War I or the period December 7, 1941, through July 1, 1955,
(2) More than 180 consecutive days of active duty (other than for training) in the Armed Forces of the U.S. any part of which occurred between Jan. 31, 1955 and Oct. 14, 1976, or (3) Award of a campaign badge or service medal
☐ Your status as (1) a disabled veteran or a veteran who was awarded the purple heart for wounds or injuries received in action, (2) a veteran's widow who has not remarried, (3) the wife of an ex serviceman who has a service connected disability which disqualifies him for civil service appointment, or (4) the widowed, divorced or separated mother of an ex-service son or daughter who died in action or who is totally and permanently disabled

Print or Type Your Name and Address ⟶

Name (First, Middle, Last)

Address (House, Apt. No. & Street)

City, State, ZIP Code (ZIP Code must be included)

PS Form 2479-B, April 1987

ADMISSION CARD
Do Not Write In This Space

This card will be returned to you. Bring it, along with personal identification bearing your picture or description, with you when you report for the test. ID's will be checked, and a fingerprint or signature specimen may be required.

SAMPLE USPS APPLICATION CARD

Instructions to Applicants

Furnish all the information requested on these cards. The attached card will be returned to you with sample questions and necessary instructions, including the time and place of the written test.

TYPEWRITE OR PRINT IN INK. DO NOT SEPARATE THESE CARDS. FOLD ONLY AT PERFORATION.

Mail or Take This Form—Both Parts—to The Postmaster of the Post Office Where You Wish to Be Employed.

PS Form 2479-A, April 1987 *(Reverse)*

Final Eligibility in This Examination is Subject to Suitability Determination

The collection of information on this form is authorized by 39 U.S.C. 401.1001; completion of this form is voluntary. This information will be used to determine qualification, suitability, and availability of applicants for USPS employment, and may be disclosed to relevant Federal Agencies regarding eligibility and suitability for employment, law enforcement activities when there is an indication of a potential violation of law, in connection with private relief legislation (to Office of Management and Budget); to a congressional office at your request, to a labor organization as required by the NLRA, and where pertinent, in a legal proceeding to which the Postal Service is a party. If this information is not provided, you may not receive full consideration for a position.

Disclosure by you of your Social Security Number (SSN) is mandatory to obtain the services, benefits, or processes that you are seeking. Solicitation of the SSN by the United States Postal Service is authorized under provisions of Executive Order 9397, dated November 22, 1943. The information gathered through the use of the number will be used only as necessary in authorized personnel administration processes.

PS Form 2479-B, April 1987 *(Reverse)*

Applicant	Fingerprint
Make no marks on this side of the card unless so instructed by examiner.	
Signature of Applicant	

Political Recommendations Prohibited

The law (39 U.S. Code 1002) prohibits political and certain other recommendations for appointments, promotions, assignments, transfers, or designations of persons in the Postal Service. Statements relating solely to character and residence are permitted, but every other kind of statement or recommendation is prohibited unless it either is requested by the Postal Service and consists solely of an evaluation of the work performance, ability, aptitude, and general qualifications of an individual or is requested by a Government representative investigating the individual's loyalty, suitability, and character. Anyone who requests or solicits a prohibited statement or recommendation is subject to disqualification from the Postal Service and anyone in the Postal Service who accepts such a statement may be suspended or removed from office.

Have You Answered All Questions on the Reverse of This Form?

in order to present it to you on a single page, however the USPS will not accept cards separated as such.) If you don't know the name of the post office, ask the clerk when you pick up the card or call the personnel office at the post office or district you're applying to. If you're a veteran, be sure to fill out your dates of service, and if you claim veteran's preference, check the appropriate box (see the section entitled "Veteran's Preference" for more information).

You can either mail in the completed application card or bring it to the Postmaster of the post office you're applying to. You might consider filling out the card right there at the post office and handing it in directly. Completing the application process in one fell swoop, rather than taking the card home, filling it out, and mailing it in, saves time and trouble, and gets the whole thing over within a few minutes.

Upon receipt of your application card, the post office will mail part of the card back to you along with a sample answer sheet, an instructional packet with sample questions, and the time and location of the exam. Make sure you hold on to the part of the card that is returned to you because it will serve as your "admission ticket" to the written test. You must fill out the sample answer sheet and bring it with you to the examination, or you will not be admitted. For more information on the sample answer sheet and the instructional packet with sample questions, see Chapter 6.

The 470 Battery Examination

The 470 Battery Examination is a national standardized test given by the USPS to evaluate the skill levels of applicants to the following entry-level positions:

- Window Clerk
- City Carrier
- Mail Handler
- Mark-Up Clerk
- Mail Processor
- Flat-Sorting Machine Operator
- Distribution Clerk

The test, implemented in 1994, was designed to replace a set of different exams for these positions and to streamline the testing process.

The 470 Battery Examination tests memory, attention to detail, reasoning, and ability to follow directions, and is broken into four sections:

- Part A: Address Checking (95 questions, six minutes)

    Task: Determine if two addresses are alike or different
- Part B: Memory for Addresses (88 questions, five minutes)

    Task: Memorize the locations of 25 addresses in five minutes
- Part C: Number Series (24 questions, 20 minutes)

    Task: Determine the series in sets of numbers
- Part D: Following Oral Directions (20–25 questions, 25 minutes)

    Task: Mark test booklet and answer sheet based on oral directions

A score of 70 percent is considered passing, though unlikely to get you hired. Due to the intense competition for postal jobs, you'll want to aim for a score in the high eighties or nineties. To help you score your best, Chapters 5–11 cover the 470 Battery Exam in detail, including three full-length practice exams and instructional chapters for each of the four sections of the exam.

IMPORTANT

In order to be admitted to the examination you must bring with you:

- Admission Card (the part of the application card that was mailed back to you)
- Completed Sample Answer Sheet
- Photo ID
- Two No. 2 Pencils

If you don't have these four things, you will not be allowed into the exam room.

Veteran's Preference

The Postal Reorganization Act of 1970 gives veterans of the U.S. military special privileges and preferences in scoring and selection. Veterans are granted an additional five or ten points on the postal exam, making for a best possible score of 110. In addition, veterans entitled to the ten point preference are allowed to "re-open" exams not open to the general public, and any veteran who misses an exam because of engagement in active military service is allowed to file an application for an exam within 120 days prior to or after discharge.

The scores of veterans from re-opened or delayed examinations are merged with the scores of all other test takers—except "compensable disabled veterans" (i.e. veterans who are eligible to be compensated for a disability). Their scores are ranked against each other and placed above *all* other scores. Contact your local post office's personnel department for more information.

STEP THREE: REGISTER

After having taken the 470 Battery Examination, you will receive notification of how you did in the mail. If you scored 70 or better on the exam, you will be told your actual score; if you scored below 70, however, you will just receive a notice stating that you did not pass (with determination and study, hopefully you won't ever see one of these). The names of all applicants who scored 70 or above are placed on what is known as a register, a list used by the USPS to rank all eligible applicants in order of score, from highest to lowest.

Registers remain valid for two years and may be extended beyond that depending on hiring needs and the availability of applicants on other registers. When local postal facilities need to fill positions, they turn to their registers, starting from the top, and continue the screening process by selecting several names from the list.

When offering an exam, a postal facility usually has already determined that it has a need for new employees, so the top names are selected immediately. This is not always the case however. Names can be selected from a register a year, or more, after the test has been given, for as long as the register is valid. When you take an exam, the first round of hiring will probably take place as soon as the tests are scored, and hopefully your name will be among those selected. If not, your name will remain on the register, and the next time positions open up, the postal facility or district that tested you will turn to that register for its next group of applicants.

It's important to remember that names on the register are ranked by score. When a postal facility takes names from a register, it starts at the top and moves down through the list. Let's say a post office has ten positions to fill. It may take 50 names off the register to start the selection process with. The person ranked 51st won't even be considered, no matter what his or her other qualifications. However, if the post office goes through those 50 names and finds it needs still more applicants to fill those or other positions, it will start with number 51, even two years later. Also, as mentioned earlier, keep in mind that veterans with compensable disabilities who passed the exam are ranked against each other, and their names are placed on top of the entire register, before all other applicants. The bottom line is, it's super-important to score as high as possible; even one point can make a difference.

If You're Selected from the Register

If your name is selected from the register, you will receive an application package from the postal facility that will be evaluating your suitability for employment. This package will inform you of the position you are being considered for and will include a four-page Application for Employment (PS Form 2591). If you're being considered for a position that requires driving, you'll also receive a form to detail your driving history.

The application package will tell you the category of employment for which you are being evaluated. Generally, entry-level applicants are hired for positions that are Part-Time Flexible, or "Flexis," as they're called. Part-Time Flexible positions are just that, part-time; you won't be guaranteed 40 hours a week, but many Flexis work that and more. Part-Time Flexible employees bid, based on seniority and performance, for Part-Time Regular and Full-Time Regular positions (for more information, see the section on employment categories in Chapter 1).

The Application for Employment asks for basic information (name, address, etc.), as well as for your education and employment history. In addition, the form asks you to answer brief questions about your personal history, including whether or not you have a criminal record and are currently using any illegal drugs. Be sure to complete the form completely and return it to the postal facility to which you are applying. Above all, answer all questions <u>honestly</u>, as this form will be used in the USPS's suitability screening, outlined below.

STEP FOUR: SUITABILITY & SELECTION

Once the USPS has put out the word and *recruited* applicants, once it has screened the basic skills of those applicants and narrowed the group through an *examination*, and once the names of those who have passed the examination have been ranked on a *register*, it's time to evaluate the *suitability* of those applicants.

As the final step of the hiring process, the postal facility considering you for employment must determine your ability to become part of a team and your fit with the tasks and duties of a postal worker. To do this, the USPS has developed a three-stage process:

- Suitability
- Selection
- Appointment

By evaluating applicants all the way up to a job offer and even into the early days of employment, the suitability screening process helps ensure that the USPS will continue to be able to meet its legally mandated duties of protecting the mail and its own high delivery standards by hiring the best people for the job.

Suitability

After receiving your completed application, the personnel office of the postal facility that is considering you for employment will review your application and begin a **Background Investigation**. As part of this investigation, the personnel department will contact former places of employment and schools you have attended to determine what kind of worker you have been and what kind of employee you will be. In addition the department does a criminal records check and military records check, and verifies your citizenship/resident alien status.

In this process there are no "automatic" disqualifiers; however, because the USPS is legally bound to protect the security of the mail, a violent or criminal past, a poor work record, or previous drug use may be of concern to the hiring department. The USPS needs reliable persons to make sure the millions of pieces of mail that are handled every day get to their destinations. If you have shown yourself to be unreliable through past behavior, you may have difficulty finding employment with the USPS.

At the same time, problems in the past don't necessarily put you out of the running for a job with the USPS. For instance, the Drug Abuse Offense and Treatment Act of 1972 ensures that no person may be denied federal employment on the sole basis of prior drug use. Although the USPS is not bound by this act, it has enacted policies in line with it and recognizes that many drug users can recover and become productive members of society. What is most important, however, is that you answer all questions on the Application for Employment honestly. Discrepancies between your answers and the truth will only make you look worse.

In addition to the background investigation, the hiring postal facility will ask you in for a **Personal Interview**. This face-to-face meeting is an opportunity for the hiring personnel to get to know you and, of course, to further evaluate your suitability for postal employment. This is your opportunity to shine, to let the USPS know why you want to work for them and why you think you're right for the job. You and the interviewer will also go over any questions that have come up regarding your application and background investigation and any discrepancies between the two.

As with the background investigation, honesty is the best policy in the personal interview. Telling an interviewer what you think he or she wants to hear will probably come across as false. Be confident and be yourself; the interviewer wants to get to know you.

After the personal interview, you may be required to pass a **Physical Agility Test**. While tests for different positions vary, remember that postal work can be arduous. Standing or walking for hours, carrying heavy sacks of mail, and moving containers all require physical strength and stamina (to familiarize yourself with the duties specific to the different entry-level jobs, read the job descriptions on page 16 in Chapter 1). If you can comfortably lift 70 pounds and have a full range of motion in your fingers and limbs, you should be ready for the test. It's a good idea, however, to contact your local personnel office once you have received your application package to get the specific requirements for the position you are being considered for.

Finally, you will be required to pass a **Drug Test**. Failure to pass the drug test may result in disqualification from the selection process.

Selection

The background investigation, personal interview, physical ability test, and drug test are all used by the hiring facility to judge your suitability for employment with the USPS. Once an applicant has been determined to be suitable, he or she is selected for employment, meaning that they are given a conditional offer of employment, the condition being a satisfactory medical review.

In accordance with the Rehabilitation Act of 1973, the USPS cannot make any examination of your medical state until a job offer has been made. Therefore, once you have passed all stages of the hiring process and have been found to be otherwise suitable, you will be offered employment on the condition you are medically fit to accept it. The **Medical Examination**, separate from the physical agility test, is used to confirm your ability to withstand the hard work often required of postal employees. Carriers must walk several miles every day, mail sorters must be able to hear over bustling machinery—like a general physical, the medical examination gauges your overall physical health and your fitness for postal employment.

Appointment

Once you have passed the medical examination and have fulfilled the condition of your offer of employment, you will be appointed to a position with the USPS. As the first order of business, all postal employees are required to take an oath of office. Next up is Employee Orientation, a period usually lasting a few days, in which you'll learn about postal policy, including attendance, pay schedules, and other rules.

After the orientation period you will report to your work location and begin on-the-job training. You'll work under supervision, and your daily duties will be explained to you. If the position for which you've been hired requires special skills, you'll receive that training first and then move on to your work location.

During your initial appointment, your performance will be evaluated as a continuation of the suitability screening process. In addition, your fingerprints will be submitted to the Office of Personnel Management for a special agency check to make sure nothing was missed during the background investigation. As you gain experience and seniority, you'll be able to bid for better shifts or other positions, including full-time regular positions.

THE HIRING PROCESS REVISITED

The hiring process at the USPS is a tough one. Much effort is made to ensure that the most suitable individuals are hired. That means that a lot of people are screened out, and only the best of the bunch are left.

To do this, the USPS must first *recruit* applicants, through newspaper announcements or Job Information Lines. Second, those applicants must take and pass an *examination* to show they have the basic skills required of postal employees. Those individuals that pass the examination are ranked on a *register,* in order of score. Applicants are chosen from the register, starting from the top, and their *suitability* for postal employment is

determined in a three-stage process: suitability, selection, and appointment.

This process ensures that the USPS can continue to meet its high service and delivery standards. To make sure you're among those that make it, you need to be prepared. As you read through the rest of this book, you may want to return to this chapter and read through it again to keep clear what will be expected of you in the hiring process. Going into the hiring process with confidence will put you, and your prospective employer, at ease.

It's important to remember that no matter how much confidence or skill you may have, no one will ever get to see it if you don't score well on the exam. To get the job, you need to be considered; to be considered, you need to score high! Chapters 5–11 will help you score your best on the 470 Battery Examination.

The final section of this chapter tells you about other opportunities with the USPS that you should know about.

OTHER OPPORTUNITIES

Besides the seven major entry-level jobs discussed in Chapter 1 that are the focus of this book, many other employment opportunities are available to the entry-level applicant at the USPS. Some of these positions require tests other than the 470 Battery Examination but otherwise follow the same hiring process. Some positions require no testing at all and have their own hiring procedures. The following sections present three alternative paths to employment with the USPS that the reader should be familiar with:

- Casual Employment
- Rural Carrier and Rural Carrier Associate
- Remote Encoding Centers and other Administrative Positions

These positions may or may not be available in your specific location. The list of postal district phone numbers and addresses at the end of this chapter will help you identify the opportunities that *are* available in your area.

CASUAL EMPLOYMENT

One of the most overlooked opportunities with the USPS is Casual Employment. Officially categorized as part of the USPS's supplemental workforce, Casual Employees fill short-term demands in postal facilities all over the U.S.

Casual Employees are limited to one 90-day period of employment, plus an additional 21-day period during the Christmas season, per calendar year. However, many "casuals" string appointments together for a full year, working from July–December (a 90-day appointment), through Christmas (a 21-day appointment), and then January–June (a 90-day appointment in new calendar year). Hours worked are dependent upon need; however, many casuals work the equivalent of full time for their entire appointment.

While these positions offer no benefits and no guarantee of hours, they are an opportunity to take seriously. Often a test may not be open in a given district, yet a significant number of casual positions are open. A casual position is an opportunity to gain valuable experience with the USPS and to get the inside word on future opportunities. While former Casual Employees gain no official preference in the hiring process, a boss usually remembers a good employee and working as a casual may be an opportunity to get yourself remembered. Further, many individuals find the flexibility of Casual Employment—a few months on, a few months off—fits their schedule perfectly.

Casual Employees are usually hired directly from the public, with openings being announced on local Job Information Lines or in Employment Offices. Occasionally, to fill demand, a postal facility may turn to its register of applicants to recruit casuals, meaning that individuals awaiting review may find temporary employment as casuals while continuing to have their name on an active register. There are no tests or examinations for Casual Employment, unless specific skills are required. If the position requires driving, for example, you'll need a valid driver's license and a clean driving record.

To find our about Casual Employment opportunities in your area, check the listings at your local post office or call your district's Job Information Line.

RURAL CARRIER AND RURAL CARRIER ASSOCIATE

The Rural Carrier position is held by many to be one of the most desirable positions available with the USPS. Away from the hustle and bustle of the city, the Rural Carrier spends many hours alone, traversing the countryside, breathing in fresh air, delivering mail door to door (see the Job Descriptions section of Chapter 1 for a rundown on what the Rural Carrier's job entails).

However, the road to becoming a Rural Carrier is not an easy one. First, you must become a Rural Carrier Associate (RCA), a non-career appointment, whose primary duty is to provide relief to Rural Carriers for vacations, holidays, and illnesses. Many RCAs, as they are known, work just one or two days a week, filling in for other Rural Carriers as the need arises. After one year of employment as an RCA, you become eligible to bid for the Career position of Rural Carrier. However, this bidding process is based on seniority. If a route opens up, Rural Carriers from other routes have the first opportunity to bid on the open route; then RCAs can bid, in order of seniority. This highly desirable position requires a commitment, and sometimes a bit of a wait, especially for the more desirable routes, where the line of interested parties can be quite long.

Because of the commitment, and because of the irregular hours, the recruiting for RCAs is often more active than for other positions with the USPS. As this book goes to press, there are over 70 locations across the country that have openings for RCAs. The hiring process is the same as for the other major entry-level jobs. The required test is the 460 Examination, which is *identical* to the 470 Battery Examination, but because of the special nature of the RCA position it is classified separately.

To find out about RCA opportunities in your area, check the listings at your local post office or call the Job Information Line for your district.

ADMINISTRATIVE POSITIONS

The second largest group of entry-level postal positions, after the 470 Battery Examination positions, is a group known as the Administrative Positions, all of which require passing a separate exam: the Clerical Abilities, or 710, Examination. These positions which are clerical in nature, include Data Conversion Operator, Clerk-Stenographer, and Clerk-Typist.

Apart from the exam, the hiring process for administrative positions is the same as for the 470 Battery Examination positions. The Clerical Abilities (710) Examination tests your skills in the following areas:

- **Clerical Aptitude**—insert names and/or numbers alphabetically or numerically into lists provided
- **Address Checking**—compare three addresses or names to see if they are alike or different (similar to the "Address Checking" section of the 470 Battery Examination)
- **Spelling**—choose the correctly spelled version of a word from a list of five options
- **Math**—perform mathematical computations: addition, subtraction, multiplication, and division

- **Verbal Abilities**—follow directions (similar to the "Following Oral Directions" section of the 470 Battery Examination)
- **Vocabulary**—determine the meaning of a particular word in a sentence
- **Reading Comprehension**—read a paragraph and answer questions based on what you have read

As with the 470 Battery Examination, when you apply for an administrative position you will receive a set of sample questions to help you prepare. With sample questions in hand, and having pinpointed the opportunities in your area with the help of this book, administrative positions are an option that you may want to consider. One last pointer: many of these positions require a typing test. Don't show up without preparing; sit yourself down in front of a computer or typewriter!

Remote Encoding Centers: An Opportunity Worth Exploring

An emerging opportunity available to those interested in the administrative side of postal work is the result of a new technology being implemented by the USPS called "remote encoding." Currently, as discussed in Chapter 1, optical recognition computers read mail as it is sorted and apply bar-codes to individual pieces of mail. However, many handwritten addresses can't be read by computers—that's where Remote Encoding Centers (RECs) come in.

Data Conversion Operators located at an REC read the handwritten addresses, which are piped in over computer lines from sorting facilities, and electronically send the appropriate bar-code back to the post office, where a sticker is then applied to the piece of mail. Data Conversion Operators must be able to quickly read an address, and then type into a computer terminal the correct information.

As this book goes to press, many Remote Encoding Centers are still hiring as they gear up for capacity. As computers become more advanced and are able to read more handwritten addresses, the USPS hopes the need for such centers will diminish. For this reason, hiring at these centers is part career employee and part long-term temporary or transitional employee. Nevertheless, RECs constitute an immediate employment opportunity worth exploring!

USPS POSTAL AREAS AND POSTAL DISTRICTS

What follows is a list of every postal district in the U.S., organized alphabetically by state within each postal *area* (you'll remember, from Chapter 1, that the U.S. is divided into ten postal areas which consist of approximately eight postal districts each). This list is a valuable resource for anyone searching for employment with the USPS, as it provides you with the contact information you need to initiate a job search, especially Job Information Lines.

The postal districts listed below usually encompass several cities, but have their central office in a major city within the district. To find your postal district, look through the list below to find the postal area that includes your state (or appropriate portion of your state), and then look for the district in which you fall, usually centered in the nearest major city. For example, if you live in Ft. Smith, Arkansas, you'll find the state of Arkansas listed under the Southwest Area; the Arkansas Customer Service District, centered in Little Rock, is the postal district that includes Ft. Smith.

ALLEGHENY AREA
The Allegheny Area includes Delaware (included in the South Jersey Customer Service District), southern New Jersey, Ohio, and Pennsylvania.

South Jersey Customer Service District
501 Benigno Blvd.
Bellmawr, NJ 08099
Job Information Line
609-933-4314

Akron Customer Service District
Employment Office
675 Wolfledges Pkwy.
Akron, OH 44309
330-996-9501
Job Information Line
330-996-9530

Cincinnati Customer Service District
Personnel Services
1591 Dalton Ave., 2nd Floor
Cincinnati, OH 45234
516-684-5451

Cleveland Customer Service District
Examinations Office
2200 Orange Ave.
Cleveland, OH 44101
216-443-4231
Job Information Line
216-443-4878

Columbus Customer Service District
Personnel Office
850 Twin Rivers Dr.
Columbus, OH 43216
614-469-4357
Job Information Line
614-469-4356

Erie Customer Service District
Examinations Office
2108 East 38th St.
Erie, PA 16515
814-898-7323
Job Information Line
814-899-0354

Harrisburg Customer Service District
Personnel Office
1425 Crooked Hill Rd.
Harrisburg, PA 17107
717-257-2250
Job Information Line
717-257-22191

Lancaster Customer Service District
Personnel Office
1905 Old Philadelphia Pike
Lancaster, PA 17602
717-390-7460
Job Information Line
717-390-7400

Philadelphia Customer Service District
Examinations Office
2970 Market St., Room 216
Philadelphia, PA 19104
215-895-8830
Job Information Line
800-276-5627

Pittsburgh Customer Service District
Human Resources Department
1001 California Ave.
Pittsburgh, PA 15290
412-359-7688
Job Information Line
412-359-7516

GREAT LAKES AREA

The Great Lakes Area includes Illinois, Indiana, and Michigan.

Central Illinois Customer Service District
Examinations Office
6801 West 73rd St.
Bedford Park, IL 60499
708-563-7493
Job Information Line
708-563-7496

North Illinois Customer Service District
Personnel Services
500 East Fullerton Ave.
Carol Stream, IL 60199
630-260-5153
Job Information Line
630-260-5200

Chicago Customer Service District
Personnel Office
433 West Van Buren St., Room 40202A
Chicago, IL 60607
312-983-8542

Greater Indiana Customer Service District
Personnel Office
3939 Biencennes Rd.
Indianapolis, IN 46298
317-870-8551
Job Information Line
317-870-8500

Detroit Customer Service District
Personnel Office
1401 West Fort St., Room 201
Detroit, MI 48223-9992
313-226-8259
Job Information Line
313-226-8490

Greater Michigan Customer Service District
Personnel Office
222 Michigan St., NW
Grand Rapids, MI 49599
616-776-1426
Job Information Line
616-776-1835

Royal Oak Customer Service District
Personnel Office
200 West 2nd St.
Royal Oak, MI 48068
810-546-7106
Job Information Line
810-546-7104

MID-ATLANTIC AREA

The Mid-Atlantic Area includes Kentucky, Maryland, North Carolina, South Carolina, Virginia, Washington D.C., and West Virgina.

Kentuckiana Customer Service District
Human Resources
1420 Gardiner Ln., Room 320
Louisville, KY 40231
502-454-1817
Job Information Line
502-454-1625

Baltimore Customer Service District
Personnel Office
900 East Fayette St.
Baltimore, MD 21233
410-347-4278
Job Information Line
410-347-4320

Mid-Carolinas Customer Service District
Personnel Services
2901 South Interstate 85 Service Road
Charolette, NC 28228
704-393-4495
Job Information Line
704-393-4490

Greensboro Customer Service District
Personnel Office
900 Market St., Room 232
Greensboro, NC 27498
910-669-1214
Job Information Line
910-271-5573

Columbia Customer Service District
Hiring and Testing Office
2001 Dixiana Rd.
Casey, SC 29292
803-926-6437
Job Information Line
803-926-6400

Northern Virginia Customer Service District
Personnel Office
84-09 Lee Highway
Merrifield, VA 22081
703-698-6438
Job Information Line
703-698-6561

Richmond Customer Service District
Personnel Office
1801 Brook Rd.
Richmond, VA 23232
804-775-6196
Job Information Line
804-321- 5927

Capital Customer Service District
Hiring and Testing Office
3300 V St., NE
Washington, DC 20002
202-523-2940
Job Information Line
202-636-1537

Appalachian Customer Service District
Personnel Office
10002 Lee St., E
Charleston, WV 25301
304-340-2742
Job Information Line
304-357-0648

MIDWEST AREA

The Midwest Area includes Iowa, Kansas (included in
the Central Plains Customer Service District in
Nebraska), Minnesota, Missouri, Nebraska, North
Dakota, South Dakota, and Wisconsin.

Hawkeye Customer Service District
Employment Office
1165 2nd Ave.
Des Moines, IA 50318
515-251-2201
Job Information Line
515-251-2061

Minneapolis Customer Service District
Personnel Office
180 East Kellog Blvd.
St. Paul, MN 554101
612-293-3036
Job Information Line
612-293-3364

Mid-America Customer Service District
Employment Office
315 W Pershing Rd., Room 576
Kansas City, MO 64108
816-374-9310
Job Information Line
816-374-9346

Gateway Customer Service District
Employment Office
1720 Market St., Room 1003
St. Louis, MO 63115
314-436-3852
Job Information Line
314-436-3855

Central Plains Customer Service District
Personnel Office
1124 Pacific St., Room 325
Omaha NE 68124
402-348-2506
Job Information Line
402-348-2523

Dakotas Customer Service District
Personnel Office
320 South Second Ave.
Sioux Falls, SD 57104
605-357-5032

Milwaukee Customer Service District
Personnel Services
340 West Saint Paul Ave., 5th Floor
Milwaukee, WI 53203
414-287-1834
Job Information Line
414-287-1835

NEW YORK METRO AREA

The New York Metro Area includes Long Island, cent-tral and northern New Jersey, New York City and Westchester County, and Puerto Rico.

Central New Jersey Customer Service District
Personnel Office
21 Kilmer Rd.
Edison, NJ 08899
908-819-3272

Northern New Jersey Customer Service District
Newark Main Post Office
2 Federal Sq.
Newark, NJ 07102
201-693-5200

Triboro Customer Service District
Personnel Office
142-02 20th Ave.
Flushing, NY 11351
718-321-5170
Job Information Line
718-529-7000

Long Island Customer Service District
Examinations Office
1377 Motor Pkwy.
Hauppauge, NY 11760
516-582-7416
Job Information Line
516-582-7530

New York City Customer Service District
(Manhattan and Bronx)
Examinations Office
421 8th Ave.
New York, NY 10199
212-330-3600

Westchester Customer Service District
Examinations Office
1000 Westchester Ave.
White Plains, NY 10610
914-697-7190

Caribbean Customer Service District
Personnel Office
585 Roosevelt Ave.
San Juan, PR 00936
787-767-3351

NORTHEAST AREA

The Northeast Area includes Connecticut, Maine, Massachusetts, New Hampshire, upstate New York, Rhode Island, and Vermont (included in the Spring-field Customer Service District in Massachusetts).

Connecticut Customer Service District
Personnel Office
141 Weston St., Room 235
Hartford, CT 06101
860-524-6110

Maine Customer Service District
Examinations Office
380 Riverside St.
Portland, ME 04103
Job Information Line
207-828-8520

Boston Customer Service District
Human Resources
25 Dorchester Ave.
Boston, MA 02205
617-654-5500
Job Information Line
617-654-5569

Middlesex Central Customer Service District
Personnel Offices
74 Main St.
North Reading, MA 01889
508-664-7634
Job Information Line
508-664-7665

Springfield Customer Service District
Human Resources
1883 Main St.
Springfield, MA 01101
413-785-6263
Job Information Line
413-731-0425

New Hampshire Customer Service District
Personnel Office
955 Goffs Falls Rd.
Manchester, NH 03103
603-644-4061
Job Information Line
603-644-4065

Albany Customer Service District
Personnel Office
30 Old Karner Rd.
Albany, NY 12288
518-452-2450
Job Information Line
518-452-2445

Western NY Customer Service District
Personnel Office
1200 William St.
Buffalo, NY 14240
716-846-2470
Job Information Line
716-846-2478

Providence Customer Service District
Personnel Office
24 Corliss St.
Providence, RI 02904
401-276-6845
Job Information Line
401-276-6844

PACIFIC AREA

The Pacific Area includes California and Hawaii.

Long Beach Customer Service District
Examinations Office
300 Long Beach Blvd.
Long Beach, CA 90802
310-983-3072
Job Information Line
310-435-4529

Los Angeles Customer Service District
Personnel Office
7001 South Central Ave.
Los Angeles, CA 90052
213-586-1340
Job Information Line
213-586-1351

Oakland Customer Service District
Personnel Office
1675 7th St.
Oakland, CA 94615
510-874-8344
Job Information Line
510-251-3040

San Diego Customer Service District
Personnel Office
11251 Rancho Carmel Dr.
San Diego, CA 92199
619-674-0430
Job Information Line
619-221-3351

San Francisco Customer Service District
Personnel Office
1300 Evans Ave.
San Francisco, CA 94188
415-550-5014
Job Information Line
415-550-5534

San Jose Customer Service District
Personnel Office
1750 Lundy Ave.
San Jose, CA 95101
408-437-6925
Job Information Line
408-437-6986

Santa Ana Customer Service District
Human Resources
3101 West Sunflower Ave.
Santa Ana, CA 92799
714-662-6384
Job Information Line
714-662-6375

Van Nuys Customer Service District
Personnel Office
28201 Franklin Pkwy.
Santa Clarita, CA 91383
805-294-7040
Job Information Line
805-294-7680

Sacramento Customer Service District
Personnel Office
3775 Industrial Blvd.
West Sacramento, CA 95799
916-373-8686
Job Information Line
916-373-8448

Honolulu Customer Service District
Human Resources
3600 Aolele St.
Honolulu, HI 96824
808-423-3712
Job Information Line
808-423-3690

SOUTHEAST AREA

The Southeat Area includes Alabama, Florida, Georgia, Mississippi, and Tennessee.

Alabama Customer Service District
Personnel Office
351 24th St., N
Room 273
Birmingham, AL 35203
205-521-0251
Job Information Line
205-521-0214

North Florida Customer Service District
Personnel Services
1100 Kings Rd.
Jacksonville, FL 32203
904-359-2921
Job Information Line
904-359-2737

Central Florida Customer Service District
Personnel Office
800 Rinehart Rd.
Mid Florida, Fl 32799
407-444-2012
Job Information Line
407-444-2029

South Florida Customer Service District
Personnel Office
2200 North West 72nd Ave.
Pembroke Pines, FL 33082
305-470-0705
Job Information Line
305-470-0412

Sun Coast Customer Service District
Personnel Services
5201 West Spruce St.
Tampa, FL 33630
813-877-0318
Job Information Line
813-877-0381

Atlanta Customer Service District
Personnel Office
3900 Crown Rd.
Atlanta, GA 30304
404-765-7560

South Georgia Customer Service District
Examinations Office
451 College St., Room 219
Macon, GA 31213
912-752-8467
Job Information Line
912-752-8465

Mississippi Customer Service District
Personnel
405 East South St.
Jackson, MS 39201
601-351-7270
Job Information Line
601-351-7099

Tennessee Customer Service District
Human Resources
525 Royal Pkwy., Room 207
Nashville, TN 37229
615-885-9212
Job Information Line
615-885-9190

SOUTHWEST AREA

The Southwest Area includes Arkansas, Louisiana, Oklahoma, and Texas.

Arkansas Customer Service District
Human Resources
4700 East McCain Blvd.
Little Rock, AR, 72205
501-945-6665

New Orleans Customer Service District
Personnel Services
701 Loyola Ave.
New Orleans, LA 70113
504-589-1171
Job Information Line
504-589-1660

Oklahoma Customer Service District
Personnel Office
3030 NorthWest Expressway St.
Oklahoma City, OK 73198
405-553-6172
Job Information Line
405-553-1967

Dallas Customer Service District
Personnel Office
951 West Bethel Rd.
Coppell, TX 75099
972-393-6780
Job Information Line
214-760-4531

Fort Worth Customer Service District
Human Resources
4600 Mark IV Pkwy.
Fort Worth, TX 76161
817-317-3350
Job Information Line
817-317-3366

Houston Customer Service District
Personnel Services
1002 Washington Ave.
Houston, TX 77202
713-226-3917
Job Information Line
713-226-3872

San Antonio Customer Service District
Personnel Office
10410 Perrinbeital Rd.
San Antonio, TX 78284
210-657-8412
Job Information Line
210-657-8400

WESTERN AREA

The Western Area includes Alaska, Arizona, Colorado, Montana, New Mexico, Nevada, Oregon, Utah, Washington, and Wyoming (included in the Denver Customer Service District in Colorado).

Anchorage Customer Service District
Personnel Office
41-41 Postmark Drive
Anchorage, AK 99599
907-266-3255
Job Information Line
907-266-3228

Phoenix Customer Service District
Personnel Office
14-41 East Buckeye Rd.
Phoenix, AZ 85026
602-223-3631
Job Information Line
602-223-3624

Denver Customer Service District
Human Resources
7500 East 53rd Pl.
Denver, CO 80266
303-853-6132
Job Information Line
303-853-6060

Billings Customer Service District
Personnel Office
841 South 26th St.
Billings, MT 59101
406-255-6427
Job Information Line
406-657-5763

Albuquerque Customer Service District
Personnel Office
1135 Broadway Blvd., NE
Room 230
Albuquerque, NM 87102
505-245-9518
Job Information Line
505-245-9517

Las Vegas Customer Service District
Personnel Office
1001 East Sunset Rd.
Las Vegas, NV 89199
702-361-9375
Job Information Line
702-361-9385

Portland Customer Service District
Personnel Office
715 NW Hoyt St.
Portland, OR 97208
503-294-2277
Job Information Line
503-294-2270

Salt Lake City Customer Service District
Personnel Office
1760 West 2100, S
Salt Lake City, UT 84199
801-974-2210
Job Information Line
801-974-2209

Seattle Customer Service District
Personnel Office
412 First Ave., N
Seattle, WA 98109
206-442-6236
Job Information Line
206-442-6240

Spokane Customer Service District
Personnel Office
707 West Main Ave.
Spokane, WA 99299
509-626-6824
Job Information Line
509-626-6896

C·H·A·P·T·E·R

EASYSMART TEST PREPARATION SYSTEM

3

CHAPTER SUMMARY

The Postal Worker Exam is one tough nut to crack. It demands a lot of preparation if you want to be one of the few who achieve a top score and reach the next stage in the hiring process. The EasySmart Test Preparation System, developed exclusively for LearningExpress by leading test experts, gives you the discipline and attitude you need to be a winner.

 irst, the bad news: Taking the Postal Worker Exam is no picnic, and neither is getting ready for it. Your future career as a postal worker depends on your getting a high score, but there are all sorts of pitfalls that can keep you from doing your best on this all-important exam. Here are some of the obstacles that can stand in the way of your success:

- Being unfamiliar with the unusual format of this exam
- Being paralyzed by test anxiety
- Leaving your preparation to the last minute
- Not preparing at all!
- Not knowing vital test-taking skills: how to pace yourself through the exam, how to use the process of elimination, and when to guess

- Not being in tip-top mental and physical shape
- Messing up on test day by arriving late at the test site, having to work on an empty stomach, or shivering through the exam because the room is cold

What's the common denominator in all these test-taking pitfalls? One word: *control*. Who's in control, you or the exam?

Now the good news: The EasySmart Test Preparation System puts *you* in control. In just nine easy-to-follow steps, you will learn everything you need to know to make sure that *you* are in charge of your preparation and your performance on the exam. *Other* test-takers may let the test get the better of them; *other* test-takers may be unprepared or out of shape, but not *you*. *You* will have taken all the steps you need to take to get a high score on the Postal Worker Exam.

Here's how the EasySmart Test Preparation System works: Nine easy steps lead you through everything you need to know and do to get ready to master your exam. Each of the steps listed below includes both reading about the step and one or more activities. It's important that you do the activities along with the reading, or you won't be getting the full benefit of the system. Each step tells you approximately how much time that step will take you to complete.

Step 1. Get Information	30 minutes
Step 2. Conquer Test Anxiety	20 minutes
Step 3. Make a Plan	50 minutes
Step 4. Learn to Manage Your Time	10 minutes
Step 5. Learn to Use the Process of Elimination	20 minutes
Step 6. Know When to Guess	20 minutes
Step 7. Reach Your Peak Performance Zone	10 minutes
Step 8. Get Your Act Together	10 minutes
Step 9. Do It!	5 minutes
Total	**3 hours**

We estimate that working through the entire system will take you approximately three hours, though it's perfectly OK if you work faster or slower than the time estimates assume. If you can take a whole afternoon or evening, you can work through the whole EasySmart Test Preparation System in one sitting. Otherwise, you can break it up, and do just one or two steps a day for the next several days. It's up to you—remember, *you're* in control.

STEP 1: GET INFORMATION

Time to complete: 30 minutes

Activities: Read Chapter 4, "Sample Answer Sheet and Questions" and take a Pop Quiz on the content of Test 470

Knowledge is power. The first step in the EasySmart Test Preparation System is finding out everything you can about the Postal Worker Exam. Once you have your information, the next steps in the EasySmart Test Preparation System will show you what to do about it.

Part A: Straight Talk About Test 470

Why do you have to take this exam, anyway? The fact is that way too many people want a secure job with the USPS, far more than can ever be hired—far more, in fact, than the USPS can even afford to process in a conventional application-resume-interview process. The USPS needs a way to dramatically cut the number of applicants they have to consider. That's where the exam comes in.

Like any civil service test, Test 470 is a screening device. It enables the USPS to rank candidates according to their exam score and then to pull only from the top of that list to get applicants to go through the rest of the selection process. Since Test 470 assesses job-related skills—abilities you actually have to have to be a good postal worker—there's a rough correlation between how well a person does on the test and how good a postal employee that person will make. But it's only a rough correlation. There are all sorts of things a written exam like this can't test: whether you can get along with the public, fellow employees, and supervisors; whether you're likely to show up on time or call in sick a lot; and so on. But those kinds of things are hard to evaluate, while whether or not you fill in the right circle on a bubble answer sheet is easy to evaluate. So the USPS, like most government agencies, uses an exam simply to cut the number of applicants it has to deal with.

This information should help you keep some perspective on the exam and what it means. Don't make the mistake of thinking that your score determines who you are or how smart you are or whether you'll make a good employee, with the USPS or elsewhere. All it shows is whether you can fill in the little circles correctly. Of course, whether you can fill in the little circles correctly is still vitally important to you! After all, your chances of being hired depend on your getting a top score. And that's why you're here—using the EasySmart Test Preparation System to achieve control over Test 470.

Part B: What's on the Test

Test 470 consists of four parts, each of which is timed separately:

- **Part A, Address Checking:** 95 questions in 6 minutes
- **Part B, Memory for Addresses:** 88 questions in 5 minutes
- **Part C, Number Series:** 24 questions in 20 minutes
- **Part D, Following Oral Directions:** 25 questions in about 20 minutes

Stop here and read Chapter 4, which consists of instructions on filling out the sample answer sheet, as well as sample questions and answers for Test 470, all official materials supplied by the USPS. This will give you a good handle on the kinds of questions you'll be facing. After you read Chapter 4—and why not answer the sample questions there while you're at it?—take the Pop Quiz on Test 470, at the bottom of this page.

STEP 2: CONQUER TEST ANXIETY

Time to complete: 20 minutes

Activity: Take the Test Stress Test

Having complete information about the exam is the first step in getting control of the exam. Next, you have to overcome one of the biggest obstacles to test success: test anxiety. Test anxiety can not only impair your performance on the exam itself; it can even keep you from preparing! In Step 2, you'll learn stress management techniques that will help you succeed on Test 470. Learn these strategies now, and practice them as you work through the exams in this book, so they'll be second nature to you by exam day.

COMBATING TEST ANXIETY

The first thing you need to know is that a little test anxiety is a good thing. Everyone gets nervous before a big exam—and if that nervousness motivates you to prepare thoroughly, so much the better. It's said that Sir Laurence Olivier, one of the foremost British actors of this century, threw up before every performance. His stage fright didn't impair his performance; in fact, it probably gave him a little extra edge—just the kind of edge you need to do well, whether on a stage or in an examination room.

On the next page is the Test Stress Test. Stop here and answer the questions on that page, to find out whether your level of test anxiety is something you should worry about.

Pop Quiz on Test 470

The three columns below show the four parts of the Postal Worker Exam, the numbers of questions (lower-case letters), and the time limits (capital letters). In the blank before the name of each part of the exam, write the two letters that correspond to the matching number of questions and time limit.

1. Number Series   **a.** 95 questions   **A.** 20 minutes
2. Address Checking   **b.** 25 questions   **B.** 6 minutes
3. Following Oral Directions   **c.** 24 questions   **C.** about 20 minutes
4. Memory for Addresses   **d.** 88 questions   **D.** 5 minutes

Answers

How did you do? If you missed any of these questions, go back and review Chapter 4: 1. c. A.; 2. a. B.; 3. b. C.; 4. d. D.

Test Stress Test

You only need to worry about test anxiety if it is extreme enough to impair your performance. The following questionnaire will provide a diagnosis of your level of test anxiety. In the blank before each statement, write the number that most accurately describes your experience.

0 = Never   1 = Once or twice   2 = Sometimes   3 = Often

_____ I have gotten so nervous before an exam that I simply put down the books and didn't study for it.

_____ I have experienced disabling physical symptoms such as vomiting and severe headaches because I was nervous about an exam.

_____ I have simply not showed up for an exam because I was scared to take it.

_____ I have experienced dizziness and disorientation while taking an exam.

_____ I have had trouble filling in the little circles because my hands were shaking too hard.

_____ I have failed an exam because I was too nervous to complete it.

_____ **Total: Add up the numbers in the blanks above.**

Your Test Stress Score

Here are the steps you should take, depending on your score. If you scored:

- **Below 3,** your level of test anxiety is nothing to worry about; it's probably just enough to give you that little extra edge.
- **Between 3 and 6,** your test anxiety may be enough to impair your performance, and you should practice the stress management techniques listed in this section to try to bring your test anxiety down to manageable levels.
- **Above 6,** your level of test anxiety is a serious concern. In addition to practicing the stress management techniques listed in this section, you may want to seek additional, personal help. Call your local high school or community college and ask for the academic counselor. Tell the counselor that you have a level of test anxiety that sometimes keeps you from being able to take the exam. The counselor may be willing to help you or may suggest someone else you should talk to.

Stress Management Before the Test

If you feel your level of anxiety getting the best of you in the weeks before the test, here is what you need to do to bring the level down again:

- **Get prepared.** There's nothing like knowing what to expect and being prepared for it to put you in control of test anxiety. That's why you're reading this book. Use it faithfully, and remind yourself that you're better prepared than most of the people taking the test.

- **Practice self-confidence.** A positive attitude is a great way to combat test anxiety. This is no time to be humble or shy. Stand in front of the mirror and say to your reflection, "I'm prepared. I'm full of self-confidence. I'm going to ace this test. I know I can do it." Say it into a tape recorder and play it back once a day. If you hear it often enough, you'll believe it.

- **Fight negative messages.** Every time someone starts telling you how hard the exam is or how it's almost impossible to get a high score, start telling them your self-confidence messages above. If the someone with the negative messages is *you*, telling yourself *you don't do well on exams, you just can't do this*, don't listen. Turn on your tape recorder and listen to your self-confidence messages.

- **Visualize.** Imagine yourself walking your route as a postal carrier or operating a sorting machine. Think of yourself coming home with your first paycheck as a USPS employee and taking your family or friends out to celebrate. Visualizing success can help make it happen—and it reminds you of why you're going to all this work in preparing for the exam.

- **Exercise.** Physical activity helps calm your body down and focus your mind. Besides, being in good physical shape can actually help you do well on the exam. Go for a run, lift weights, go swimming—and do it regularly.

Stress Management on Test Day

There are several ways you can bring down your level of test anxiety on test day. They'll work best if you practice them in the weeks before the test, so you know which ones work best for you.

- **Deep breathing.** Take a deep breath while you count to five. Hold it for a count of one, then let it out on a count of five. Repeat several times.

- **Move your body.** Try rolling your head in a circle. Rotate your shoulders. Shake your hands from the wrist. Many people find these movements very relaxing.

- **Visualize again.** Think of the place where you are most relaxed: lying on the beach in the sun, walking through the park, or whatever. Now close your eyes and imagine you're actually there. If you practice in advance, you'll find that you only need a few seconds of this exercise to experience a significant increase in your sense of well-being.

When anxiety threatens to overwhelm you right there during the exam, there are still things you can do to manage the stress level:

- **Repeat your self-confidence messages.** You should have them memorized by now. Say them quietly to yourself, and believe them!
- **Visualize one more time.** This time, visualize yourself moving smoothly and quickly through the test answering every question right and finishing just before time is up. Like most visualization techniques, this one works best if you've practiced it ahead of time.
- **Find an easy question.** Skim over the test until you find an easy question, and answer it. Getting even one circle filled in gets you into the test-taking groove.
- **Take a mental break.** Everyone loses concentration once in a while during a long test. It's normal, so you shouldn't worry about it. Instead, accept what has happened. Say to yourself, "Hey, I lost it there for a minute. My brain is taking a break." Put down your pencil, close your eyes, and do some deep breathing for a few seconds. Then you're ready to go back to work.

Try these techniques ahead of time, and see if they don't work for you!

STEP 3: MAKE A PLAN

Time to complete: 50 minutes
Activity: Construct a study plan
Maybe the most important thing you can do to get control of yourself and your exam is to make a study plan. Too many people fail to prepare simply because they fail to plan. Spending hours on the day before the exam poring over sample test questions not only raises your level of test anxiety, it also is simply no substitute for careful preparation and practice over time.

Don't fall into the cram trap. Take control of your preparation time by mapping out a study schedule. On the following pages are four sample schedules, based on the amount of time you have before the Postal Worker Exam. If you're the kind of person who needs deadlines and assignments to motivate you for a project, here they are. If you're the kind of person who doesn't like to follow other people's plans, you can use the suggested schedules here to construct your own.

Even more important than making a plan is making a commitment. You can't improve your memory, speed, and accuracy overnight. You have to set aside some time every day for study and practice. Try for at least 20 minutes a day. Twenty minutes daily will do you much more good than two hours on Saturday.

If you have months before the exam, you're lucky. Don't put off your study until the week before the exam. Start now. A few minutes a day, with half an hour or more on weekends, can make a big difference in your score—and in your chances of getting the job!

SCHEDULE A: THE LEISURE PLAN

If no test has been announced in your postal district, you may have a year or more in which to get ready. This schedule gives you six months to sharpen your skills. If an exam is announced in the middle of your preparation, you can use one of the later schedules to help you compress your study program.

Time	Preparation
First month	Take the first practice exam in Chapter 5. Use your score on each part of the exam to help you decide where to concentrate your study.
Second month	Read Chapter 6, "Address Checking Questions," work through the exercises, and take Sample Address Checking Section 1 (but not 2). Find other people who are preparing for the test and form a study group.
Third month	Take Sample Address Checking Section 2 in Chapter 6. Then read Chapter 7, "Memory for Addresses Questions," work through the exercises, and take Sample Memory for Addresses Section 1 (but not 2).
Fourth month	Take Sample Memory for Addresses Section 2. Then read Chapter 8, "Number Series Questions," work through the exercises, and take the Sample Number Series Section.
Fifth month	Read Chapter 9, "Following Oral Directions," work through the exercises, and take the Sample Following Oral Directions Section.
Sixth month	Take the second practice test in Chapter 10. Use your score to help you decide where to concentrate your efforts this month. Go back to the relevant chapters and try the sample test sections again.
While you're waiting for the exam	Take the third practice test in Chapter 11. Periodically review Chapters 6–9, concentrating on the sections that give you the most trouble.

SCHEDULE B: THE JUST-ENOUGH-TIME PLAN

If you have two or three months before the exam, that should be enough time to prepare for the written test. This schedule assumes exactly two months; stretch it out or compress it if you have more or less time.

Time	Preparation
Exam minus 8 weeks	Take the first practice exam in Chapter 5. Use your score on each part of the exam to help you decide where to concentrate your study.
Exam minus 7 weeks	Read Chapter 6, "Address Checking Questions," work through the exercises, and take Sample Address Checking Section 1 (but not 2).
Exam minus 6 weeks	Take Sample Address Checking Section 2 in Chapter 6. Then read Chapter 7, "Memory for Addresses Questions," work through the exercises, and take Sample Memory for Addresses Section 1 (but not 2).
Exam minus 5 weeks	Take Sample Memory for Addresses Section 2. Then read Chapter 8, "Number Series Questions," work through the exercises, and take the Sample Number Series Section.
Exam minus 4 weeks	Read Chapter 9, "Following Oral Directions," work through the exercises, and take the Sample Following Oral Directions Section.
Exam minus 3 weeks	Take the second practice test in Chapter 10. Use your score to help you decide where to concentrate your efforts this week. Go back to the relevant chapters and try the sample test sections again.
Exam minus 2 weeks	Review Chapters 6–9, concentrating on the *one* section that gives you the most trouble.
Exam minus 1 week	Take the third practice exam in Chapter 11. Review the chapters on the sections of the exam that still give you trouble.
Exam minus 1 day	Relax. Do something unrelated to the postal exam. Eat a good meal and go to bed at your usual time.

SCHEDULE C: MORE STUDY IN LESS TIME

If you have just one month before the exam, you still have enough time for some concentrated study that will help you improve your score. You'll have to work hard, though, to put in enough time to do all the necessary steps.

Time	Preparation
Exam minus 4 weeks	Take the first practice exam in Chapter 5. Read Chapter 6, "Address Checking Questions," and Chapter 7, "Memory for Address Questions." Work through the exercises and take the *first* Sample Section in each chapter.
Exam minus 3 weeks	Take Sample Address Checking Section 2 in Chapter 6 and Sample Memory for Addresses Section 2 in Chapter 7. Read Chapter 8, "Number Series Questions," work through the exercises, and take the Sample Number Series Section.
Exam minus 2 weeks	Read Chapter 9, "Following Oral Directions," work through the exercises, and take the Sample Following Oral Directions section.
Exam minus 1 week	Take the second practice test in Chapter 10. Review the areas where your score is lowest.
Exam minus 3 days	Take the third practice exam in Chapter 11. Choose *one* area to review.
Exam minus 1 day	Relax. Do something unrelated to the exam. Eat a good meal and go to bed at your usual time.

SCHEDULE D: THE CRAM PLAN

If you have two weeks or less before the exam, you really have your work cut out for you. Carve an hour out of your day, *every day,* for study. This schedule assumes you have just two weeks to prepare in; if you have more or less time, you'll have to expand or compress the schedule accordingly.

Time	Preparation
Exam minus 14–12 days	Take the first practice exam in Chapter 5. Read Chapter 6, "Address Checking Questions," work through the exercises, and take Sample Address Checking Sections 1 and 2.
Exam minus 11–10 days	Read Chapter 7, "Memory for Addresses Questions," work through the exercises, and take Sample Memory for Addresses Section 1 (but not 2).
Exam minus 9–8 days	Take Sample Memory for Addresses Section 2 in Chapter 7. Read Chapter 8, "Number Series Questions," work through the exercises, and take the Sample Number Series Section.
Exam minus 7–6 days	Read Chapter 9, "Following Oral Directions," work through the exercises, and take the Sample Following Oral Directions Section.
Exam minus 5–4 days	Take the second practice test in Chapter 10. Review the areas where your score is lowest.
Exam minus 3–2 days	Take the third practice exam in Chapter 11. Choose *one* area to review.
Exam minus 1 day	Relax. Do something unrelated to the exam. Eat a good meal and go to bed at your usual time.

STEP 4: LEARN TO MANAGE YOUR TIME

Time to complete: 10 minutes to read, many hours of practice!
Activities: Practice these strategies as you take the sample tests in this book

Steps 4, 5, and 6 of the EasySmart Test Preparation System put you in charge of your exam by showing you test-taking strategies that work. Practice these strategies as you take the sample tests in this book, and then you'll be ready to use them on test day.

First, you'll take control of your time on the exam. Each of the sections of Test 470 is timed separately, and none of them allows you a whole lot of time. Thus, you should use your time wisely to avoid making errors. The chapters in this book on each part of the exam offer you time-management strategies for that section. Here are some general tips for the whole exam.

- **Listen carefully to directions.** By the time you get to the exam, you should know the directions for all four parts of the test, but listen just in case something has changed. And, of course, in Part D, Following Oral Directions, listening carefully is the whole point.
- **Keep moving.** You don't have time to dither around on one question. If you don't know the answer, skip the question and move on. Circle the number of the question in your test booklet in case you have time to come back to it later.
- **Keep track of your place on the answer sheet.** If you skip a question, make sure you skip on the answer sheet too. Check yourself every 5–10 questions to make sure the question number and the answer sheet number are still the same.
- **Don't rush.** Though you should keep moving, rushing won't help. Try to keep calm and work methodically and quickly.

STEP 5: LEARN TO USE THE PROCESS OF ELIMINATION

Time to complete: 20 minutes
Activity: Use the process of elimination on the practice questions in this section

After time management, your next most important tool for taking control of Test 470 is using the process of elimination wisely. Standard test-taking wisdom says that you should always read all the answer choices before choosing your answer and eliminate wrong answer choices to help you find the right answer. Of course, you don't actually have to read the answer choices on Parts A and B of the postal exam, where the answer choices are always the same: answer A or D for Part A and answers A–E for Part B. Still, you can use the process of elimination on all the parts except Part A, Address Checking. In Part A, since there are only two answer choices, eliminating the wrong answer is the same as finding the right answer!

The process of elimination works to some extent on Part B, Memory for Addresses, and Part D, Following Oral Directions. Where it really pays off is Part C, Number Series.

PROCESS OF ELIMINATION ON PART B

How well you can use the process of elimination on Part B, Memory for Addresses, depends, as you might expect, on how well you managed to memorize the boxes in the first place. If you're confident about the content of all five boxes, you're all set—you won't have to use the process of elimination. But suppose you ran out of time during the memorization segment and really were only able to get the contents of Boxes A, B, and C down cold; you're a little fuzzy on Boxes D and E. (Or maybe you had all five down cold a few minutes ago, but now you're starting to doubt whether you've confused some of the address elements in those last two boxes.)

So then let's say that question 5 is the name Smith. You run through your system of memorization (see Chapter 7) and find that Smith isn't among the names you memorized for Boxes A through C. But you don't know whether it's in Box D or E. You've just used the process of elimination. You know that three of the possible answers are wrong, and only two have the possibility of being right. As you'll see when you read Step 6 on guessing, if you can eliminate even one wrong answer choice, you should go ahead and mark one of the possible answers.

PROCESS OF ELIMINATION ON PART D

On Part D, Following Oral Directions, eliminating wrong answers will really work only if you miss part of the directions but hear the rest—which can happen, since the reader won't repeat the directions.

Suppose you heard part of the directions, and then got busy working on that part and missed the next part. What you see on your worksheet goes like this:

12. C   D   E   B   A

What you hear—with the part you missed indicated by an ellipsis (. . .)—is this:

Look at Line 12. If four is less than three and more than two, circle letter D as in dog. If . . . . Now, on your answer grid, find number 30. Darken the space for the letter you circled.

You were busy figuring out that, while four is more than two, it's less than three, so you didn't hear the next part of the directions. Nevertheless, you can use the process of elimination here, because you did manage to figure out that you should not circle letter D, and therefore D isn't the answer to number 30 on the answer grid. So you should simply pick another letter and fill it in.

PROCESS OF ELIMINATION ON PART C

Using the process of elimination pays off best on Part C, Number Series. For one thing, you have more time to think on this section, and for another, this is the one section that requires some serious reasoning on your part. Those two things make the process of elimination work for you.

Let's say you have a number series question that goes like this:

1. 6 14 8 28 10 42 12 . . . . **A)** 34 10   **B)** 44 14   **C)** 54 11   **D)** 6 46   **E)** 56 14

With any number series question, you should start by figuring out what the sequence is. If you figure out the sequence and find your answer among the answer choices, fine; you don't need to use the process of elimination.

But suppose, for the sake of this demonstration, that you can't figure out how this number series works. You see that there are smaller numbers alternating with greater numbers. You see that all the numbers are even numbers. But that's all the farther you can get. At that point, you could turn to the answer choices for help. And in fact the process of elimination will help you, if not find the right answer, at least come close.

You can eliminate choice C easily. It has an odd number in it. If you think a little farther, you can also eliminate choice A, because both the smaller numbers and the greater numbers in the series keep getting higher, while the numbers in A are lower than the ones already given. You can also eliminate choice D, because it reverses the order of smaller and greater numbers; it's time in the series for one of the greater numbers.

Your process of elimination has left you with only B and E as possible answer choices. At that point, you would be safe in simply taking a guess. The process of elimination leaves you in a much stronger position than you would be if you simply marked an answer at random.

The answer, by the way, is E. Starting with the first number in the series, 6, every other number increases by 2 (6, 8, 10, 12). Starting with the second number, 14, every other number increases by 14 (14, 28, 42). So you need the next number in the second series, 56, and then the next number in the first series, 14.

Now you try it. Below are two fairly hard number series questions. Pretend it's late in the exam and you don't have a lot of time left to reason out each question. See if you can use the process of elimination to narrow down your choice of answers.

23. 24 31 17 33 40 17 42 . . . . **A)** 17 49   **B)** 45 17   **C)** 49 17   **D)** 49 51   **E)** 17 51

24. 4 9 8 13 12 17 16 . . . . **A)** 21 20   **B)** 15 20   **C)** 17 13   **D)** 20 21   **E)** 20 16

Did you use the process of elimination? On question 23, you might have started by eliminating the one answer that doesn't have 17 in it, answer D. If you were really on top of things, you could eliminate all the answers that don't have 17 in the *second* position, since in the original series the repeating 17 is every *third* number and it's time for the other number, not the 17, to come first. That would knock out answers A and E as well, and you'd be left to choose between answers B and C. The correct answer is C, since the series goes: add 7, add 2, with 17 coming before each "add 2" step.

On question 24, if you noted that this is an alternating series, with the steps going "add 5, subtract 1, add 5" and so on, you didn't need to use process of elimination; you chose answer A. But if you couldn't figure that out in a short amount of time, you might at least have eliminated answer C, which repeats two numbers from a series that doesn't seem to have repeating numbers in it. If you got a little more sophisticated, you might have eliminated choice E, because it has two even numbers while the series seems to alternate odd and even numbers.

That's how process of elimination works. It's your tool for the next step, which is knowing when to guess.

STEP 6: KNOW WHEN TO GUESS

Time to complete: 20 minutes

Activity: Complete worksheet on Your Guessing Ability

Armed with the process of elimination, you're ready to take control of one of the big questions in test-taking: Should I guess? The first and main answer is Yes. Unless the exam has a so-called "guessing penalty," you have nothing to lose and everything to gain from guessing. The more complicated answer depends both on the exam and on you—your personality and your "guessing intuition."

GUESSING AND TEST 470

One reason the question of whether or not to guess depends on the exam is that some exams have what's called a "guessing penalty." Parts A and B of Test 470 have a guessing penalty, while Parts C and D have no such penalty.

How the "Guessing Penalty" Works

A "guessing penalty" really only works against *random* guessing—filling in the little circles to make a nice pattern on your answer sheet. If you can eliminate one or more answer choices, as outlined above, you're better off taking a guess than leaving the answer blank, even on the sections that have a penalty.

Here's how a "guessing penalty" works: Depending on the number of answer choices in a given section, some proportion of the number of questions you get wrong is subtracted from the total number of questions you got right. The proportion ranges from just one-fourth of your wrong answers on Part B to *all* of your wrong answers on Part A. Without a guessing penalty, your score would simply be the number of questions you got right.

On Part A of Test 470, there are two answer choices for every question. If you answered each question at random, A, B, A, B, down your answer sheet, odds are you'd get half the questions right and half wrong. The "guessing penalty" is that wrong answers are subtracted from right answers. So if, out of the 95 questions, you got 48 right and 47 wrong, you'd have a net score of 1. (If you got 47 right and 48 wrong, you'd have a negative score!)

On Part B, there are five answer choices for every question. Again, if you marked A, B, C, D, E, all the way down your answer sheet, the odds are that you would get one-fifth of the answers right out of the 88 questions, or about 18 questions. The guessing penalty is that one-fourth of your wrong answers are subtracted. One-fourth of the 70 questions you got wrong is also about 18. So your net score would be zero.

What You Should Do About the Guessing Penalty

That's how a guessing penalty works. The first thing this means for you is that marking your answer sheet at random doesn't pay. If you're running out of time on Part A or Part B, you should not use your remaining seconds to mark a pretty pattern on your answer sheet. Take those few seconds to try to answer one more question right.

But as soon as you get out of the realm of random guessing, the "guessing penalty" no longer works against you. If you can use the process of elimination to get rid of even one wrong answer choice, the odds stop being against you and start working in your favor. (Of course, this doesn't really apply to Part A; when there are two answer choices, eliminating one wrong answer is the same as finding the right answer!)

On Part B of the exam, you should not guess if you have absolutely no idea which box the given address is in. However, if you can eliminate even one wrong answer choice—you know for sure that it's not in Box A, because you remember the contents of Box A quite clearly—you should go ahead and guess from the remaining answer choices. If you eliminate one wrong choice, you have neutralized the one-fourth point penalty. If you eliminate more than one answer choice, the odds are in your favor. So if you have even the vaguest idea at all, go ahead and guess.

Sections That Don't Have a Guessing Penalty

On Part C it's always safe to guess—especially if you've been able to eliminate one or more wrong answer choices as outlined in Step 5. It's even safe to mark answers at random if you find that you are running out of time and haven't gotten to all the questions. Those wrong answers can't count against you—and you just might get one or two right, purely by chance.

On Part D, though, guessing is a little more problematic. If you're sure of the number you've been instructed to mark on your answer grid, but you aren't sure which circle to fill in, it's safe to go ahead and guess. If the answer is wrong, it won't count against you. But if you aren't sure of the number you're supposed to go to on the answer grid, you shouldn't guess unless you're near the end of the instructions. If you mark answer 22 A early on and later find that you have been instructed to mark 22 D—well, it'll bring your blood pressure up. So, at least in the early part of the test, it's safest not to mark an answer you're not sure of. If you're near the end of the instructions, though, you might as well go ahead and guess. Once again, the wrong answer won't count against you.

GUESSING AND YOU

The other factor in deciding whether or not to guess, besides the exam, is you. There are two things you need to know about yourself before you go into the exam:

- Are you a risk-taker?
- Are you a good guesser?

These questions matter most on the sections that have guessing penalties. Even if you're a play-it-safe person with lousy intuition, guessing on other sections is perfectly safe. Overcome your anxieties, and go ahead and mark an answer.

But when you know your guess could count against you when you're wrong, your own personal risk-taking temperament and guessing skill do factor in. Complete the worksheet Your Guessing Ability on the next page to get an idea of how good your intuition is.

Your Guessing Ability

The following are ten really hard questions. You're not supposed to know the answers. Rather, this is an assessment of your ability to guess when you don't have a clue. Read each question carefully, just as if you did expect to answer it. If you have any knowledge at all of the subject of the question, use that knowledge to help you eliminate wrong answer choices. Use this answer grid to fill in your answers to the questions.

ANSWER GRID

1. Ⓐ Ⓑ Ⓒ Ⓓ   5. Ⓐ Ⓑ Ⓒ Ⓓ   9. Ⓐ Ⓑ Ⓒ Ⓓ
2. Ⓐ Ⓑ Ⓒ Ⓓ   6. Ⓐ Ⓑ Ⓒ Ⓓ   10. Ⓐ Ⓑ Ⓒ Ⓓ
3. Ⓐ Ⓑ Ⓒ Ⓓ   7. Ⓐ Ⓑ Ⓒ Ⓓ
4. Ⓐ Ⓑ Ⓒ Ⓓ   8. Ⓐ Ⓑ Ⓒ Ⓓ

1. September 7 is Independence Day in
   A. India
   B. Costa Rica
   C. Brazil
   D. Australia

2. Which of the following is the formula for determining the momentum of an object?
   A. $p = mv$
   B. $F = ma$
   C. $P = IV$
   D. $E = mc^2$

3. Because of the expansion of the universe, the stars and other celestial bodies are all moving away from each other. This phenomenon is known as
   A. Newton's first law
   B. the big bang
   C. gravitational collapse
   D. Hubble flow

4. American author Gertrude Stein was born in
   A. 1713
   B. 1830
   C. 1874
   D. 1901

5. Which of the following is NOT one of the Five Classics attributed to Confucius?
   A. the I Ching
   B. the Book of Holiness
   C. the Spring and Autumn Annals
   D. the Book of History

6. The religious and philosophical doctrine that holds that the universe is constantly in a struggle between good and evil is known as
   A. Pelagianism
   B. Manichaeanism
   C. neo-Hegelianism
   D. Epicureanism

7. The third Chief Justice of the U.S. Supreme Court was
   A. John Blair
   B. William Cushing
   C. James Wilson
   D. John Jay

8. Which of the following is the poisonous portion of a daffodil?
   A. the bulb
   B. the leaves
   C. the stem
   D. the flowers

9. The winner of the Masters golf tournament in 1953 was
   A. Sam Snead
   B. Cary Middlecoff
   C. Arnold Palmer
   D. Ben Hogan

10. The state with the highest per capita personal income in 1980 was
   A. Alaska
   B. Connecticut
   C. New York
   D. Texas

Answers

Check your answers against the correct answers below.

1. C.	**5.** B.	**9.** D.
2. A.	**6.** B.	**10.** A.
3. D.	**7.** B.	
4. C.	**8.** A.	

How Did You Do?

You may have simply gotten lucky and actually known the answer to one or two questions. In addition, your guessing was more successful if you were able to use the process of elimination on any of the questions. Maybe you didn't know who the third Chief Justice was (question 7), but you knew that John Jay was the first. In that case, you would have eliminated answer **D** and therefore improved your odds of guessing right from one in four to one in three.

According to probability, you should get 2 1/2 answers correct, so getting either two or three right would be average. If you got four or more right, you may be a really terrific guesser. If you got one or none right, you may be a really bad guesser.

Keep in mind, though, that this is only a small sample. You should continue to keep track of your guessing ability as you work through the sample questions in this book. Circle the numbers of questions you guess on as you make your guess; or, if you don't have time while you take the practice tests, go back afterward and try to remember which questions you guessed at. Use the following probabilities to find out if you're a good or bad guesser. On each part of the exam, if you get more than the indicated number of questions right when you guess, you've got good intuition and should trust it to guide you in guessing on the real exam. If you get fewer than the indicated number of questions right when you guess, you are not such a good guesser and should guess on Parts A and B of the real exam only when you can eliminate a wrong answer choice.

- Part A, one out of two
- Part B, one out of five
- Part C, one of five
- Part D, one out of five

STEP 7: REACH YOUR PEAK PERFORMANCE ZONE

Time to complete: 10 minutes to read; weeks to complete!

Activity: Complete the Physical Preparation Checklist

To get ready for a challenge like a big exam, you have to take control of your physical, as well as your mental, state. Exercise, proper diet, and rest will ensure that your body works with, rather than against, your mind on test day, as well as during your preparation.

EXERCISE

If you don't already have a regular exercise program going, the time during which you're preparing for an exam is actually an excellent time to start one. And if you're already keeping fit—or trying to get that way—don't let the pressure of preparing for an exam fool you into quitting now. Exercise helps reduce stress by pumping wonderful good-feeling hormones called endorphins into your system. It also increases the oxygen supply throughout your body, including your brain, so you'll be at peak performance on test day.

A half hour of vigorous activity—enough to raise a sweat—every day should be your aim. If you're really pressed for time, every other day is OK. Choose an activity you like and get out there and do it. Jogging with a friend always makes the time go faster, or take a radio.

But don't overdo. You don't want to exhaust yourself. Moderation is the key.

DIET

First of all, cut out the junk. Go easy on caffeine and nicotine, and eliminate alcohol and any other drugs from your system at least two weeks before the exam. Promise yourself a binge the night after the exam, if need be.

What your body needs for peak performance is simply a balanced diet. Eat plenty of fruits and vegetables, along with protein and carbohydrates. Foods that are high in lecithin (an amino acid), such as fish and beans, are especially good "brain foods."

The night before the exam, you might "carbo-load" the way athletes do before a contest. Eat a big plate of spaghetti, rice and beans, or whatever your favorite carbohydrate is.

REST

You probably know how much sleep you need every night to be at your best, even if you don't always get it. Make sure you do get that much sleep, though, for at least a week before the exam. Moderation is important here, too. Extra sleep will just make you groggy.

If you're not a morning person and your exam will be given in the morning, you should reset your internal clock so that your body doesn't think you're taking an exam at 3 a.m. You have to start this process well before the exam. The way it works is to get up half an hour earlier each morning, and then go to bed half an hour earlier that night. Don't try it the other way around; you'll just toss and turn if you go to bed early without having gotten up early. The next morning, get up another half an hour earlier, and so on. How long you will have to do this depends on how late you're used to getting up.

Physical Preparation Checklist

For the week before the test, write down 1) what physical exercise you engaged in and for how long and 2) what you ate for each meal. Remember, you're trying for at least half an hour of exercise every other day (preferably every day) and a balanced diet that's light on junk food.

Exam minus 7 days
Exercise: _____ for _____ minutes
Breakfast: _____
Lunch: _____
Dinner: _____
Snacks: _____

Exam minus 6 days
Exercise: _____ for _____ minutes
Breakfast: _____
Lunch: _____
Dinner: _____
Snacks: _____

Exam minus 5 days
Exercise: _____ for _____ minutes
Breakfast: _____
Lunch: _____
Dinner: _____
Snacks: _____

Exam minus 4 days
Exercise: _____ for _____ minutes
Breakfast: _____
Lunch: _____
Dinner: _____
Snacks: _____

Exam minus 3 days
Exercise: _____ for _____ minutes
Breakfast: _____
Lunch: _____
Dinner: _____
Snacks: _____

Exam minus 2 days

Exercise: _____ for _____ minutes

Breakfast: _____

Lunch: _____

Dinner: _____

Snacks: _____

Exam minus 1 day

Exercise: _____ for _____ minutes

Breakfast: _____

Lunch: _____

Dinner: _____

Snacks: _____

STEP 8: GET YOUR ACT TOGETHER

Time to complete: 10 minutes to read; time to complete will vary

Activity: Complete Final Preparations worksheet

You're in control of your mind and body; you're in charge of test anxiety, your preparation, and your test-taking strategies. Now it's time to take charge of external factors, like the testing site and the materials you need to take the exam.

FIND OUT WHERE THE TEST IS AND MAKE A TRIAL RUN

Your kit from the USPS will tell you when and where your exam is being held. Do you know how to get to the testing site? Do you know how long it will take to get there? If not, make a trial run, preferably on the same day of the week at the same time of day. Make note, on the worksheet Final Preparations, of the amount of time it will take you to get to the exam site. Plan on arriving 10–15 minutes early so you can get the lay of the land, use the bathroom, and calm down. Then figure out how early you will have to get up that morning, and make sure you get up that early every day for a week before the exam.

GATHER YOUR MATERIALS

The night before the exam, lay out the clothes you will wear and the materials you have to bring with you to the exam. Plan on dressing in layers; you won't have any control over the temperature of the examination room. Have a sweater or jacket you can take off if it's warm. Use the checklist on the worksheet Final Preparations to help you pull together what you'll need.

Don't Skip Breakfast

Even if you don't usually eat breakfast, do so on exam morning. A cup of coffee doesn't count. Don't do dough-nuts or other sweet foods, either. A sugar high will leave you with a sugar low in the middle of the exam. A mix of protein and carbohydrates is best: cereal with milk and just a little sugar, or eggs with toast, will do your body a world of good.

Final Preparations

Getting to the Exam Site

Location of exam: _____

Date of exam: _____

Time of exam: _____

Do I know how to get to the exam site? Yes _____ No _____
If no, make a trial run.

Time it will take to get to exam site: _____

Things to lay out the night before the exam

Clothes I will wear   _____

Sweater/jacket   _____

Completed Sample Answer Sheet   _____

Admission card   _____

Photo ID   _____

2 No. 2. pencils   _____

_____   _____

_____   _____

STEP 9: DO IT!

Time to complete: 5 minutes, plus test-taking time

Activity: Ace the Postal Worker Exam!

Fast forward to exam day. You're ready. You made a study plan and followed through. You practiced your test-taking strategies while working through this book. You're in control of your physical, mental, and emotional state. You know when and where to show up and what to bring with you. In other words, you're better prepared than most of the other people taking the Postal Worker Exam with you. You're psyched.

Just one more thing. When you're done with the Postal Worker Exam, you will have earned a reward. Plan a celebration for exam night. Call up your friends and plan a party, or have a nice dinner for two—whatever your heart desires. Give yourself something to look forward to.

And then do it. Go into the Postal Worker Exam, full of confidence, armed with test-taking strategies you've practiced till they're second nature. You're in control of yourself, your environment, and your performance on the exam. You're ready to succeed. So do it. Go in there and ace the exam. And look forward to your future career as a postal worker!

C·H·A·P·T·E·R

SAMPLE ANSWER SHEET AND QUESTIONS

4

nce the 470 Battery Exam has been announced in your location, and you've sent in your application card, you'll receive a kit in the mail from the USPS. This kit will contain a sample answer sheet (2 pages) and an instructional packet with sample questions (12 pages), along with the date and time of the examination. We've reproduced both the sample answer sheet and the instructional packet with sample questions for you here, to give you an idea of what to expect.

As you read in Chapter 2, in order to be admitted to the Exam, you'll need to complete the sample answer sheet the USPS sends you (the reproduction here is for information only, it will not be accepted by the USPS in place of the actual sample answer sheet). Once you're in the exam room you won't have time to start from scratch, so you'll be asked to copy your work from the sample answer sheet to an actual answer sheet, which will be given to you when you arrive at the examination site. The test proctor will check your sample answer sheet for completion, so make sure you fill it out entirely.

At first glance, the sample answer sheet can be a bit intimidating. Don't worry, the instructional packet included in your kit has a set of detailed instructions on how to fill out each section of the answer sheet. Immediately following the sample answer sheet instructions, you'll find a section entitled "Test Instructions" which includes the sample questions and instructions on the different types of questions you'll be asked to answer on the 470 Exam. Read through the following pages carefully to familiarize yourself with the material. Remember, you'll need to complete your sample answer sheet in order to be admitted to the exam, use the reproduction provided here for practice.

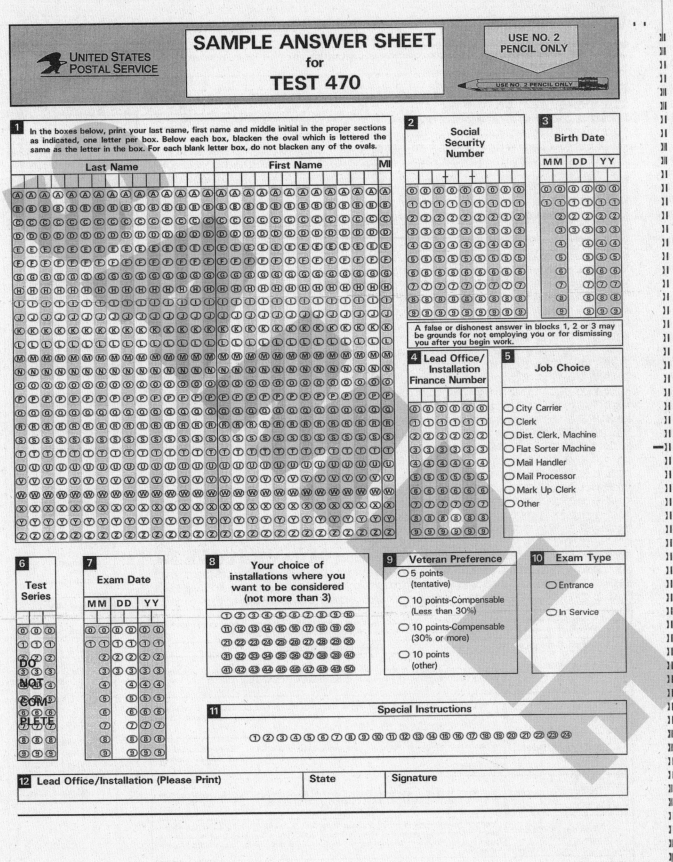

SAMPLE ANSWER SHEET
for
TEST 470

UNITED STATES POSTAL SERVICE

USE NO. 2 PENCIL ONLY

USE NO. 2 PENCIL ONLY

1 In the boxes below, print your last name, first name and middle initial in the proper sections as indicated, one letter per box. Below each box, blacken the oval which is lettered the same as the letter in the box. For each blank letter box, do not blacken any of the ovals.

Last Name   **First Name**   **MI**

2 Social Security Number

3 Birth Date

MM | DD | YY

A false or dishonest answer in blocks 1, 2 or 3 may be grounds for not employing you or for dismissing you after you begin work.

4 Lead Office/ Installation Finance Number

5 Job Choice

- ○ City Carrier
- ○ Clerk
- ○ Dist. Clerk, Machine
- ○ Flat Sorter Machine
- ○ Mail Handler
- ○ Mail Processor
- ○ Mark Up Clerk
- ○ Other

6 Test Series

DO NOT COM PLETE

7 Exam Date

MM | DD | YY

8 Your choice of installations where you want to be considered (not more than 3)

1 2 3 4 5 6 7 8 9 10
11 12 13 14 15 16 17 18 19 20
21 22 23 24 25 26 27 28 29 30
31 32 33 34 35 36 37 38 39 40
41 42 43 44 45 46 47 48 49 50

9 Veteran Preference

- ○ 5 points (tentative)
- ○ 10 points-Compensable (Less than 30%)
- ○ 10 points-Compensable (30% or more)
- ○ 10 points (other)

10 Exam Type

- ○ Entrance
- ○ In Service

11 Special Instructions

1 2 3 4 5 6 7 8 9 10 11 12 13 14 15 16 17 18 19 20 21 22 23 24

12 Lead Office/Installation (Please Print) | State | Signature

PS Form **8155-S**, July 1993

Page 1

13 Print your city and state ⟶

14 In the boxes below, print your street address or post office box (one letter, number, or symbol per box).

15 ZIP.

16 +4

[Grid of bubble-fill boxes for address containing digits 0-9, symbols (− /), and letters A through Z for each character position]

[ZIP code bubble grid: digits 0-9]

[+4 bubble grid: digits 0-9]

RESEARCH QUESTIONNAIRE

General Instructions

The U.S. Postal Service wants to make sure that its part in the recruitment and hiring of postal employees is fair for everyone. To do this we need your answers to the three questions below. Your responses are voluntary. Please answer each of the questions to the best of your ability. Your answers will be used for research purposes only and to help assure equal employment opportunity. Please provide accurate information. Your cooperation is important. Completely darken the oval corresponding to your response choice.

17 Indicate Sex

○ Male

○ Female

18 Disability Code

see page 4

[Bubble grid: digits 0-9, two columns]

19 The categories below are designed to identify your basic racial and national origin category. If you are of mixed racial and/or national origin, indicate the category with which you most closely identify yourself.

Name of Category	Definition of Category
○ American Indian or Alaskan Native	A person having origins in any of the original peoples of North America, and who maintains cultural identification through community recognition or tribal affiliation.
○ Asian or Pacific Islander	A person having origins in any of the original peoples of the Far East, Southeast Asia, the Indian subcontinent, or the Pacific Islands. This area includes, for example China, India, Japan, Korea, the Philippine Islands, Samoa, and Vietnam.
○ Black, not of Hispanic Origin	A person having origins in any of the black racial groups of Africa. Does not include persons of Mexican, Puerto Rican, Cuban, Central or South American, or other Spanish cultures or origins (see Hispanic).
○ Hispanic	A person of Mexican, Puerto Rican, Cuban, Central or South American, or other Spanish cultures or origins. Does not include persons of Portuguese culture or origin.
○ White, not of Hispanic Origin	A person having origins in any of the original peoples of Europe, North Africa, or the Middle East. Does not include persons of Mexican, Puerto Rican, Cuban, Central or South American, or other Spanish cultures or origins (see Hispanic). Also includes persons not included in other categories.

YOU MUST BRING THE FOLLOWING TO BE ADMITTED:

Completed Sample Answer Sheet,
Admission Card/Notice,
Photo ID and
2 Sharpened No. 2 Pencils

LATECOMERS WILL NOT BE ADMITTED.

No. 2 pencil,

Social Security card,

ZIP Code for current address and

ZIP+4 Code for current address.

UNITED STATES POSTAL SERVICE

These instructions will prepare you for the exam. Please take time to **carefully read ALL of the instructions. THIS IS YOUR RESPONSIBILITY.** You should read all of the instructions and complete the required items even if you have taken a Postal exam before. **We are providing you with:**

1. *A SAMPLE ANSWER SHEET TO FILL OUT AT HOME.* This will enable you to complete the Answer Sheet in the exam room.

2. *WHAT YOU CAN EXPECT DURING THE ACTUAL TEST PART OF THE EXAM SESSION.*

3. *SAMPLE QUESTIONS FOR PRACTICE.* So that you will be familiar with the type of questions on the test, sample questions are included for practice.

4. *HOW THE FOUR PARTS OF THE TEST WILL BE SCORED.*

To fill out the Sample Answer Sheet, you will need:

This booklet,

Sample Answer Sheet,

Your Admission Card/Notice,

In the exam room, you will be given 15 minutes to copy your work from the Sample Answer Sheet to the Answer Sheet. The test will begin soon thereafter. You will not have time in the exam room to become familiar with these instructions.

The Answer Sheet will be given to you in the exam room. It is processed by a high-speed scanner. It is important that you precisely complete the grids on the Sample Answer Sheet. This is so you will know exactly how to fill out the Answer Sheet in the exam room.

You are responsible for correctly completing the Sample Answer Sheet. When you report to take the test, you must bring it with you.

Your Sample Answer Sheet will be checked for accurate and total completion. You may not have time to fix any errors or complete items not filled out before the session starts. Only those who have a properly completed Sample Answer Sheet will be admitted. Those who still have an incomplete Sample Answer Sheet by the time the exam starts will NOT be admitted.

THE FOLLOWING INSTRUCTIONS EXPLAIN HOW TO FILL OUT EACH GRID ON THE SAMPLE ANSWER SHEET.

EFFECTIVE JULY 1994

Examples of correct and incorrect marks are:

CORRECT MARKS

INCORRECT MARKS

1 NAME. Use your full, legal name when completing this grid. Use the same name every time you take a postal exam. Use of a nickname could result in a delay in processing the result.

GRID 1 is divided into three parts: **Last Name, First Name** and **MI** (Middle Initial). Each part is surrounded by a border. **Each part of your name must be entered ONLY in the place for that part.**

Last Name. Enter your last name one letter to a box. **You must start with the first square box to the left.**

If you are a JR, SR, III or IV, this should be included as a part of your last name. After entering your last name, skip a box and enter the correct letters.

To help you complete the grids correctly, you will use the **EDGE** of the Admission Card/Notice or the envelope as a guide. Place the Admission Card/Notice or envelope on top of GRID 1 so that the edge is to the LEFT of the first column. For example, when the last name is "HALL III":

Last Name

EDGE

(**If you are left handed,** place the edge to the RIGHT of the first column.)

For the letter in the box, find the matching circle in the column below and darken that circle.

Next, move the edge with one hand so that it is against the next column. Darken the circle with the other hand for that letter.

Last Name

EDGE

Then proceed until you have darkened the circle for each letter you have entered in a box.

If your name has the letter "O" in it, make sure to darken the circle that comes after "N". Do not mistake the letter "Q" for the letter "O".

When you come to a blank box, do nothing.

The following is an example of a completed grid when the last name is "HALL III":

Last Name

First Name. Enter your first name one letter to a box. **You must start with the first box after the border line.**

As you did for **Last Name,** take the edge and place it on top of this grid against the first column.

Find the matching circle below and darken that circle. Next, move the edge so it is against the next column. Darken the circle for that letter. Then proceed until you have darkened the circle for each letter you have entered in a box.

Do not mistake the letter "Q" for the letter "O".

2

When you come to a blank box, do nothing.

MI (Middle Initial). Enter your middle initial and darken the circle for the letter. If you do not have a middle initial, do not enter anything in the box or darken a circle.

2 SOCIAL SECURITY NUMBER. Look at your Social Security card. Compare the number with the one on the Admission Card/Notice. If the number on the Admission Card/Notice is not correct, draw a line through it and make the correction.

Enter your correct Social Security Number in GRID 2 on the Sample Answer Sheet.

Using the edge, darken the matching numerical circles.

3 BIRTH DATE. For GRID 3, in the box labeled "MM", enter the two numbers for your birth month, one number to a box. If you were born in January through September, you would enter a "0" in the first box and the number for the month in the second box. Using the edge, darken the matching circles.

In the box labeled "DD", enter the two numbers for your day of birth, one number to a box. If your day of birth is from one to nine, enter a "0" in the first box and the number for the day in the second box. Using the edge, darken the matching circles.

In the box labeled "YY", enter the last two numbers of the year in which you were born, one number to a box. Do not use the current year. Using the edge, darken the matching circles.

WHEN YOU FINISH GRID 3, YOU SHOULD HAVE ENTERED AND GRIDDED SIX NUMBERS.

4 LEAD OFFICE/INSTALLATION FINANCE NUMBER. Look at the Admission Card/Notice. On it there is a six digit number and the name of the office for which you have applied. With your pencil, enter this number in GRID 4, one number to a box. Using the edge, darken the matching numerical circles.

5 JOB CHOICE. Refer to the Choice Sheet for instructions.

6 TEST SERIES. Do nothing with GRID 6.

7 EXAM DATE. Look at the Admission Card/Notice for the date you are scheduled to take this exam. For GRID 7, in the box labeled"MM", enter the two numbers for the exam month, one number to a box. If the exam is in January through September, you would

enter a "0" in the first box and the number for the month in the second box. Using the edge, darken the matching circles.

In the box labeled "DD", enter the two numbers for your day of exam, one number to a box. If your day of exam is from one to nine, enter a "0" in the first box and the number for the day in the second box. Using the edge, darken the matching circles.

In the box labeled "YY", enter the last two numbers of the year of the exam, one number to a box. Using the edge, darken the matching circles.

WHEN YOU FINISH GRID 7, YOU SHOULD HAVE ENTERED AND GRIDDED SIX NUMBERS.

IMPORTANT NOTE. If you are a current career Postal employee OR your Admission Card/Notice is stamped "INSERVICE", DO NOT COMPLETE GRIDS 8, 9, 17, 18 AND 19.

8 YOUR CHOICE OF INSTALLATIONS. Refer to the Choice Sheet for instructions.

9 VETERAN PREFERENCE. If you are not eligible to claim Veteran Preference, do nothing with GRID 9. The following is an explanation of the different types of Veteran Preference:

5 Points (tentative). This preference is usually given to honorably separated veterans who served on active duty in the Armed Forces of the United States under one of the following conditions:

a. During a declared war (the last one was World War II); or

b. During the period April 28, 1952 to July 1, 1955; or

c. During the period February 1, 1955 through October 14, 1976 for which any part of more than 180 consecutive days was served. (An initial period of active duty for training under the 6-month Reserve or National Guard Program does not count.)

d. In any campaign or expedition for which a campaign badge was authorized.

Veterans who served in Southwest Asia or in the surrounding contiguous waters or air space on or after August 2, 1990 AND who were awarded the Southwest Asia Service Medal can claim five points.

10 Points - Compensable (Less than 30%). This preference is given to honorably separated veterans who served on active duty in the Armed Forces at any

time and have a service-connected disability for which compensation is provided at 10% or more, but less than 30%.

10 Points - Compensable (30% or more). This preference is given to honorably separated veterans who served on active duty in the Armed Forces at any time and have a service-connected disability for which compensation is provided at 30% or more.

10 Points (other). This preference is claimed by a variety of people:

a. Veterans who were awarded the Purple Heart; or

b. Veterans who have a recognized disability for which no compensation is received; or

c. An unremarried widow or widower of an honorably separated veteran, provided the deceased veteran served in active duty during a war, or the veteran died while in the Armed Forces.

Darken only one circle in GRID 9 if you wish to claim Veteran Preference. Do not darken more than one circle. Points claimed will be added to your score ONLY if you pass the exam with a score of 70 or better.

10 EXAM TYPE. In GRID 10, for:

Entrance, darken this circle if you applied for this exam in response to a public announcement or are taking the test for other reasons (see 11 below). Current career Postal employees do NOT darken this circle.

Inservice, darken this circle if you are a current career Postal employee. Also, darken this circle if you are taking this exam on a noncompetitive basis -- your Admission Card/Notice will be stamped "INSERVICE."

11 SPECIAL INSTRUCTIONS. If you do not have "DELAYED" or "REOPENED" stamped on your Admission Card/Notice, do nothing with GRID 11. This grid is only for people who are taking this exam because they either:

a. missed an opportunity to take the exam when last opened to the public because they were on active military duty, "DELAYED" status OR

b. entitled to 10 point Veteran Preference, "REOPENED" status.

Grid the circle labeled "3" for "DELAYED", or the circle labeled "4" for "REOPENED."

12 LEAD OFFICE (Name). Look at the right side of the Admission Card/Notice for the name of the installation for which you are applying. Print the name in the block labeled: "Lead Office/Installation (Please Print)". Print the two letter abbreviation for the state in the block labeled "State."

Sign your name in the block labeled "Signature."

13 PRINT YOUR CITY AND STATE. Turn to Page 2 of the Sample Answer Sheet. Print the city and state of your current mailing address.

14 STREET ADDRESS. This is for the one line address that will be used to deliver your test result. If you pass and later your score is reached for consideration, the address you grid will be used to notify you. The address you grid must meet Postal standards. Study the following examples:

1234 MAIN ST APT 999

45678 MADISON BLVD S

33 1/2 IVY DR SW

4329-02 MONTGOMERY PL

2342 NW SMITH RD

RR 2 BOX 50

PO BOX 4502

You must use the correct shortened format for your one line address. Also, such an address will be easier and quicker to grid.

This grid is different from the other ones because it contains numbers, special symbols and letters. Enter your one line address in the boxes. You must start with the first box to the left. Skip a blank box where there needs to be a space. By using the edge and starting with the first column to the left, darken the circles.

Do not mistake the letter "Q" for the letter "O".

When you come to a blank box, do nothing.

15 ZIP (Code). You must have your correct ZIP Code to complete this grid. An incorrect ZIP Code will result in a delay in sending your rating to you. Your ZIP Code is found on magazines, utility bills and other business mail you receive at home. Enter your correct

five digit ZIP Code in the boxes. Then use the edge to darken the matching numerical circles.

16 +4 (Code). You must have your correct ZIP+4 Code to complete this grid. Your ZIP+4 is usually found on mail you receive at home. This four digit number appears after the five digit ZIP Code. Enter this number in GRID 16. Use the edge and darken the numerical circles.

FOR GRIDS 17, 18 AND 19, read the General Instructions for the RESEARCH QUESTIONNAIRE on Page 2 of the Sample Answer Sheet.

17 SEX. Darken the appropriate circle in GRID 17.

18 DISABILITY CODE. If you do **n o t** have a disability, enter 0 in the first box and 5 in the second box in GRID 18. Code "05" indicates "No Disability." Using the edge, darken the numerical circles.

A disability refers to a physical or mental disability or history of such disability which is likely to cause difficulty in obtaining, maintaining, or advancing in employment. On Page 4, you will find a list of various disabilities. Each of the disabilities has a number. If you have a disability, read the list carefully and select the code that best describes your disability. If you have multiple disabilities, choose the code for the one that is most disabling. Enter the two numbers of the disability code in the boxes at the top of GRID 18. If your disability is not listed, enter zero in the first column and six in the second column. Using the edge, darken the numerical circles.

19 RACIAL AND NATIONAL ORIGIN. This grid is for the collection of your racial and national origin. Darken the circle for the category that applies to you. If you are of mixed racial and/or national origin, you should identify yourself by the one category for which you most closely associate yourself by darkening the appropriate circle in GRID 19.

Checking your work. After you have finished, go back and check your work. For a letter or number in a box, you should have only one circle darkened in the column found directly below. Make sure that you have completed all items as requested.

After checking your work, go back to Page 1 of the Sample Answer Sheet. In the upper left corner is the United States Postal Service eagle. Draw a circle around the eagle.

Get someone else to check your work. Since the scanner that reads the Answer Sheet only picks up what is gridded, you should have someone else check your work. Let them tell you if you made a mistake so that you can correct it. This will help make sure that you do the best job you possibly can on the Answer Sheet in the exam room.

TEST INSTRUCTIONS

During the test session, it will be your responsibility to pay close attention to what the examiner has to say and to follow all instructions. One of the purposes of the test is to see how quickly and accurately you can work. Therefore, each part of the test will be carefully timed. You will not START until being told to do so. Also, when you are told to STOP, you must immediately STOP answering the questions. When you are told to work on a particular part of the examination, regardless of which part, you are to work on that part ONLY. If you finish a part before time is called, you may review your answers for that part, but you will not go on or back to any other part. Failure to follow ANY directions given to you by the examiner may be grounds for disqualification. Instructions read by the examiner are intended to ensure that each applicant has the same fair and objective opportunity to compete in the examination.

SAMPLE QUESTIONS

Study carefully before the examination.

The following questions are like the ones that will be on the test. Study these carefully. This will give you practice with the different kinds of questions and show you how to mark your answers.

Part A: Address Checking

In this part of the test, you will have to decide whether two addresses are alike or different. If the two addresses are exactly *Alike* in every way, darken circle A for the question. If the two addresses are *Different* in any way, darken circle D for the question.

Mark your answers to these sample questions on the Sample Answer Grid at the right.

1...2134 S 20th St   2134 S 20th St

Since the two addresses are exactly alike, mark A for
question 1 on the Sample Answer Grid.

2...4608 N Warnock St   4806 N Warnock St

3...1202 W Girard Dr   1202 W Girard Rd

4...Chappaqua NY 10514   Chappaqua NY 10514

5...2207 Markland Ave   2207 Markham Ave

Sample Answer Grid
1 Ⓐ Ⓓ
2 Ⓐ Ⓓ
3 Ⓐ Ⓓ
4 Ⓐ Ⓓ
5 Ⓐ Ⓓ

The correct answers to questions 2 to 5 are: 2D, 3D, 4A, and 5D.

Your score on Part A of the actual test will be based on the number of wrong answers as well as on the number of
right answers. Part A is scored right answers minus wrong answers. Random guessing should not help your score.
For the Part A test, you will have six minutes to answer as many of the 95 questions as you can. It will be to your
advantage to work as quickly and as accurately as possible. You will not be expected to be able to answer all the
questions in the time allowed.

Part B: Memory for Addresses

In this part of the test, you will have to memorize the locations (A, B, C, D, or E) of 25 addresses shown in five
boxes, like those below. For example, "Sardis" is in Box C, "6800-6999 Table" is in Box B, etc. (The addresses in
the actual test will be different.)

A	B	C	D	E
4700-5599 Table	6800-6999 Table	5600-6499 Table	6500-6799 Table	4400-4699 Table
Lismore	Kelford	Joel	Tatum	Ruskin
5600-6499 West	6500-6799 West	6800-6999 West	4400-4699 West	4700-5599 West
Hesper	Musella	Sardis	Porter	Nathan
4400-4699 Blake	5600-6499 Blake	6500-6799 Blake	4700-5599 Blake	6800-6999 Blake

Study the locations of the addresses for five minutes. As you study, silently repeat these to yourself. Then cover
the boxes and try to answer the questions below. Mark your answers for each question by darkening the circle as
was done for questions 1 and 2.

1. Musella   5. 4400-4699 Blake   9. 6500-6799 Blake   13. Porter
2. 4700-5599 Blake   6. Hesper   10. Joel   14. 6800-6999 Blake
3. 4700-5599 Table   7. Kelford   11. 4400-4699 Blake
4. Tatum   8. Nathan   12. 6500-6799 West

Sample Answer Grid			
1 Ⓐ●ⒸⒹⒺ	5 ⒶⒷⒸⒹⒺ	9 ⒶⒷⒸⒹⒺ	13 ⒶⒷⒸⒹⒺ
2 ⒶⒷⒸ●Ⓔ	6 ⒶⒷⒸⒹⒺ	10 ⒶⒷⒸⒹⒺ	14 ⒶⒷⒸⒹⒺ
3 ⒶⒷⒸⒹⒺ	7 ⒶⒷⒸⒹⒺ	11 ⒶⒷⒸⒹⒺ	
4 ⒶⒷⒸⒹⒺ	8 ⒶⒷⒸⒹⒺ	12 ⒶⒷⒸⒹⒺ	

The correct answers for questions 3 to 14 are: 3A, 4D, 5A, 6A, 7B, 8E, 9C, 10C, 11A, 12B, 13D, and 14E.

During the examination, you will have three practice exercises to help you memorize the location of addresses shown in five boxes. After the practice exercises, the actual test will be given. Part B is scored right answers minus one-fourth of the wrong answers. Random guessing should not help your score. But, if you can eliminate one or more alternatives, it is to your advantage to guess. For the Part B test, you will have five minutes to answer as many of the 88 questions as you can. It will be to your advantage to work as quickly and as accurately as you can. You will not be expected to be able to answer all the questions in the time allowed.

Part C: Number Series

For each *Number Series* question there is at the left a series of numbers which follow some definite order and at the right five sets of two numbers each. You are to look at the numbers in the series at the left and find out what order they follow. Then decide what the next two numbers in that series would be if the same order were continued. Mark your answers on the Sample Answer Grid.

1. 1 2 3 4 5 6 7.................. A) 1 2   B) 5 6   C) 8 9   D) 4 5   E) 7 8

The numbers in this series are increasing by 1. If the series were continued for two more numbers, it would read: 1 2 3 4 5 6 7 8 9. Therefore the correct answer is 8 and 9 and you should have darkened C for question 1.

2. 15 14 13 12 11 10 9............ A) 2 1   B) 17 16   C) 8 9   D) 8 7   E) 9 8

The numbers in this series are decreasing by 1. If the series were continued for two more numbers, it would read: 15 14 13 12 11 10 9 8 7. Therefore the correct answer is 8 and 7 and you should have darkened D for question 2.

3. 20 20 21 21 22 22 23........... A) 23 23   B) 23 24   C) 19 19   D) 22 23   E) 21 22

Each number in this series is repeated and then increased by 1. If the series were continued for two more numbers, it would read: 20 20 21 21 22 22 23 23 24. Therefore the correct answer is 23 and 24 and you should have darkened B for question 3.

4. 17 3 17 4 17 5 17.............. A) 6 17   B) 6 7   C) 17 6   D) 5 6   E) 17 7

This series is the number 17 separated by numbers increasing by 1, beginning with the number 3. If the series were continued for two more numbers, it would read: 17 3 17 4 17 5 17 6 17. Therefore the correct answer is 6 and 17 and you should have darkened A for question 4.

5. 1 2 4 5 7 8 10................. A) 11 12   B) 12 14   C) 10 13   D) 12 13   E) 11 13

The numbers in this series are increasing first by 1 (plus 1) and then by 2 (plus 2). If the series were continued for two more numbers, it would read: 1 2 4 5 7 8 10 (plus 1) 11 and (plus 2) 13. Therefore the correct answer is 11 and 13 and you should have darkened E for question 5.

Now read and work sample questions 6 through 10 and mark your answers on the Sample Answer Grid.

6. 21 21 20 20 19 19 18........... A) 18 18   B) 18 17   C) 17 18   D) 17 17   E) 18 19

7. 1 22 1 23 1 24 1............... A) 26 1   B) 25 26   C) 25 1   D) 1 26   E) 1 25

8. 1 20 3 19 5 18 7............... A) 8 9   B) 8 17   C) 17 10   D) 17 9   E) 9 18

9. 4 7 19 13 16 19 22............. A) 23 26   B) 25 27   C) 25 26   D) 25 28   E) 24 27

10. 30 2 28 4 26 6 24............. A) 23 9   B) 26 8   C) 8 9   D) 26 22   E) 8 22

8

The correct answers to sample questions 6 to 10 are: 6B, 7C, 8D, 9D and 10E. Explanations follow.

6. Each number in the series repeats itself and then decreases by 1 or minus 1; *21* (repeat) *21* (minus 1) *20* (repeat) *20* (minus 1) *19* (repeat) *19* (minus 1) *18* (repeat) *?* (minus 1) *?*

7. The number 1 is separated by numbers which begin with 22 and increased by 1; *1 22 1* (increase 22 by 1) *23 1* (increase 23 by 1) *24 1* (increase 24 by 1) *?*

8. This is best explained by two alternating series — one series starts with 1 and increases by 2 or plus 2; the other series starts with 20 and decreases by 1 or minus 1.

$$1 \quad \overset{1}{\wedge} \quad 3 \quad \overset{}{\wedge} \quad 5 \quad \overset{}{\wedge} \quad 7 \quad \overset{}{\wedge} \quad ?$$
$$20 \qquad 19 \qquad 18 \qquad ?$$

9. This series of numbers increases by 3 (plus 3) beginning with the first number — *4 7 10 13 16 19 22 ? ?*

10. Look for two alternating series — one series starts with 30 and decreases by 2 (minus 2); the other series starts with 2 and increases by 2 (plus 2).

Now try questions 11 to 15.

11. 5 6 20 7 8 19 9 . . . . A) 10 18   B) 18 17   C) 10 17   D) 18 19   E) 10 11

12. 4 6 9 11 14 16 19 . . . . A) 21 24   B) 22 25   C) 20 22   D) 21 23   E) 22 24

13. 8 8 1 10 10 3 12 . . . . A) 13 13   B) 12 5   C) 12 4   D) 13 5   E) 4 12

14. 10 12 50 15 17 50 20 . . . . A) 50 21   B) 21 50   C) 50 22   D) 22 50   E) 22 24

15. 20 21 23 24 27 28 32 33 38 39 . A) 45 46   B) 45 52   C) 44 45   D) 44 49   E) 40 46

Sample Answer Grid			
11 Ⓐ Ⓑ Ⓒ Ⓓ Ⓔ	13 Ⓐ Ⓑ Ⓒ Ⓓ Ⓔ	14 Ⓐ Ⓑ Ⓒ Ⓓ Ⓔ	15 Ⓐ Ⓑ Ⓒ Ⓓ Ⓔ
12 Ⓐ Ⓑ Ⓒ Ⓓ Ⓔ			

The correct answers to the sample questions above are: 11A, 12A, 13B, 14D and 15A.

It will be to your advantage to answer every question in Part C that you can, since your score on this part of the test will be based on the number of questions that you answer correctly. Answer first those questions which are easiest for you. For the Part C test, you will have 20 minutes to answer as many of the 24 questions as you can.

Part D: Following Oral Directions

In this part of the test, you will be told to follow directions by writing in a test booklet and then on an answer sheet. The test booklet will have lines of material like the following five samples:

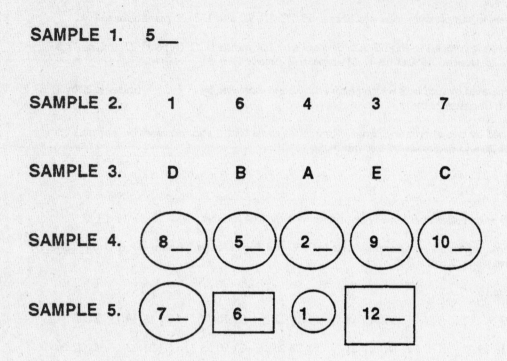

SAMPLE 1.   5 __

SAMPLE 2.   1   6   4   3   7

SAMPLE 3.   D   B   A   E   C

SAMPLE 4.   (8__)   (5__)   (2__)   (9__)   (10__)

SAMPLE 5.   (7__)   [6__]   (1__)   [12 __]

To practice this part of the test, tear off page 12. Then have somebody read the instructions to you and you follow the instructions. When he or she tells you to darken the space on the Sample Answer Grid, use the one on this page.

	Sample Answer Grid		
1 Ⓐ Ⓑ Ⓒ Ⓓ Ⓔ	4 Ⓐ Ⓑ Ⓒ Ⓓ Ⓔ	7 Ⓐ Ⓑ Ⓒ Ⓓ Ⓔ	10 Ⓐ Ⓑ Ⓒ Ⓓ Ⓔ
2 Ⓐ Ⓑ Ⓒ Ⓓ Ⓔ	5 Ⓐ Ⓑ Ⓒ Ⓓ Ⓔ	8 Ⓐ Ⓑ Ⓒ Ⓓ Ⓔ	11 Ⓐ Ⓑ Ⓒ Ⓓ Ⓔ
3 Ⓐ Ⓑ Ⓒ Ⓓ Ⓔ	6 Ⓐ Ⓑ Ⓒ Ⓓ Ⓔ	9 Ⓐ Ⓑ Ⓒ Ⓓ Ⓔ	12 Ⓐ Ⓑ Ⓒ Ⓓ Ⓔ

Your score for Part D will be based on the number of questions that you answer correctly. Therfore, if you are not sure of an answer, it will be to your advantage to guess. Part D will take about 25 minutes.

KEEP THESE INSTRUCTIONS FOR FUTURE REFERENCE. YOUR PARTICIPATION AND COOPERATION IN THIS POSTAL EXAM IS APPRECIATED.

Instructions to be read (the words in parentheses should NOT be read aloud)

You are to follow the instructions that I shall read to you. I cannot repeat them.

Look at the samples. Sample 8 has a number and a line beside it. On the line write an A. (Pause 2 seconds.) Now on the Sample Answer Grid, find number 5 (pause 2 seconds) and darken the space for the letter you just wrote on the line. (Pause 2 seconds.)

Look at Sample 9. (Pause slightly.) Draw a line under the third number. (Pause 2 seconds.) Now look on the Sample Answer Grid, find the number under which you just drew a line and darken space B as in baker for that number. (Pause 5 seconds.)

Look at the letters in Sample 10. (Pause slightly.) Draw a line under the third letter in the line. (Pause 2 seconds.) Now on your Sample Answer Grid, find number 9 (pause 2 seconds) and darken the space for the letter under which you drew a line. (Pause 5 seconds.)

Look at the five circles in Sample 11. (Pause slightly.) Each circle has a number and a line in it. Write D as in dog on the blank in the last circle. (Pause 2 seconds.) Now on the Sample Answer Grid, darken the space for the number-letter combination that is in the circle you just wrote in. (Pause 5 seconds.)

Look at Sample 12. (Pause slightly.) There are two circles and two boxes of different sizes with numbers in them. (Pause slightly.) If 4 is more than 2 and if 5 is less than 3, write A in the smaller circle. (Pause slightly.) Otherwise write C in the larger box. (Pause 2 seconds.) Now on the Sample Answer Grid, darken the space for the number-letter combination in the box or circle in which you just wrote. (Pause 5 seconds.)

Now look at the Sample Answer Grid. (Pause slightly.) You should have darkened spaces 4B, 5A, 9A, 10D, and 12C on the Sample Answer Grid. (If the person preparing to take the examination made any mistakes, try to help him or her see why he or she made wrong marks.)

C·H·A·P·T·E·R

POSTAL EXAM 1

5

CHAPTER SUMMARY

This is the first of two practice exams in this book based on the 470 Battery Exam, which the U.S. Postal Service uses to assess applicants for most entry-level jobs. Use this test to see how you would do if you had to take the exam today.

This chapter presents a complete sample Test 470, sometimes referred to as the 470 Battery Examination, constructed on the basis of information provided by the U.S. Postal Service. If you're applying for a job as a clerk, carrier, mail handler, markup clerk, mail processor, flat-sorting machine operator, or distribution clerk, this is the exam you'll have to take. (Applicants for entry-level clerical jobs take the 710 Exam.)

Test 470 has four sections, each of which is timed separately. Make sure you have a stopwatch or alarm clock available before you take this sample test, so that you can time yourself accurately. Read the following descriptions and instructions for each part of the test carefully before you proceed.

Part A: Address Checking tests your ability to discern whether two given addresses are alike, for which you mark circle A on your answer grid, or different, circle D. You have six minutes to answer 95 questions.

Part B: Memory for Addresses is exactly what it sounds like, a test of your ability to memorize addresses. You will be given five minutes, plus three to six more minutes of practice sessions, to memorize 25 addresses in five boxes. Then, during the actual test section, you will have five minutes to identify which box (A–E) each of 88 addresses was in. The sample test in this chapter does not include the practice sessions that will be part of the real test. Thus, you should give yourself **ten minutes** to memorize the boxes, which is approximately the amount of time you will have during the memorization session and the practice sessions combined. Then give yourself just five minutes for the 88 questions.

Part C: Number Series tests your ability to reason using numbers. For each question, you will be given a series of seven numbers. Your job is to choose, from among five answer choices, the choice that represents the two numbers that would come next if the series were continued. You have 20 minutes for 24 questions.

Part D: Following Oral Directions is also what it sounds like, a test of your ability to follow instructions that are given orally. An examiner reads instructions as to how you should mark first a worksheet and then the answer grid. The examiner will pause to allow you to work but will not repeat the instructions. As you mark the answer grid, you will not be going in order beginning from number 1; instead, you should follow the examiner's instructions exactly. For this sample test, get a friend to read the instructions to you, pausing where noted in the script. **Do not attempt to do this section by reading the instructions yourself.** That would not be an accurate representation of what the real test will be like. There are 25 scored questions in this practice section, and the process of answering them should take approximately 20 minutes.

Before you begin this test, find yourself a quiet place to work and get together your equipment: some pencils for marking the answer grid, your stopwatch or alarm clock, and your reader for Part D. Make sure that you have enough time to complete the whole exam at one sitting—about an hour and ten minutes, with a couple minutes' break between each section.

The answer sheet you should use for answering the questions is on the following page. Then comes the exam itself, and after that is the answer key. The answer key is followed by a section on how to score your exam.

PART A: ADDRESS CHECKING

1. Ⓐ Ⓓ		20. Ⓐ Ⓓ		39. Ⓐ Ⓓ		58. Ⓐ Ⓓ		77. Ⓐ Ⓓ	
2. Ⓐ Ⓓ		21. Ⓐ Ⓓ		40. Ⓐ Ⓓ		59. Ⓐ Ⓓ		78. Ⓐ Ⓓ	
3. Ⓐ Ⓓ		22. Ⓐ Ⓓ		41. Ⓐ Ⓓ		60. Ⓐ Ⓓ		79. Ⓐ Ⓓ	
4. Ⓐ Ⓓ		23. Ⓐ Ⓓ		42. Ⓐ Ⓓ		61. Ⓐ Ⓓ		80. Ⓐ Ⓓ	
5. Ⓐ Ⓓ		24. Ⓐ Ⓓ		43. Ⓐ Ⓓ		62. Ⓐ Ⓓ		81. Ⓐ Ⓓ	
6. Ⓐ Ⓓ		25. Ⓐ Ⓓ		44. Ⓐ Ⓓ		63. Ⓐ Ⓓ		82. Ⓐ Ⓓ	
7. Ⓐ Ⓓ		26. Ⓐ Ⓓ		45. Ⓐ Ⓓ		64. Ⓐ Ⓓ		83. Ⓐ Ⓓ	
8. Ⓐ Ⓓ		27. Ⓐ Ⓓ		46. Ⓐ Ⓓ		65. Ⓐ Ⓓ		84. Ⓐ Ⓓ	
9. Ⓐ Ⓓ		28. Ⓐ Ⓓ		47. Ⓐ Ⓓ		66. Ⓐ Ⓓ		85. Ⓐ Ⓓ	
10. Ⓐ Ⓓ		29. Ⓐ Ⓓ		48. Ⓐ Ⓓ		67. Ⓐ Ⓓ		86. Ⓐ Ⓓ	
11. Ⓐ Ⓓ		30. Ⓐ Ⓓ		49. Ⓐ Ⓓ		68. Ⓐ Ⓓ		87. Ⓐ Ⓓ	
12. Ⓐ Ⓓ		31. Ⓐ Ⓓ		50. Ⓐ Ⓓ		69. Ⓐ Ⓓ		88. Ⓐ Ⓓ	
13. Ⓐ Ⓓ		32. Ⓐ Ⓓ		51. Ⓐ Ⓓ		70. Ⓐ Ⓓ		89. Ⓐ Ⓓ	
14. Ⓐ Ⓓ		33. Ⓐ Ⓓ		52. Ⓐ Ⓓ		71. Ⓐ Ⓓ		90. Ⓐ Ⓓ	
15. Ⓐ Ⓓ		34. Ⓐ Ⓓ		53. Ⓐ Ⓓ		72. Ⓐ Ⓓ		91. Ⓐ Ⓓ	
16. Ⓐ Ⓓ		35. Ⓐ Ⓓ		54. Ⓐ Ⓓ		73. Ⓐ Ⓓ		92. Ⓐ Ⓓ	
17. Ⓐ Ⓓ		36. Ⓐ Ⓓ		55. Ⓐ Ⓓ		74. Ⓐ Ⓓ		93. Ⓐ Ⓓ	
18. Ⓐ Ⓓ		37. Ⓐ Ⓓ		56. Ⓐ Ⓓ		75. Ⓐ Ⓓ		94. Ⓐ Ⓓ	
19. Ⓐ Ⓓ		38. Ⓐ Ⓓ		57. Ⓐ Ⓓ		76. Ⓐ Ⓓ		95. Ⓐ Ⓓ	

PART B: MEMORY FOR ADDRESSES

1. Ⓐ Ⓑ Ⓒ Ⓓ Ⓔ	25. Ⓐ Ⓑ Ⓒ Ⓓ Ⓔ	49. Ⓐ Ⓑ Ⓒ Ⓓ Ⓔ
2. Ⓐ Ⓑ Ⓒ Ⓓ Ⓔ	26. Ⓐ Ⓑ Ⓒ Ⓓ Ⓔ	50. Ⓐ Ⓑ Ⓒ Ⓓ Ⓔ
3. Ⓐ Ⓑ Ⓒ Ⓓ Ⓔ	27. Ⓐ Ⓑ Ⓒ Ⓓ Ⓔ	51. Ⓐ Ⓑ Ⓒ Ⓓ Ⓔ
4. Ⓐ Ⓑ Ⓒ Ⓓ Ⓔ	28. Ⓐ Ⓑ Ⓒ Ⓓ Ⓔ	52. Ⓐ Ⓑ Ⓒ Ⓓ Ⓔ
5. Ⓐ Ⓑ Ⓒ Ⓓ Ⓔ	29. Ⓐ Ⓑ Ⓒ Ⓓ Ⓔ	53. Ⓐ Ⓑ Ⓒ Ⓓ Ⓔ
6. Ⓐ Ⓑ Ⓒ Ⓓ Ⓔ	30. Ⓐ Ⓑ Ⓒ Ⓓ Ⓔ	54. Ⓐ Ⓑ Ⓒ Ⓓ Ⓔ
7. Ⓐ Ⓑ Ⓒ Ⓓ Ⓔ	31. Ⓐ Ⓑ Ⓒ Ⓓ Ⓔ	55. Ⓐ Ⓑ Ⓒ Ⓓ Ⓔ
8. Ⓐ Ⓑ Ⓒ Ⓓ Ⓔ	32. Ⓐ Ⓑ Ⓒ Ⓓ Ⓔ	56. Ⓐ Ⓑ Ⓒ Ⓓ Ⓔ
9. Ⓐ Ⓑ Ⓒ Ⓓ Ⓔ	33. Ⓐ Ⓑ Ⓒ Ⓓ Ⓔ	57. Ⓐ Ⓑ Ⓒ Ⓓ Ⓔ
10. Ⓐ Ⓑ Ⓒ Ⓓ Ⓔ	34. Ⓐ Ⓑ Ⓒ Ⓓ Ⓔ	58. Ⓐ Ⓑ Ⓒ Ⓓ Ⓔ
11. Ⓐ Ⓑ Ⓒ Ⓓ Ⓔ	35. Ⓐ Ⓑ Ⓒ Ⓓ Ⓔ	59. Ⓐ Ⓑ Ⓒ Ⓓ Ⓔ
12. Ⓐ Ⓑ Ⓒ Ⓓ Ⓔ	36. Ⓐ Ⓑ Ⓒ Ⓓ Ⓔ	60. Ⓐ Ⓑ Ⓒ Ⓓ Ⓔ
13. Ⓐ Ⓑ Ⓒ Ⓓ Ⓔ	37. Ⓐ Ⓑ Ⓒ Ⓓ Ⓔ	61. Ⓐ Ⓑ Ⓒ Ⓓ Ⓔ
14. Ⓐ Ⓑ Ⓒ Ⓓ Ⓔ	38. Ⓐ Ⓑ Ⓒ Ⓓ Ⓔ	62. Ⓐ Ⓑ Ⓒ Ⓓ Ⓔ
15. Ⓐ Ⓑ Ⓒ Ⓓ Ⓔ	39. Ⓐ Ⓑ Ⓒ Ⓓ Ⓔ	63. Ⓐ Ⓑ Ⓒ Ⓓ Ⓔ
16. Ⓐ Ⓑ Ⓒ Ⓓ Ⓔ	40. Ⓐ Ⓑ Ⓒ Ⓓ Ⓔ	64. Ⓐ Ⓑ Ⓒ Ⓓ Ⓔ
17. Ⓐ Ⓑ Ⓒ Ⓓ Ⓔ	41. Ⓐ Ⓑ Ⓒ Ⓓ Ⓔ	65. Ⓐ Ⓑ Ⓒ Ⓓ Ⓔ
18. Ⓐ Ⓑ Ⓒ Ⓓ Ⓔ	42. Ⓐ Ⓑ Ⓒ Ⓓ Ⓔ	66. Ⓐ Ⓑ Ⓒ Ⓓ Ⓔ
19. Ⓐ Ⓑ Ⓒ Ⓓ Ⓔ	43. Ⓐ Ⓑ Ⓒ Ⓓ Ⓔ	67. Ⓐ Ⓑ Ⓒ Ⓓ Ⓔ
20. Ⓐ Ⓑ Ⓒ Ⓓ Ⓔ	44. Ⓐ Ⓑ Ⓒ Ⓓ Ⓔ	68. Ⓐ Ⓑ Ⓒ Ⓓ Ⓔ
21. Ⓐ Ⓑ Ⓒ Ⓓ Ⓔ	45. Ⓐ Ⓑ Ⓒ Ⓓ Ⓔ	69. Ⓐ Ⓑ Ⓒ Ⓓ Ⓔ
22. Ⓐ Ⓑ Ⓒ Ⓓ Ⓔ	46. Ⓐ Ⓑ Ⓒ Ⓓ Ⓔ	70. Ⓐ Ⓑ Ⓒ Ⓓ Ⓔ
23. Ⓐ Ⓑ Ⓒ Ⓓ Ⓔ	47. Ⓐ Ⓑ Ⓒ Ⓓ Ⓔ	71. Ⓐ Ⓑ Ⓒ Ⓓ Ⓔ
24. Ⓐ Ⓑ Ⓒ Ⓓ Ⓔ	48. Ⓐ Ⓑ Ⓒ Ⓓ Ⓔ	72. Ⓐ Ⓑ Ⓒ Ⓓ Ⓔ

PART B: MEMORY FOR ADDRESSES CONT.

73. Ⓐ Ⓑ Ⓒ Ⓓ Ⓔ
74. Ⓐ Ⓑ Ⓒ Ⓓ Ⓔ
75. Ⓐ Ⓑ Ⓒ Ⓓ Ⓔ
76. Ⓐ Ⓑ Ⓒ Ⓓ Ⓔ
77. Ⓐ Ⓑ Ⓒ Ⓓ Ⓔ
78. Ⓐ Ⓑ Ⓒ Ⓓ Ⓔ

79. Ⓐ Ⓑ Ⓒ Ⓓ Ⓔ
80. Ⓐ Ⓑ Ⓒ Ⓓ Ⓔ
81. Ⓐ Ⓑ Ⓒ Ⓓ Ⓔ
82. Ⓐ Ⓑ Ⓒ Ⓓ Ⓔ
83. Ⓐ Ⓑ Ⓒ Ⓓ Ⓔ
84. Ⓐ Ⓑ Ⓒ Ⓓ Ⓔ

85. Ⓐ Ⓑ Ⓒ Ⓓ Ⓔ
86. Ⓐ Ⓑ Ⓒ Ⓓ Ⓔ
87. Ⓐ Ⓑ Ⓒ Ⓓ Ⓔ
88. Ⓐ Ⓑ Ⓒ Ⓓ Ⓔ

PART C: NUMBER SERIES

1. Ⓐ Ⓑ Ⓒ Ⓓ Ⓔ
2. Ⓐ Ⓑ Ⓒ Ⓓ Ⓔ
3. Ⓐ Ⓑ Ⓒ Ⓓ Ⓔ
4. Ⓐ Ⓑ Ⓒ Ⓓ Ⓔ
5. Ⓐ Ⓑ Ⓒ Ⓓ Ⓔ
6. Ⓐ Ⓑ Ⓒ Ⓓ Ⓔ
7. Ⓐ Ⓑ Ⓒ Ⓓ Ⓔ
8. Ⓐ Ⓑ Ⓒ Ⓓ Ⓔ

9. Ⓐ Ⓑ Ⓒ Ⓓ Ⓔ
10. Ⓐ Ⓑ Ⓒ Ⓓ Ⓔ
11. Ⓐ Ⓑ Ⓒ Ⓓ Ⓔ
12. Ⓐ Ⓑ Ⓒ Ⓓ Ⓔ
13. Ⓐ Ⓑ Ⓒ Ⓓ Ⓔ
14. Ⓐ Ⓑ Ⓒ Ⓓ Ⓔ
15. Ⓐ Ⓑ Ⓒ Ⓓ Ⓔ
16. Ⓐ Ⓑ Ⓒ Ⓓ Ⓔ

17. Ⓐ Ⓑ Ⓒ Ⓓ Ⓔ
18. Ⓐ Ⓑ Ⓒ Ⓓ Ⓔ
19. Ⓐ Ⓑ Ⓒ Ⓓ Ⓔ
20. Ⓐ Ⓑ Ⓒ Ⓓ Ⓔ
21. Ⓐ Ⓑ Ⓒ Ⓓ Ⓔ
22. Ⓐ Ⓑ Ⓒ Ⓓ Ⓔ
23. Ⓐ Ⓑ Ⓒ Ⓓ Ⓔ
24. Ⓐ Ⓑ Ⓒ Ⓓ Ⓔ

PART D: FOLLOWING ORAL DIRECTIONS

1. Ⓐ Ⓑ Ⓒ Ⓓ Ⓔ
2. Ⓐ Ⓑ Ⓒ Ⓓ Ⓔ
3. Ⓐ Ⓑ Ⓒ Ⓓ Ⓔ
4. Ⓐ Ⓑ Ⓒ Ⓓ Ⓔ
5. Ⓐ Ⓑ Ⓒ Ⓓ Ⓔ
6. Ⓐ Ⓑ Ⓒ Ⓓ Ⓔ
7. Ⓐ Ⓑ Ⓒ Ⓓ Ⓔ
8. Ⓐ Ⓑ Ⓒ Ⓓ Ⓔ
9. Ⓐ Ⓑ Ⓒ Ⓓ Ⓔ
10. Ⓐ Ⓑ Ⓒ Ⓓ Ⓔ
11. Ⓐ Ⓑ Ⓒ Ⓓ Ⓔ
12. Ⓐ Ⓑ Ⓒ Ⓓ Ⓔ
13. Ⓐ Ⓑ Ⓒ Ⓓ Ⓔ
14. Ⓐ Ⓑ Ⓒ Ⓓ Ⓔ
15. Ⓐ Ⓑ Ⓒ Ⓓ Ⓔ
16. Ⓐ Ⓑ Ⓒ Ⓓ Ⓔ
17. Ⓐ Ⓑ Ⓒ Ⓓ Ⓔ

18. Ⓐ Ⓑ Ⓒ Ⓓ Ⓔ
19. Ⓐ Ⓑ Ⓒ Ⓓ Ⓔ
20. Ⓐ Ⓑ Ⓒ Ⓓ Ⓔ
21. Ⓐ Ⓑ Ⓒ Ⓓ Ⓔ
22. Ⓐ Ⓑ Ⓒ Ⓓ Ⓔ
23. Ⓐ Ⓑ Ⓒ Ⓓ Ⓔ
24. Ⓐ Ⓑ Ⓒ Ⓓ Ⓔ
25. Ⓐ Ⓑ Ⓒ Ⓓ Ⓔ
26. Ⓐ Ⓑ Ⓒ Ⓓ Ⓔ
27. Ⓐ Ⓑ Ⓒ Ⓓ Ⓔ
28. Ⓐ Ⓑ Ⓒ Ⓓ Ⓔ
29. Ⓐ Ⓑ Ⓒ Ⓓ Ⓔ
30. Ⓐ Ⓑ Ⓒ Ⓓ Ⓔ
31. Ⓐ Ⓑ Ⓒ Ⓓ Ⓔ
32. Ⓐ Ⓑ Ⓒ Ⓓ Ⓔ
33. Ⓐ Ⓑ Ⓒ Ⓓ Ⓔ
34. Ⓐ Ⓑ Ⓒ Ⓓ Ⓔ

35. Ⓐ Ⓑ Ⓒ Ⓓ Ⓔ
36. Ⓐ Ⓑ Ⓒ Ⓓ Ⓔ
37. Ⓐ Ⓑ Ⓒ Ⓓ Ⓔ
38. Ⓐ Ⓑ Ⓒ Ⓓ Ⓔ
39. Ⓐ Ⓑ Ⓒ Ⓓ Ⓔ
40. Ⓐ Ⓑ Ⓒ Ⓓ Ⓔ
41. Ⓐ Ⓑ Ⓒ Ⓓ Ⓔ
42. Ⓐ Ⓑ Ⓒ Ⓓ Ⓔ
43. Ⓐ Ⓑ Ⓒ Ⓓ Ⓔ
44. Ⓐ Ⓑ Ⓒ Ⓓ Ⓔ
45. Ⓐ Ⓑ Ⓒ Ⓓ Ⓔ
46. Ⓐ Ⓑ Ⓒ Ⓓ Ⓔ
47. Ⓐ Ⓑ Ⓒ Ⓓ Ⓔ
48. Ⓐ Ⓑ Ⓒ Ⓓ Ⓔ
49. Ⓐ Ⓑ Ⓒ Ⓓ Ⓔ
50. Ⓐ Ⓑ Ⓒ Ⓓ Ⓔ

POSTAL EXAM #1

PART A: ADDRESS CHECKING

Below are 95 pairs of addresses. Look at each pair and decide if the two addresses are alike or different in any way. It they are exactly ALIKE, darken circle A on your answer sheet; if they are DIFFERENT in any way, darken circle D. You will have six minutes to answer the 95 questions.

1.	1617 Ellis Dr	1617 Ellis Dr
2.	710 Holloway St	710 Holloday St
3.	4220 E Morgan St	4220 E Morgan St
4.	363 Cornwallis Dr	363 Cornwallis Cr
5.	1417 Alexander Ave	1471 Alexander Ave
6.	Denver CO 80201	Denver CO 80201
7.	3584 Hemlock Ln	3584 Hemlock Ln
8.	1290 Brannon Rd	1290 Brennon Rd
9.	626 Weaver Dairy Rd	626 Weaver Dairy Rt
10.	5103 Meadowview Rd	5103 Meadowview Rd
11.	7883 W Foster Dr	7883 W Foster Dr
12.	826 S Farmington St	826 S Farmington St
13.	Auburn AL 38630	Auburn AL 36830
14.	4913 Penbrook Ave	4913 Penbrook Ave
15.	727 Housman St	727 Housman St
16.	923 Williams Circle	932 Williams Circle
17.	Winston-Salem NC 27106	Winston-Salem NC 27706
18.	2821 Wesleyan Ln	2821 Wesleyan Ln
19.	Boise ID 83708	Boise IL 83708
20.	4164 Lytchfield Ct	4164 Litchfield Ct

21. 4745 Schooner Blvd   4745 Schooner Blvd

22. Roxbury NY 12474   Roxbury NY 12747

23. Spencer IA 51301   Spencer ID 51301

24. 11745 Anderson Ridge Rd   11745 Anderson Ridge Rd

25. Annapolis MT 21401   Annapolis MD 21401

26. 31 Abington Ave   31 Abington Ave

27. 2110 37th St   2110 37th St

28. 8838 Vermont St NW   8838 Vermont St NW

29. 9119 Coachway Dr   9191 Coachway Dr

30. Taylorsville NC 28681   Taylorsville NC 28681

31. 2002 Westminister Dr   2002 Westminister Cr

32. 5511 W Glenwood Ave   5511 W Glenwood Ave

33. 732 Moorefield St   732 Morefield St

34. 2958 Home Ave   2598 Home Ave

35. 1618 Smith Level Rd   1618 Smith Level Dr

36. Rockville MD 20851   Rockville MD 20581

37. 10320 Hickory Ridge   10320 Hickory Ridge

38. 231 Park Place #32   231 Park Place #32

39. 203 E Quailwood Court   203 S Quailwood Court

40. 87 East 23rd St   87 East 23rd St

41. Tulsa OK 74104   Tulsa OK 71404

42. Altamont NY 12009   Altamont NJ 12009

43. 6619 10th St   6619 10th St

44. 601 N Channel Dr   601 E Channel Dr

45. 211 Watkins Place   211 Watkins Place

46.	600 Audobon Lake Dr	600 Audobon Lake Dr
47.	21 Westview Dr #31	21 Westview Dr #37
48.	Niskayuna NY 12309	Niskayuna NY 12309
49.	608 South 5th St	608 South 6th St
50.	Flagstaff AZ 86004	Flagstaff AZ 86004
51.	2626 Southeast Dr	2626 Southwest Dr
52.	1980 W 34th St	1890 W 34th St
53.	171 Springton Parkway	171 Springton Parkway
54.	398 Valley Mills Ln	398 Valley Hills Ln
55.	Danville VA 24541	Danville MA 24541
56.	7244 Clearwater Cr	7244 Clearwater Cr
57.	5608 Maplewood Dr	5806 Maplewood Dr
58.	3552 University Dr SE	3552 University Dr SW
59.	1914 Turnpike Dr	1914 Turnpike Dr
60.	Washington DC 20035-5200	Washington DC 20053-5200
61.	23903 Flamenco Ct	23903 Flamenco Ct
62.	218 Williamson Ave	218 Williamston Ave
63.	Santa Fe NM 87501	Sante Fe NM 85701
64.	416 N Oakhurst Dr	416 N Oakhurst Dr
65.	7471 Pine Island Rd	7471 Pine Island Rd
66.	220 East 26th St	220 East 26th St
67.	Bowling Green OH 43402	Bowling Green OK 43402
68.	2211 Redford Ave	2211 Radford Ave
69.	55 N Lakeshore Dr	55 N Lakeshore Dr
70.	Texarkana TX 75501	Texarkana TX 75701

71. 6013 E Windsor Ave   6013 E Windsor Ave

72. 515 Summit Ave NW   515 Summit Ave NE

73. 9236 Water St   9236 Walter St

74. 2202 Del Casa Dr   2202 Del Casa Dr

75. 4462 Woodson Trace   4462 Woodson Place

76. 8701 E McCarty Lane   8707 E McCarty Lane

77. Warren RI 02885   Warren RI 02885

78. 9560 W Broadway St   9560 W Broadway Ct

79. 117 Corner Bend Terrace   117 Corner Bend Terrace

80. 6348 Leicester Hwy   6348 Leicester Hwy

81. 2029 Reynolda Rd   2029 Reynolds Rd

82. Mankato MN 56001   Mankato MN 56001

83. 432 N Southfields Ave   432 N Southfields Ave

84. 1520 N St NW   1520 M St NW

85. 7483 W Market St   7483 W Market St

86. Albany CA 94706   Albany CA 97406

87. 16774 SW Shelby Court   16774 SW Shelby Court

88. 2521 Meredith Turnpike   2521 Meredith Turnpike

89. Greensboro NC 27405   Greensboro NC 27405

90. 7801 Foxcove Ct   7801 Foxgrove Ct

91. 5206 Newburgh Hts   5206 Newburgh St

92. 3832 Glen Burnie Hwy   3832 Glen Burnie Hwy

93. St Louis MO 63112   St Louis MO 62112

94. Wilkes-Barre PA 18701   Wilkes-Barre PA 18701

95. 147 Schuykill Ave   147 Schuykill Ave

PART B: MEMORY FOR ADDRESSES

Below are five boxes labeled A, B, C, D, and E. Each box contains three sets of addresses (which include street names with number ranges) and two single names. Study the boxes for **ten minutes** and memorize the location (A, B, C, D, or E) of each of the numbered addresses and single names. Then answer the 88 questions on the next page by darkening the circle (A, B, C, D, or E) that corresponds to the box in which the address or name appears. You will have **five minutes** to answer the 88 questions.

A	B	C	D	E
5200–6299 Broad	7200–8399 Broad	4100–5199 Broad	2400–4099 Broad	6300–7199 Broad
Garcia	Newton	Owens	Truitt	Harris
4100–5199 Maple	1200–2199 Maple	5200–6299 Maple	3100–4099 Maple	2200–3099 Maple
Sanderson	Harper	Chen	Shipp	Woodward
6300–7199 Alpine	5200–6299 Alpine	7200–8399 Alpine	8400–9799 Alpine	4100–5199 Alpine

1. 1200–2199 Maple
2. 5200–6299 Broad
3. 5200–6099 Alpine
4. Woodward
5. Shipp
6. 8400–9799 Alpine
7. 4100–5199 Maple
8. Truitt
9. 2200–3099 Maple
10. Harper
11. Newton
12. 4100–5199 Alpine
13. 4100–5199 Maple
14. Owens
15. 2400–4099 Broad
16. Chen
17. 4100–5199 Broad
18. Garcia
19. 1200–2199 Maple
20. 7200–8399 Alpine
21. 3100–4099 Maple
22. Sanderson
23. 6300–7199 Broad
24. 5200–6299 Alpine
25. 7200–8399 Broad
26. 2200–3099 Maple
27. 8400–9799 Alpine
28. 2200–2399 Maple
29. 5200–6299 Broad
30. 3100–4099 Maple
31. Woodward
32. 2400–4099 Broad
33. Garcia
34. 6300–7199 Broad
35. Shipp
36. 3100–4099 Maple
37. 6300–7199 Alpine
38. Harper
39. 5200–6299 Broad
40. Owens
41. Truitt
42. Sanderson
43. 1200–2199 Maple
44. Harris
45. 7200–8399 Broad
46. 4100–5199 Alpine
47. Newton
48. 5200–6299 Maple
49. 6300–7199 Alpine
50. 4100–5199 Broad

51. Woodward

52. 6300–7199 Broad

53. 7200–8399 Alpine

54. 6300–7199 Broad

55. Chen

56. Harper

57. 4100–5199 Alpine

58. 7200–8399 Broad

59. Harris

60. 2400–4099 Broad

61. Newton

62. 5200–6299 Maple

63. 8400–9799 Alpine

64. 4100–5199 Broad

65. Shipp

66. Owens

67. Chen

68. Harris

69. Harper

70. 4100–5199 Broad

71. 5200–6299 Maple

72. Truitt

73. 7200–8399 Broad

74. 3100–4099 Maple

75. Garcia

76. Woodward

77. Truitt

78. 6300–7199 Alpine

79. 2400–4099 Broad

80. 7200–8399 Alpine

81. Sanderson

82. 5200–6299 Alpine

83. Shipp

84. Harper

85. 5200–6299 Broad

86. 4100–5199 Maple

87. Harris

88. Garcia

PART C: NUMBER SERIES

Below, on the left, you will see a series of numbers that follow some definite order. On the right are five sets of two numbers each, labeled A, B, C, D, and E. Look at the number series to find its pattern, and then darken the circle for the answer pair that would come next in the series, if the same pattern were followed. You have 20 minutes for this section.

1. 66 59 52 45 38 31 24 . . . . **A)** 17 10 **B)** 16 9 **C)** 17 11 **D)** 17 9 **E)** 16 10

2. 7 10 19 14 17 19 21 . . . . **A)** 24 17 **B)** 24 19 **C)** 24 27 **D)** 25 28 **E)** 19 22

3. 74 66 58 50 42 34 26 . . . . **A)** 20 12 **B)** 18 8 **C)** 20 10 **D)** 18 10 **E)** 16 8

4. 50 5 40 10 30 15 20 . . . . **A)** 25 15 **B)** 20 10 **C)** 20 25 **D)** 10 5 **E)** 10 15

5. 19 19 17 17 15 15 13 . . . . **A)** 11 11 **B)** 13 13 **C)** 13 15 **D)** 11 12 **E)** 13 11

6. 21 24 30 21 36 42 21 . . . . **A)** 54 21 **B)** 50 56 **C)** 48 21 **D)** 46 54 **E)** 48 54

7. 9 11 33 13 15 33 17 . . . . **A)** 19 33 **B)** 33 35 **C)** 33 19 **D)** 15 33 **E)** 19 21

8. 2 7 12 17 22 27 32 . . . . **A)** 38 42 **B)** 37 42 **C)** 37 43 **D)** 36 42 **E)** 32 37

9. 33 31 27 25 21 19 15 . . . . **A)** 9 7 **B)** 17 11 **C)** 13 9 **D)** 11 7 **E)** 9 13

10. 28 25 5 21 18 5 14 . . . . **A)** 11 5 **B)** 10 7 **C)** 11 8 **D)** 5 10 **E)** 10 5

11. 9 12 11 14 13 16 15 . . . . **A)** 14 13 **B)** 18 21 **C)** 14 17 **D)** 12 13 **E)** 18 17

12. 44 44 50 50 56 56 62 . . . . **A)** 68 68 **B)** 62 70 **C)** 62 68 **D)** 68 74 **E)** 62 66

13. 75 65 85 55 45 85 35 . . . . **A)** 25 15 **B)** 25 85 **C)** 35 25 **D)** 85 35 **E)** 25 85

14. 1 10 7 20 13 30 19 . . . . **A)** 26 40 **B)** 29 36 **C)** 40 25 **D)** 25 31 **E)** 40 50

15. 2 8 14 20 26 32 38 . . . . **A)** 42 46 **B)** 44 50 **C)** 42 48 **D)** 40 42 **E)** 32 26

16. 10 20 25 35 40 50 55 . . . . **A)** 70 65 **B)** 60 70 **C)** 60 75 **D)** 60 65 **E)** 65 70

17. 40 40 31 31 22 22 13 . . . . **A)** 13 4   **B)** 13 5   **C)** 4 13   **D)** 9 4   **E)** 4 4

18. 17 17 34 20 20 31 23 . . . . **A)** 26 23   **B)** 34 20   **C)** 23 33   **D)** 27 28   **E)** 23 28

19. 2 3 4 5 6 4 8 . . . . **A)** 9 10   **B)** 4 8   **C)** 10 4   **D)** 9 4   **E)** 8 9

20. 61 57 50 61 43 36 61 . . . . **A)** 29 61   **B)** 27 20   **C)** 31 61   **D)** 22 15   **E)** 29 22

21. 9 16 23 30 37 44 51 . . . . **A)** 59 66   **B)** 56 62   **C)** 58 66   **D)** 58 65   **E)** 54 61

22. 8 22 12 16 22 20 24 . . . . **A)** 28 32   **B)** 28 22   **C)** 22 28   **D)** 32 36   **E)** 22 26

23. 2 22 4 18 6 14 8 . . . . **A)** 10 12   **B)** 10 6   **C)** 12 8   **D)** 10 10   **E)** 18 6

24. 13 17 21 25 29 33 37 . . . . **A)** 42 46   **B)** 41 46   **C)** 42 47   **D)** 41 45   **E)** 41 55

PART D: FOLLOWING ORAL DIRECTIONS

Listen closely to the instructions the examiner gives you. The examiner will refer you to the following lines. Write whatever the examiner tells you on the lines, and then fill in the answer grid as the examiner directs you. The examiner will not repeat the instructions.

Line 1. 31 E   23 B   15 D

Line 2. b   e   a   C   d

Line 3. _____ C   _____ A   _____ E   _____ D   _____ B

Line 4. 13 _____   24 _____   32 _____   41 _____   14 _____

Line 5. 40 _____   29 _____   47 _____   35 _____   21 _____

Line 6. 3 _____   E _____   35 _____   A _____   17 _____

Line 7. ┌──┐ ┌──┐ ┌──┐ ┌──┐ ┌──┐
          │14│ │17│ │13│ │19│ │15│
          └──┘ └──┘ └──┘ └──┘ └──┘

Line 8. 8-Dog   18-Cat   9-Bird   19-Elk   6-Antelope

Line 9. 2630/38-A   6570/2-D   8810/12-E   5140/25-B   3290/46-C

Line 10.
┌─────────────┐
│ 3-B   29-C │
│ 31-D 12-A │
└─────────────┘

Line 11. 41 _____   27 _____

Line 12. A   A   B   E   A

Line 13. April 13 _____   July 10 _____   June 16 _____   March 30 _____   May 25 _____

Line 14. 48 ☐   > ☐   & ☐   % ☐   28 ☐

Line 15. ! _____   # _____   + _____   * _____ $ _____

Line 16. C-cherry/10-E   A-apple/25-B   D-date/50-A   E-apricot/25-D   B-banana/4-C

Line 17. 29 29   10 10   45 35   48 48   2 2

Line 18. +31   −44   +18   +1   +22

EXAMINER INSTRUCTIONS

Look at Line 1. (**Pause slightly.**) Circle the middle number-letter combination. (**Pause two seconds.**) On your answer grid, find the combination you circled and darken the appropriate space. (**Pause five seconds.**)

Look at the letters in Line 2. (**Pause slightly.**) Draw a line under the letter that is a capital letter. (**Pause two seconds.**) On your answer grid, find number 7. (**Pause two seconds.**) Darken the space that matches the letter you underlined. (**Pause five seconds.**)

Look at Line 3. (**Pause slightly.**) Write the number 43 on the line that precedes the second letter. (**Pause two seconds.**) Now, on your answer grid, find the number-letter combination you just wrote and darken the appropriate space. (**Pause five seconds.**)

Look at the numbers in Line 4. (**Pause slightly.**) Draw a line under the fourth number on the line. (**Pause two seconds.**) Now, reverse the digits of that number and write the resulting number on the blank to the right of the number you underlined. (**Pause two seconds.**) Then, on your answer grid, find the number you just wrote. (**Pause two seconds.**) Now, darken space C as in cat for that number.

Look at Line 5. (**Pause slightly.**) Write the letter A as in apple to the right of the *lowest* number. (**Pause two seconds.**) Then, on your answer grid, darken the space for the number-letter combination you just wrote. (**Pause five seconds.**)

Look at the row of numbers and letters in Line 6. (**Pause slightly.**) Draw a line under the fourth letter or number in this line. (**Pause two seconds.**) Write the number 39 on the blank line to the right of the letter or number you just underlined. (**Pause two seconds.**) Then, on your answer grid, darken the space for the number-letter combination you just wrote. (**Pause five seconds.**)

Look at Line 7. (**Pause slightly.**) Write the letter B as in boy next to the number in the second box from the left. (**Pause two seconds.**) Then, on your answer grid, darken the space for the number-letter combination you just wrote. (**Pause five seconds.**)

Look at Line 5 again. (**Pause two seconds.**) Draw a circle around the even number. (**Pause two seconds.**) Next, write the letter D as in dog on the line to the right of that number. (**Pause two seconds.**) Now, on your answer grid, darken the space for the number-letter combination you just wrote. (**Pause five seconds.**)

Look at Line 8. (**Pause two seconds.**) Each number in the line is followed by a word. (**Pause slightly.**) Draw a circle around the word that begins with the letter E as in elephant. (**Pause two seconds.**) Now, underline the number next to the word you just circled. (**Pause two seconds.**) Then, on your answer grid, find the number you just underlined. Darken the letter A as in apple next to that number. (**Pause five seconds.**)

Look at Line 9. (**Pause slightly.**) Draw a line under the highest four-digit number in this line. (**Pause three seconds.**) Then, draw a circle around the number-letter combination immediately to the right of the number you underlined. (**Pause two seconds.**) On your answer grid, darken the space for the combination you circled. (**Pause five seconds.**)

Look at the box in Line 10. (**Pause slightly.**) Draw a line under the number-letter combination located in the lower left corner of the box. (**Pause two seconds.**) Now, on your answer grid, find the space for the combination you just underlined and darken that space. (**Pause five seconds.**)

Look at Line 11. (**Pause slightly.**) If the first number is less than the second, write the letter B as in boy on the line next to the first number. (**Pause slightly.**) If the second number is less than the first, write the letter C as in cat on the line next to the second number. (**Pause two seconds.**) Now, on your answer grid, darken the space for the number-letter combination you just wrote. (**Pause five seconds.**)

Look at Line 12. (**Pause slightly.**) Find the letter that appears the most times and draw a circle around the last appearance of that letter in the line. (**Pause two seconds.**) Then, on your answer grid, find number 33. (**Pause two seconds.**) Now, darken the space for the letter you just circled. (**Pause five seconds.**)

Look at Line 10 again. (**Pause two seconds.**) Find the number-letter combination in the lower left corner. (**Pause two seconds.**) Now, move clockwise two places and draw a circle around that number-letter combination. (**Pause two seconds.**) On your answer grid, darken the space for the number-letter combination you just circled. (**Pause five seconds.**)

Look at Line 6 again. (**Pause two seconds.**) Find the lowest number and write the letter D as in dog next to it. (**Pause two seconds.**) Now, on your answer grid, darken the space for the number-letter combination you just created. (**Pause five seconds.**)

Look at the dates in Line 13. (**Pause two seconds.**) Draw a line under the *earliest* of the five dates. (**Pause three seconds.**) Write the letter B as in boy on the line next to the date you underlined. (**Pause two seconds.**) Now, on your answer grid, find the number of the date you underlined (**pause two seconds**) and darken the space for the letter you wrote. (**Pause five seconds.**)

Look at Line 14. (**Pause slightly.**) Draw a line under the number to the right of the percent sign. (**Pause two seconds.**) Then, write the letter E as in elephant in the box next to the number you underlined. (**Pause two seconds.**) Now, on your answer grid, find the number-letter combination you wrote and darken that space. (**Pause five seconds.**)

Look at the symbols in Line 15. (**Pause slightly.**) If the fifth symbol is a dollar sign, find number 15 on your answer grid and darken the letter E as in elephant. (**Pause three seconds.**) If the symbol is *not* a dollar sign, find the number 16 on your answer grid and darken the letter E as in elephant. (**Pause five seconds.**)

Look at Line 16. (**Pause slightly.**) Find the letter that does *not* match the first letter of the type of fruit it is next to, and underline that letter and word. (**Pause three seconds.**) Then, draw a circle around the number-letter combination next to the word you underlined. (**Pause two seconds.**) Now, on your answer grid, darken the space for the combination you just circled. (**Pause five seconds.**)

Look at the pairs of numbers in Line 17. (**Pause slightly.**) Draw a line under the pair in which the numbers are not the same. (**Pause two seconds.**) Then, circle the *lower* of the two numbers you underlined. (**Pause two seconds.**) Now, on your answer grid, find the number you just circled and darken the space E as in elephant for that number. (**Pause five seconds.**)

Look at Line 15 again. (**Pause two seconds.**) Find the exclamation point and write a 37 on the blank line to the right of it. (**Pause two seconds.**) Then, on your answer grid, find the number you just wrote (**pause slightly**), and darken space A as in apple. (**Pause five seconds.**)

Look at Line 18. (**Pause two seconds.**) Draw a line under the number that is preceded by a minus sign. (**Pause two seconds.**) Now, on your answer grid, find the number you underlined and darken space B as in boy. (**Pause five seconds.**)

Look at Line 7 again. (**Pause two seconds.**) Find the numbers in the second and third boxes. (**Pause slightly.**) Then, find the lower of those two numbers and draw a circle around it. (**Pause two seconds.**) Now, on your answer grid, find the number you just circled and darken space A as in apple. (**Pause five seconds.**)

Look at Line 16 again. (**Pause two seconds.**) Draw a line under the word "date." (**Pause two seconds.**) Now, draw a square around the number-letter combination next to the word you just underlined. (**Pause two seconds.**) Now, on your answer grid, darken the space for the number-letter combination in the square you drew. (**Pause five seconds.**)

Look at Line 18 again. (**Pause two seconds.**) Draw a circle around the fourth number in the line. (**Pause two seconds.**) Now, on your answer grid, find the number you circled. (**Pause two seconds.**) If the number was preceded by a plus sign, darken space A as in apple. (**Pause two seconds.**) If the number was preceded by a minus sign, darken space B as in baker. (**Pause five seconds.**)

ANSWERS

PART A: ADDRESS CHECKING

1. A	25. D	49. D	73. D
2. D	26. A	50. A	74. A
3. A	27. A	51. D	75. D
4. D	28. A	52. D	76. D
5. D	29. D	53. A	77. A
6. A	30. A	54. D	78. D
7. A	31. D	55. D	79. A
8. D	32. A	56. A	80. A
9. D	33. D	57. D	81. D
10. A	34. D	58. D	82. A
11. A	35. D	59. A	83. A
12. A	36. D	60. D	84. D
13. D	37. A	61. A	85. A
14. A	38. A	62. D	86. D
15. A	39. D	63. D	87. A
16. D	40. A	64. A	88. A
17. D	41. D	65. A	89. A
18. A	42. D	66. A	90. D
19. D	43. A	67. D	91. D
20. D	44. D	68. D	92. A
21. A	45. A	69. A	93. D
22. D	46. A	70. D	94. A
23. D	47. D	71. A	95. A
24. A	48. A	72. D	

PART B: MEMORY FOR ADDRESSES

1. B	23. E	45. B	67. C
2. A	24. B	46. E	68. E
3. B	25. B	47. B	69. B
4. E	26. E	48. C	70. C
5. D	27. D	49. A	71. C
6. D	28. E	50. C	72. D
7. A	29. A	51. E	73. B
8. D	30. D	52. E	74. D
9. E	31. E	53. C	75. A
10. B	32. D	54. E	76. E
11. B	33. A	55. C	77. D
12. E	34. E	56. B	78. A
13. A	35. D	57. E	79. D
14. C	36. D	58. B	80. C
15. D	37. A	59. E	81. A
16. C	38. B	60. D	82. B
17. C	39. A	61. B	83. D
18. A	40. C	62. C	84. B
19. B	41. D	63. D	85. A
20. C	42. A	64. C	86. A
21. D	43. B	65. D	87. E
22. A	44. E	66. C	88. A

PART C: NUMBER SERIES

1. **A.** In this simple subtraction series, each number is 7 less than the previous number.

2. **B.** This is an alternating addition series, with a random number, 19, interpolated as every third number. The addition series alternates between adding 3 and adding 4. The number 19 appears after each number arrived at by adding 3.

3. **D.** In this simple subtraction series, each number is 8 less than the previous number.

4. **B.** This is an alternating addition and subtraction series. In the first pattern, 10 is subtracted from each number to arrive at the next. In the second, 5 is added to each number to arrive at the next.

5. **E.** This is a simple subtraction with repetition series. It begins with 19, which is repeated, then 2 is subtracted, resulting in 17, which is repeated, and so on.

6. **E.** This is a simple addition series with a random number, 21, interpolated as every third number. In the series, 6 is added to each number except 21, to arrive at the next number.

7. **A.** In this alternating repetition series, a random number, 33, is interpolated every third number into a simple addition series, in which each number increases by 2.

8. **B.** In this simple addition series, each number is 5 greater than the previous number.

9. **C.** This is an alternating subtraction series. First 2 is subtracted, then 4, then 2, and so on.

10. **A.** This is an alternating subtraction series with the interpolation of a random number, 5, as every third number. In the subtraction series, 3 is subtracted, then 4, then 3, and so on.

11. **E.** This is a simple alternating addition and subtraction series. First, 3 is added, then 1 is subtracted; then 3 is added, 1 subtracted, and so on.

12. **C.** This is an alternation with repetition series, in which each number repeats itself, then increases by 6.

13. **B.** This is a simple subtraction series in which a random number, 85, is interpolated as every third number. In the subtraction series, 10 is subtracted from each number to arrive at the next.

14. **C.** Here every other number follows a different pattern. In the first series, 6 is added to each number to arrive at the next. In the second series, 10 is added to each number to arrive at the next.

15. **B.** This is a simple addition series, which begins with 2 and adds 6.

16. **E.** This is an alternating addition series, in which 10 is added, then 5, then 10, and so on.

17. **A.** This is a subtraction series with repetition. Each number repeats itself and then decreases by 9.

18. **E.** This is an alternating subtraction series with repetition. There are two different patterns here. In the first, a number repeats itself; then 3 is added to that number to arrive at the next number, which also repeats. This gives the series 17, 17, 20, 20, 23, and so on. Every third number follows a second pattern, in which 3 is subtracted from each number to arrive at the next: 34, 31, 28.

19. **D.** This is an alternating addition series, with a random number, 4, interpolated as every third number. In the main series 1 is added, then 2 is added, then 1, then 2, and so on.

20. E. This is an alternating repetition series, in which a random number, 61, is interpolated as every third number into an otherwise simple subtraction series. Starting with the second number, 57, each number (except 61) is 7 less than the previous number.

21. D. Here is a simple addition series, which begins with 9 and adds 7.

22. C. This is an alternating repetition series, with a random number, 22, interpolated as every third number into an otherwise simple addition series. In the addition series, 4 is added to each number to arrive at the next number.

23. D. This is an alternating addition and subtraction series. In the first pattern, 2 is added to each number to arrive at the next; in the alternate pattern, 4 is subtracted from each number to arrive at the next.

24. D. In this simple addition series, each number is 4 more than the previous number.

PART D: FOLLOWING ORAL DIRECTIONS

You should have filled in only the numbers listed below with the answers indicated. The rest of the numbers on your answer grid should be blank. However, filling in a number that should have been blank does not count, as only questions you got right are scored.

1. A	**17.** B	**29.** C	**40.** D
3. D	**19.** A	**30.** B	**43.** A
7. C	**21.** A	**31.** D	**44.** B
12. E	**23.** B	**33.** A	**50.** A
13. A	**25.** D	**35.** E	
14. C	**27.** C	**37.** A	
15. E	**28.** E	**39.** A	

SCORING

The USPS uses a complicated formula to convert your raw score—the number of questions you got right, minus a fraction of the number you got wrong for some parts of the exam—to a scaled score. The scaled score is on a scale of 1 to 100, and that's the score the USPS will use to rank you against other applicants. Before you can approximate your scaled score, however, you have to figure out your raw score.

YOUR RAW SCORE

Parts A and B of the postal exam are scored in a way that makes random guessing work against you: A fraction of your wrong answer score is subtracted from your right answer score. Parts C and D are scored by counting right answers only. So here's how to determine your raw score for each part.

Part A: Address Checking

First, count the questions you got right. Then, count the number of questions you got wrong. Subtract your wrong answers from your right answers to get your raw score. Questions you didn't answer don't count either way.

1. Number of questions right: _____

2. Number of questions wrong: _____

3. Subtract number 2 from number 1: _____

The result of number 3 above is your raw score on Part A.

Part B: Memory for Addresses

Count the questions you got right. Then, count the number of questions you got wrong and divide by four. Subtract the results of the division from the number you got right to determine your raw score. Questions you didn't answer don't count either way.

4. Number of questions right: _____

5. Number of questions wrong: _____

6. Divide number 5 by 4: _____

7. Subtract number 6 from number 4: _____

The result of number 7 above is your raw score on Part B.

Part C: Number Series and Part D: Following Oral Directions

Your raw scores on Part C and Part D are simply the number of questions you got right. Nothing is subtracted for wrong answers or questions you left blank.

8. Number of questions right on Part C: _____

9. Number of questions right on Part D: _____

Total Raw Score

For your total raw score, add together the four numbers in blanks 3, 7, 8, and 9 above.

10. Total raw score: _____

SCALED SCORE

Now that you have your raw score, use the table below to convert it to an approximate score on a scale of 1 to 100.

RAW SCORE TO SCALED SCORE CONVERSION

Raw Score	Scaled Score
220 or above	100
200–219	95–99
180–199	90–94
160–179	85–89
140–159	80–84
120–139	75–79
100–119	70–74
below 100	below 70

NEXT STEPS

How did you do? You need a score of 70 to pass the exam. However, just passing isn't good enough to get you a job. The competition is so fierce that you need a much higher score than 70 to have a good chance of being chosen. A score in the high 90s is the best insurance.

If you *did* score in the high 90s, you're lucky—as well as fast, accurate, smart, and a good listener. That doesn't mean that you shouldn't practice any more, but it does mean that you can go into your preparation for the postal worker exam with confidence. You can use the tips in this book and the practice questions to help you gain an edge—a point or two can mean the difference in whether you get hired or not.

If your score isn't what you'd like, don't throw in the towel just yet. The 470 Battery Exam is a tough exam, but you can learn how to conquer it. That's what this book is for. Analyze the reasons for your difficulties to help you decide on a plan of attack.

- **Did the unfamiliar format of the questions throw you for a loop?** These *are* unusual questions, unlike what you've probably encountered on standardized exams in the past. You can read more complete descriptions of each part of the test, including the kinds of questions you're likely to encounter, in the chapters that follow.
- **Did the short amount of time allowed, particularly for Parts A and B, give you trouble?** Practice is the best way to get better at answering these questions quickly. Chapters 8–11 of this book offer you lots of opportunities for practice, and there's also another complete practice exam in Chapter 12.
- **Did you do pretty well on some parts and not on others?** Maybe you did all right on Parts A, B, and C but really fell down on Part D. Or maybe Part D was easy for you, but you had trouble memorizing the boxes in Part B. Whatever your weakest point, choose that part to work on most diligently in the weeks ahead.

Use this book to its fullest extent. Familiarity and practice with the kinds of questions given on the exam are the key to your success.

C·H·A·P·T·E·R
ADDRESS CHECKING QUESTIONS
6

CHAPTER SUMMARY

Working quickly and accurately is the key to doing well on Part A of the postal exam, Address Checking. This chapter shows you how. It includes two complete sample Address Checking sections for you to practice with.

For many United States Postal Service employees, accuracy in the area of address checking is crucial. If a clerk or carrier misreads an address, the consequences to the customer can be dire. We have all heard stories of the fateful letter delivered to the wrong address, where it languished forever, causing a great fortune—or even a great love—to be lost. And efficiency is as important as accuracy. The clerk or carrier must work swiftly so that the mail can go through on time.

That's why the postal exam includes a section on checking addresses. At first glance, the Address Checking section would seem to be the easiest part of the exam. However, the time constraint makes it more difficult than it appears on the surface. On the actual exam, you will have only six minutes to work on 95 questions. You're not expected to finish them all, but the more you finish accurately, the better your score will be. So it will be to your advantage to practice as hard on this portion of the exam as on the others—preferably with stopwatch in hand.

WHAT THE ADDRESS CHECKING SECTION IS LIKE

In the Address Checking section, each question consists of a pair of addresses that are either identical or very nearly so. Your task is to decide whether the addresses are alike (A) or different (D). Two basic types of address will be represented on the test:

- Street names and numbers, occasionally with apartment numbers or "compass" directions—N, S, E, W, NW, SE, and so on—before or after the address
- Cities and states with zip codes

The differences between addresses may be subtle: There may be slight variations in the spellings of cities, towns, or street names, for example, or state and other abbreviations may be similar but not alike. Consider, for example, the differences between Ct and St, between KS and KY, between Schaeffer and Shaeffer, or between 2109 and 2190.

Sample Questions

Try your hand at the following brief example of Address Checking questions. Scan the following five pairs of addresses and determine whether the two addresses in each pair are alike or different. Next to each one, circle A if the two addresses are alike or D if they are different. Take **no more than 15 seconds** to finish the problem:

1.	9698 Hawthorne Ln	9689 Hawthorne Ln	A	D
2.	Brewster MA 18180	Brewster WA 16330	A	D
3.	41202 Geirrod NW	41202 Geirrod NW	A	D
4.	Iowa City IA 52245	Iowa City IA 52242	A	D
5.	2121 Roselinde Ct	2121 Roselinde Ct	A	D

Numbers 3 and 5 are alike; numbers 1, 2, and 4 are different. If you missed any of the answers, look closely now to see where you went wrong.

HOW TO PREPARE

The best way to prepare is to practice. There are two sample test sections at the end of this chapter, in addition to the complete tests in Chapters 7 and 12.

Differences to Look For

The most common differences you can expect to see include the following:

- Variations in spelling, due to missing or added letters

Blair Ferry Rd	Blaire Ferry Rd
Hartford Wy	Harford Wy
Rondell Street	Rondel Street

- Variations in spelling, often with the same pronunciation

Dyersburg	Dyersberg
Hadlyville	Hadleyville
Gare Blvd	Gair Blvd

- Variations in abbreviations

Cir	Ct
WA	MA
St	Dr

- Variations in compass abbreviations

450 NE Warwick Way	450 NW Warwick Way
916 SW Lupe Cir	916 SE Lupe Cir
9637 W Narcisa Ln	9637 Narcisa Ln W

- Transposed numbers in street addresses or zip codes

9889 - 7th St NW	9898 - 7th St NW
Iowa City, IA 52242	Iowa City, IA 52422
4334 Inocencia Blvd	4343 Inocencia Blvd

- Variations in number of digits

9673	967
34437	3447

- Replacement of one digit by another

63947	63647
4088	4080
9669	9689

Try looking for these variations as you work through the practice materials in this book.

TAKING THE TEST

On test day, you'll need all your wits about you in order to do well on this section of the exam. Here are a few pointers.

Listen to the Instructions

This may seem elementary advice, but under the stress of test taking it's easy to become distracted. So at the beginning, be very careful to *pay close attention to the examiner's instructions.* Because the abilities being tested are speed and accuracy, the test will be carefully timed. You must not **start** until you are told to; and you must **stop** when you are told to. When you are directed to work on a particular part of the exam—as you will be for the Address Checking section—work **only** on that part. If you finish a section before the time is up, you may review your answers, but you may not move on. Failure to follow directions can result in disqualification. And that would be depressing!

Keep Your Place

A simple, but often overlooked, factor that is crucial to your score is to *make sure you do not lose your place on the answer sheet.* Because of the speed with which you have to work, you can easily skip a number or even a column on the answer sheet and mark a whole series of answers incorrectly before you discover your error. In this portion of the test, seconds count, and you don't want to have to take time to erase.

You will not be allowed to use a straight-edge ruler or any other tool in the test itself, so as you work, be sure to **use both hands.** Hold your pencil in your writing hand and use the index finger of your other hand to run along under the addresses being compared, or use the index finger on one column and little finger on the other. (If you have two pencils in the exam, you could use one as a straight edge, but it's not very reliable, as a pencil can slip or roll.)

Read What You See

Be sure to *read what you see,* not what you expect to see. It is natural, when you see the word "Ct" to read it as "Court"; similarly, when you see "Pkwy" you will instinctively think "Parkway." However, it is best to **sound out the syllables in your mind,** rather than reading complete words: KY should be read "kay-wy," rather than "Kentucky"; 919 should be read "nine-one-nine," rather than "nine-nineteen"; "St" should be read "es-tee," rather than "street," and so on.

One Thing at a Time

One way to approach the address pairs is to *focus on only one element at a time.* For street addresses, try checking first street numbers, then abbreviations, then street names, and then apartment numbers (if any).

First, check for differences in street numbers:

1. **36747** Blair Ferry Rd   **37647** Blaire Ferry Rd
2. **976** Rodham Way, #3   **976** Rodham Way, #8
3. **4774** Marguerite Cir   **4774** Marguarite Cir
4. **9309** Gier Park Ct   **9309** Gier Park Cir

In example 1, there is a difference in the two street numbers, so **stop right there**. It does not matter that there is a difference in the street names—**one difference is enough** to mark D and move on. In examples 2, 3, and 4, the street numbers are alike.

Second, check for differences in street names:

2. 976 **Rodham** Way, #3   976 **Rodham** Way, #8
3. 4774 **Marguerite** Cir   4774 **Marguarite** Cir
4. 9309 **Gier Park** Ct   9309 **Gier Park** Cir

In example 3, the street names are spelled differently—though you would probably pronounce the two spellings the same. Mark D and move on. In the other two examples, the street names are spelled the same.

Third, check for differences in abbreviations and street designations:

2. 976 Rodham **Way,** #3   976 Rodham **Way,** #8
4. 9309 Gier Park **Ct**   9309 Gier Park **Cir**

In example 2, the street designation is the same. In example 4, there is the difference between "Ct" and "Cir," so mark D and move on.

Finally, check for differences in apartment numbers:

2. 976 Rodham Way, **#3**   976 Rodham Way, **#8**

In this remaining example, the apartment numbers are different. The digits "3" and "8" are easy to confuse, so remember to silently **sound everything out**: In this case, say silently "three" and "eight," rather than depending on your eye alone.

Continue this method for city names, state abbreviations and zip codes, again checking only **one element at a time.** For example:

1. **Ada** MI 18000   **Ada** MN 17080
      Ada **MI** 18000   Ada **MN** 18000
2. **Jamestown** NC 26000   **Jamesville** NC 61200
3. **Iowa City** IA 52245   **Iowa City** IA 52242
      Iowa City **IA** 52245   Iowa City **IA** 52242
      Iowa City IA **52245**   Iowa City IA **52242**

In example 1, the town names are the same, so check the state names next; these are different, so choose D and move on. In example 2, the town names, though very similar, are different, so choose D and move on. In example 3, the town and state names are the same, so move to the zip codes; these are different, so choose D.

STRATEGIES FOR SUCCESS

Remember: There has only to be **ONE difference** for you to mark D, so as soon as you see a difference, mark your answer and **MOVE ON**. Under no circumstances should you continue to peruse that particular address pair. Seconds count.

Some people believe that **working in a reverse order** from the one you are used to in reading will help you spot differences you might otherwise overlook. In your practice sessions, try working from right to left: first checking apartment numbers, then street names, then street numbers; or first checking zip codes, then checking state abbreviations. Again with this technique, focus on the separate elements one at a time. For example:

6077 Wesley Dr **NW**   6877 Weslyn Dr **NW**

The compass directions are the same, so move backwards to street abbreviation:

6077 Wesley **Dr** NW   6877 Weslyn **Dr** NW

The street abbreviations are the same, so move backwards to street name:

6077 **Wesley** Dr NW   6877 **Weslyn** Dr NW

Ah ha! The street names are different; mark D and move on. The number does not matter, as only one difference is necessary.

As you practice and get better at spotting differences quickly, you may find that you can **combine two steps** in one sweep of the eye. For instance, you might be able to deal with the street number and the compass direction at the same time, or the city name and state abbreviation. Try it out with the practice materials in this book to see if you can combine any steps without sacrificing accuracy. However, if you find that you miss too many differences by trying to combine steps, go back to checking one element at a time.

It is **all right to skip,** as you are not expected to answer all 95 questions in the six minutes. In this part of the test, you will be penalized for wrong answers, so it is **not** to your advantage to guess or just randomly mark A or D. Your score on this part of the test will be based on right answers minus wrong answers.

What your elders told you when you were a kid about practicing the clarinet or shooting hoops is of special use here: PRACTICE, PRACTICE, PRACTICE. Each time you check an address pair, you'll be better on the next ones. So relax. Although this section of the exam requires speed and close attention to detail, it really is not difficult.

How to Answer Address Checking Questions

- Don't expect to answer all the questions in the time allowed.
- Be sure you do not lose your place on the answer sheet—**use both hands.**
- Read what you see, not what you expect to see—**sound the words out silently** (KY is "kay-wy," St is "es-tee," and so on).
- Focus on only **one element at a time:** numbers, then abbreviations, then street or city names; or you may go in reverse order.
- As soon as you spot a difference, mark D and **move on.**
- **Do not guess**—you will be penalized for wrong answers.
- **PRACTICE, PRACTICE, PRACTICE.**

What follows are two sample test sections, each complete with 95 questions. First comes an answer grid for you to use in taking each test. Then come the questions themselves, followed by the answer key. As you take these practice sections, time yourself with a stopwatch, to see how many you can complete in the six minutes. With practice, your efficiency and accuracy will improve. The two practice exams in Chapters 7 and 12 also feature complete address checking sections.

PART A: ADDRESS CHECKING

1.	Ⓐ	Ⓓ		20.	Ⓐ	Ⓓ		39.	Ⓐ	Ⓓ		58.	Ⓐ	Ⓓ		77.	Ⓐ	Ⓓ
2.	Ⓐ	Ⓓ		21.	Ⓐ	Ⓓ		40.	Ⓐ	Ⓓ		59.	Ⓐ	Ⓓ		78.	Ⓐ	Ⓓ
3.	Ⓐ	Ⓓ		22.	Ⓐ	Ⓓ		41.	Ⓐ	Ⓓ		60.	Ⓐ	Ⓓ		79.	Ⓐ	Ⓓ
4.	Ⓐ	Ⓓ		23.	Ⓐ	Ⓓ		42.	Ⓐ	Ⓓ		61.	Ⓐ	Ⓓ		80.	Ⓐ	Ⓓ
5.	Ⓐ	Ⓓ		24.	Ⓐ	Ⓓ		43.	Ⓐ	Ⓓ		62.	Ⓐ	Ⓓ		81.	Ⓐ	Ⓓ
6.	Ⓐ	Ⓓ		25.	Ⓐ	Ⓓ		44.	Ⓐ	Ⓓ		63.	Ⓐ	Ⓓ		82.	Ⓐ	Ⓓ
7.	Ⓐ	Ⓓ		26.	Ⓐ	Ⓓ		45.	Ⓐ	Ⓓ		64.	Ⓐ	Ⓓ		83.	Ⓐ	Ⓓ
8.	Ⓐ	Ⓓ		27.	Ⓐ	Ⓓ		46.	Ⓐ	Ⓓ		65.	Ⓐ	Ⓓ		84.	Ⓐ	Ⓓ
9.	Ⓐ	Ⓓ		28.	Ⓐ	Ⓓ		47.	Ⓐ	Ⓓ		66.	Ⓐ	Ⓓ		85.	Ⓐ	Ⓓ
10.	Ⓐ	Ⓓ		29.	Ⓐ	Ⓓ		48.	Ⓐ	Ⓓ		67.	Ⓐ	Ⓓ		86.	Ⓐ	Ⓓ
11.	Ⓐ	Ⓓ		30.	Ⓐ	Ⓓ		49.	Ⓐ	Ⓓ		68.	Ⓐ	Ⓓ		87.	Ⓐ	Ⓓ
12.	Ⓐ	Ⓓ		31.	Ⓐ	Ⓓ		50.	Ⓐ	Ⓓ		69.	Ⓐ	Ⓓ		88.	Ⓐ	Ⓓ
13.	Ⓐ	Ⓓ		32.	Ⓐ	Ⓓ		51.	Ⓐ	Ⓓ		70.	Ⓐ	Ⓓ		89.	Ⓐ	Ⓓ
14.	Ⓐ	Ⓓ		33.	Ⓐ	Ⓓ		52.	Ⓐ	Ⓓ		71.	Ⓐ	Ⓓ		90.	Ⓐ	Ⓓ
15.	Ⓐ	Ⓓ		34.	Ⓐ	Ⓓ		53.	Ⓐ	Ⓓ		72.	Ⓐ	Ⓓ		91.	Ⓐ	Ⓓ
16.	Ⓐ	Ⓓ		35.	Ⓐ	Ⓓ		54.	Ⓐ	Ⓓ		73.	Ⓐ	Ⓓ		92.	Ⓐ	Ⓓ
17.	Ⓐ	Ⓓ		36.	Ⓐ	Ⓓ		55.	Ⓐ	Ⓓ		74.	Ⓐ	Ⓓ		93.	Ⓐ	Ⓓ
18.	Ⓐ	Ⓓ		37.	Ⓐ	Ⓓ		56.	Ⓐ	Ⓓ		75.	Ⓐ	Ⓓ		94.	Ⓐ	Ⓓ
19.	Ⓐ	Ⓓ		38.	Ⓐ	Ⓓ		57.	Ⓐ	Ⓓ		76.	Ⓐ	Ⓓ		95.	Ⓐ	Ⓓ

SAMPLE ADDRESS CHECKING SECTION 1

Below are 95 pairs of addresses. Look at each pair and decide if the two addresses are alike or different in any way. If they are exactly ALIKE, darken circle A on your answer sheet; if they are DIFFERENT, darken circle D. You will have six minutes to answer the 95 questions.

1.	4007 W Nineteeth St	4007 W Ninetieth St
2.	33321 Fowler NE	33321 Flower NE
3.	4112 Mont St	4112 Mont St
4.	997 Woodcrest Dr	997 Woodcrest Rd
5.	419 S Dunsbar	419 S Dunsbar
6.	N Liberty IA 53217	N Liberty IA 52317
7.	4370 McCollogh Way	4370 McCollough Way
8.	Boulder CO 80302	Boulder CO 80302
9.	79 McGee St	79 McGhee St
10.	Montgomery AL 36103	Montgomery AR 36103
11.	Box 29610	Box 29610
12.	St Albany NY 12207	St Albany NY 12027
13.	Dallas TX 75275	Dallas TX 75275
14.	9772 Sharon Center Rd	9772 Sharon Center Ct
15.	4647 Chaloupek	4647 Chaloupek
16.	6771 Southhampton Ct	6771 Southhamton Ct
17.	55 5th Ave	55 5th Ave
18.	4337 Nguyen Wy	4737 Nguyen Wy
19.	Marlboro MA 01752	Marlboro MA 01752
20.	26 Naaktgeboren St	26 Naaktgeboren Ct
21.	437 Potwin Ln	437 Potwyn Ln

22.	420 Bulkley St	420 Bulkley St
23.	47 Francisco Ln	47 Francisca Ln
24.	2142 Windsor Way	2142 Windsor Way
25.	1003 Denbigh Drive	1003 Denhigh Drive
26.	2030 Westridge #407	2030 Westbridge #407
27.	96 Sachem Village	96 Sachem Village
28.	New York NY 10308	New York NY 10038
29.	881 14th St	881 14th St
30.	9401 Steindler Blvd #42	9401 Steindler Blvd #42
31.	438 Aubry	438 Aubrey
32.	P.O. Box 9642-C	P.O. Box 9642-C
33.	9732 Kaczinski St	9732 Kaczinsky St
34.	4949 Rathjen Ct	4994 Rathjen Ct
35.	Ann Harbor MI 48106	Ann Arbor MI 48106
36.	7710 NE Blvd N	7710 NE Blvd W
37.	7142 No Chavez Cir	7142 No Chavez Cir
38.	404 Trinity Medical Plaza	404 Trinity Medical Plaza
39.	960 Leheigh Rd	960 Leheigh Ct
40.	Champaign IL 61820	Champaign IL 61820
41.	2835 Friendship Ln	2385 Friendship Ln
42.	P.O. Box 8939-E	P.O. Box 8989-E
43.	Wichita KS 67203	Wichita KS 67203
44.	210 Pittman Rd	210 Pittmann Rd
45.	Springfield IL 67294	Springfield IL 62794
46.	3290 S Lake Road	3290 S Lake Road

47.	Napa CA 95458	Napa CA 94558
48.	Zapata TX 78076	Zapata TX 78076
49.	Edwardsville IL 62026	Edwardsville IL 62206
50.	9246 Setting Sun Way	9246 Setting Sun Way
51.	3030 Prairie Rd NE	3030 Prairie Rd NW
52.	Laquey MO 65534	Laquey MO 65534
53.	San Mateo CA 94402	San Mateo CA 94402
54.	9008 Schaeffer St	9008 Shaeffer St
55.	32232 Miettlinen	32232 Miettlinen
56.	Cedar Rapids IA 52403	Cedar Rapids IA 52304
57.	9667 Ferndale Ln	9667 Ferndale Ln
58.	4330 Querida Wy	4030 Querida Wy
59.	1717 Stevens Ct	1771 Stevens Ct
60.	Columbia MO 65203	Columbia MO 65203
61.	4969 Myers Blvd	4996 Myers Blvd
62.	Laramie WY 82070	Laramie WY 82070
63.	Paxton MA 01612	Paxon MA 01612
64.	916 McMurray Ct	916 MacMurray Ct
65.	7614 Brown Deer Rd, #17	7641 Brown Deer Rd, #17
66.	5005 S Christofides Ave	5005 S Christofides Ave
67.	Orlando FL 32803	Orlando FL 32308
68.	Richmond VA 23241	Richmond VA 23241
69.	961 Old Post Hwy	916 Old Post Hwy
70.	Mtn Grove MO 65711	Mtn Grove MO 65711
71.	9669 Reingold Ct	9696 Reingold Ct

72.	709 20th Ave	709 20th Ave
73.	West Lebanon NH 03784	West Lebanon NH 03784
74.	777 W Minnie Ct	777 N Minnie Ct
75.	3043 Rowena Ave #104	3043 Rowena Ave #104
76.	Grayslake IL 60030	Greystoke IL 60030
77.	9669 McClellan Dr	9669 McClelland Dr
78.	London NW3 England	London NW3 England
79.	2277 Rondell Wy	2272 Rondell Wy
80.	437 Mt Veeder Rd	437 Mt Veeder Rd
81.	916 Marlboro Wy	619 Marlboro Wy
82.	Helena MT 59624	Helena MT 56924
83.	Shawnee KS 66203	Shawnee KS 66203
84.	San Francisco CA 94109	San Francisco CA 94109
85.	2039 Westridge Drive	2039 Westridge Drive
86.	1115 Lexington Way	1151 Lexington Way
87.	17 S Takeri Way #4470	17 E Takeri Way #4470
88.	49703 Clark St	49703 Clarke St
89.	Albuquerque NM 87102	Albuquerque NM 87102
90.	Iowa City IA 52245	Iowa City IA 52242
91.	916 Woodside Dr	916 Woodside Dr
92.	9969 Western Blvd	9699 Western Blvd
93.	2922 Skyline Ct	2922 Skyview Ln
94.	1631 1 Av	1631 1 Av
95.	907 E Caspari	907 E Caspari

ANSWERS TO SAMPLE ADDRESS CHECKING SECTION 1

1. D	25. D	49. D	73. A
2. D	26. D	50. A	74. D
3. A	27. A	51. D	75. A
4. D	28. D	52. A	76. D
5. A	29. A	53. A	77. D
6. D	30. A	54. D	78. A
7. D	31. D	55. A	79. D
8. A	32. A	56. D	80. A
9. D	33. D	57. A	81. D
10. D	34. D	58. D	82. D
11. A	35. D	59. D	83. A
12. D	36. D	60. A	84. A
13. A	37. A	61. D	85. A
14. D	38. A	62. A	86. D
15. A	39. D	63. D	87. D
16. D	40. A	64. D	88. D
17. A	41. D	65. D	89. A
18. D	42. D	66. A	90. D
19. A	43. A	67. D	91. A
20. D	44. D	68. A	92. D
21. D	45. D	69. D	93. D
22. A	46. A	70. A	94. A
23. D	47. D	71. D	95. A
24. A	48. A	72. A	

PART A: ADDRESS CHECKING

1.	Ⓐ Ⓓ	20.	Ⓐ Ⓓ	39.	Ⓐ Ⓓ	58.	Ⓐ Ⓓ	77.	Ⓐ Ⓓ
2.	Ⓐ Ⓓ	21.	Ⓐ Ⓓ	40.	Ⓐ Ⓓ	59.	Ⓐ Ⓓ	78.	Ⓐ Ⓓ
3.	Ⓐ Ⓓ	22.	Ⓐ Ⓓ	41.	Ⓐ Ⓓ	60.	Ⓐ Ⓓ	79.	Ⓐ Ⓓ
4.	Ⓐ Ⓓ	23.	Ⓐ Ⓓ	42.	Ⓐ Ⓓ	61.	Ⓐ Ⓓ	80.	Ⓐ Ⓓ
5.	Ⓐ Ⓓ	24.	Ⓐ Ⓓ	43.	Ⓐ Ⓓ	62.	Ⓐ Ⓓ	81.	Ⓐ Ⓓ
6.	Ⓐ Ⓓ	25.	Ⓐ Ⓓ	44.	Ⓐ Ⓓ	63.	Ⓐ Ⓓ	82.	Ⓐ Ⓓ
7.	Ⓐ Ⓓ	26.	Ⓐ Ⓓ	45.	Ⓐ Ⓓ	64.	Ⓐ Ⓓ	83.	Ⓐ Ⓓ
8.	Ⓐ Ⓓ	27.	Ⓐ Ⓓ	46.	Ⓐ Ⓓ	65.	Ⓐ Ⓓ	84.	Ⓐ Ⓓ
9.	Ⓐ Ⓓ	28.	Ⓐ Ⓓ	47.	Ⓐ Ⓓ	66.	Ⓐ Ⓓ	85.	Ⓐ Ⓓ
10.	Ⓐ Ⓓ	29.	Ⓐ Ⓓ	48.	Ⓐ Ⓓ	67.	Ⓐ Ⓓ	86.	Ⓐ Ⓓ
11.	Ⓐ Ⓓ	30.	Ⓐ Ⓓ	49.	Ⓐ Ⓓ	68.	Ⓐ Ⓓ	87.	Ⓐ Ⓓ
12.	Ⓐ Ⓓ	31.	Ⓐ Ⓓ	50.	Ⓐ Ⓓ	69.	Ⓐ Ⓓ	88.	Ⓐ Ⓓ
13.	Ⓐ Ⓓ	32.	Ⓐ Ⓓ	51.	Ⓐ Ⓓ	70.	Ⓐ Ⓓ	89.	Ⓐ Ⓓ
14.	Ⓐ Ⓓ	33.	Ⓐ Ⓓ	52.	Ⓐ Ⓓ	71.	Ⓐ Ⓓ	90.	Ⓐ Ⓓ
15.	Ⓐ Ⓓ	34.	Ⓐ Ⓓ	53.	Ⓐ Ⓓ	72.	Ⓐ Ⓓ	91.	Ⓐ Ⓓ
16.	Ⓐ Ⓓ	35.	Ⓐ Ⓓ	54.	Ⓐ Ⓓ	73.	Ⓐ Ⓓ	92.	Ⓐ Ⓓ
17.	Ⓐ Ⓓ	36.	Ⓐ Ⓓ	55.	Ⓐ Ⓓ	74.	Ⓐ Ⓓ	93.	Ⓐ Ⓓ
18.	Ⓐ Ⓓ	37.	Ⓐ Ⓓ	56.	Ⓐ Ⓓ	75.	Ⓐ Ⓓ	94.	Ⓐ Ⓓ
19.	Ⓐ Ⓓ	38.	Ⓐ Ⓓ	57.	Ⓐ Ⓓ	76.	Ⓐ Ⓓ	95.	Ⓐ Ⓓ

SAMPLE ADDRESS CHECKING SECTION 2

Below are 95 pairs of addresses. Look at each pair and decide if the two addresses are alike or different in any way. If they are exactly ALIKE, darken circle A on your answer sheet; if they are DIFFERENT, darken circle D. You will have six minutes to answer the 95 questions.

1. 1121 Y Ave   1121 Y Ave

2. 2912 Losey St   9212 Losey St

3. Pago Pago AS 96799   Pogo Pago AS 96799

4. Portland ME 04104   Portland ME 04104

5. 2553 Cemetery Rd   2553 Cemetery Dr

6. 4569 Vanderbilt Dr   4569 Vanderlilt Dr

7. Honolulu HI 96813   Honolulu HI 96813

8. Bismarck ND 58502   Bismark ND 58502

9. 4512 Russell St   4512 Russell St

10. 1234 Amana Rd NW   1234 Amana Rd NE

11. 3715 Angel Falls Bl   3715 Angel Falls Bl

12. 1118 Church St   1818 Church St

13. Boise ID 83703   Boise IA 83703

14. Annapolis MD 21401   Annapolis MD 21401

15. 5704 Derby Av   5074 Derby Av

16. 1590 Nutmeg Dr   1590 Nutmeg Dr

17. Baton Rouge LA 70821   Baton Rouge LA 70021

18. 2340 150 St   2340 15 St

19. 1287 Main St NE   1287 Main St NE

20. Honolulu HI 96813   Honolulu HA 96813

21. 1551 Larch Av   5151 Larch Av

22. 1927 Chambers Av SW   1927 Chalmers Av SW

23.	Tallahassee FL 32399	Tallahassee FL 32399
24.	1107 N Adams Dr	1107 N Adams Dr
25.	Helena MT 59624	Helena MT 59824
26.	2349 Dogwood St	2349 Dogwood St
27.	1212 N Green Av	1212 S Green Av
28.	3312 N Fulton Rd	3312 N Fulton Rd
29.	Camp Hill PA 17011	Camp Hill PA 17711
30.	Montpelier VT 05601	Montpelier VA 05601
31.	2201 SE Baker Rd	2201 SE Baker Dr
32.	1170 Hwy 92	1170 Hwy 92
33.	St Croix VI 00820	St Croix VI 00820
34.	1705 Prairie du Chien Rd	1507 Prairie du Chien Rd
35.	2324 McLean Rd NW	2423 McLean Rd NW
36.	1957 Fullerton Pkwy	1957 Fullerton Pkwy
37.	New Haven CT 06510	New Heaven CT 06510
38.	4563 Mesa Dr SE	4563 Mesa Dr SW
39.	2403 Towncrest Dr	2413 Towncrest Dr
40.	Carson City NV 89701	Carson City NV 89701
41.	4409 Kodiak Ct	4409 Kodiak Cr
42.	1654 Winston Ln	1654 Winston Ln
43.	Salem OR 97308	Salem ON 97308
44.	3627 Industrial Hwy	3627 Industrial Wy
45.	1354 Westwinds Dr	1354 Westwinds Dr
46.	Phoenix AZ 85012	Phenix AZ 85012
47.	1303 Chamberlain Rd	1303 Chamberlain Rd

48.	San Antonio TX 78217	San Antonio TX 78217
49.	1111 Wakefield Ct	1111 Wakefield Ct
50.	Denver CO 80264	Denver CO 88264
51.	1526 Terrace Rd	1526 Terrace Rd
52.	Providence RI 02908	Providence RH 02908
53.	5753 Alpine Dr NW	5753 Alpine Rd NW
54.	4744 Vincent Av SE	4744 Vincent Av SE
55.	Boston MA 02114	Boston MA 12114
56.	2720 Muscatine Av	2720 Muscatine Av
57.	4518 Bowery Rd	4418 Bowery Rd
58.	Springfield IL 62701	Springfield IL 62701
59.	2303 Cameron Wy	2303 Cameron Wy
60.	Pierre SD 57501	Pierre SD 57501
61.	Dover DE 19901	Dover DE 19991
62.	4539 Penn Cr	4539 Penn Cr
63.	1931 Arbor Dr	1931 Arber Dr
64.	Atlanta GA 30303	Atlanta GA 30333
65.	2427 Shady Glen Ct	2424 Shady Glen Ct
66.	5519 Park Ridge Dr	5519 Park Ridge Rd
67.	Lexington KY 40503	Lexington KY 40503
68.	2167 Keokuk St	2176 Keokuk St
69.	4606 Bartelt Rd	4606 Bartlet Rd
70.	3304 Oberlin St	3304 Oberlin St
71.	Santa Fe NM 87501	Santa Ana NM 87501
72.	2719 Puffer Dr	2791 Puffer Dr

73. 1327 Highland Ct   1327 Highland Ct

74. Jackson MS 39201   Jackson MS 39201

75. 3350 Vista Park Dr   3350 Vista Park Rd

76. 3004 Forest Gate Cr NE   3004 Forest Gate Cr NE

77. Nashville TN 37219   Nashville TX 37219

78. Charleston WV 25311   Charleston WV 25311

79. Jefferson City MO 65109   Jefferson City MO 65109

80. 2012 Union Rd   2012 Onion Rd

81. 2713 Windram Bluff NE   2731 Windram Bluff NE

82. Indianapolis IN 46204   Indianapolis IN 46304

83. 2714 Fairway Ln   2714 Fairway Ln

84. 1260 Devon Dr   1206 Devon Dr

85. Manchester NH 03109   Manchester NH 03109

86. Cheyenne WY 82003   Cheyanne WY 82003

87. 1605 Lightening Av   1605 Lightning Av

88. 3319 Ridgeland Dr   3119 Ridgeland Dr

89. Agana Guam 96910   Agana Guam 96910

90. 2712 Dearborn St   2712 Deerborn St

91. 5419 Crestview Dr   5419 Crestview Dr

92. Olympia WA 98501   Olympia WA 98501

93. 1949 Potsdam Bl   1499 Potsdam Bl

94. 1850 Sterling Ct   1850 Sterling Cr

95. Salt Lake City UT 84102   Salt Lake City UT 84102

ANSWERS TO SAMPLE ADDRESS CHECKING SECTION 2

1. A	25. D	49. A	73. A
2. D	26. A	50. D	74. A
3. D	27. D	51. A	75. D
4. A	28. A	52. D	76. A
5. D	29. D	53. D	77. D
6. D	30. D	54. A	78. A
7. A	31. D	55. D	79. A
8. D	32. A	56. A	80. D
9. A	33. A	57. D	81. D
10. D	34. D	58. A	82. D
11. A	35. D	59. A	83. A
12. D	36. A	60. A	84. D
13. D	37. D	61. D	85. A
14. A	38. D	62. A	86. D
15. D	39. D	63. D	87. D
16. A	40. A	64. D	88. D
17. D	41. D	65. D	89. A
18. D	42. A	66. D	90. D
19. A	43. D	67. A	91. A
20. D	44. D	68. D	92. A
21. D	45. A	69. D	93. D
22. D	46. D	70. A	94. D
23. A	47. A	71. D	95. A
24. A	48. A	72. D	

C·H·A·P·T·E·R 7

MEMORY FOR ADDRESSES QUESTIONS

CHAPTER SUMMARY
Part B, Memory for Addresses, is the part of the postal exam many people find most challenging. This chapter gives you crucial tools to help you memorize the addresses and answer the questions quickly and accurately.

orrect mail sorting is extremely important to postal customers, whether they be Joe Jobst and Sherry Shippit down the street or a government agency with 10,000 employees. Everyone depends on accurate mail sorting. Without it, the country, and peoples' individual lives, might well grind to a halt. Consequently, Part B, Memory for Addresses, is a crucial part of the postal service exam.

WHAT THE MEMORY FOR ADDRESSES SECTION IS LIKE

In this part of the test, you will be shown five boxes like those in the sample problem below and asked to memorize the locations (A, B, C, D, or E) of information in those boxes. The information in each box will consist of three street addresses with ranges of numbers (for example, 4900–4399 Market) and two single names (for example, Astor and Southward). You will be given five minutes to study the boxes. There is a set of short practice exercises based on the boxes, each of which will take one to three minutes. In some of the practice exercises and in the actual test, you will be asked to identify the locations (Box A, B, C, D, or E) of the addresses or names without referring back to the boxes.

It's a difficult chore, keeping all these names and numbers in your head. This part of the exam is demanding. How, you may ask yourself, will I ever be able to solve the following problems?

SAMPLE PROBLEMS

Your task is to memorize the locations (A, B, C, D, or E) of the 25 address elements shown in the five boxes below. For example, Kelso is in Box C, 6800–6999 Fargo is in Box B, and so on. (The addresses in the actual test will of course be different.)

A	B	C	D	E
4700–5599 Fargo	6800–6999 Fargo	5600–6499 Fargo	6500–6799 Fargo	4400–4699 Fargo
Lynn	Morris	Marietta	Argo	Hawthorne
5600–6499 East	6500–6799 East	6800–6999 East	4400–4699 East	4700–5599 East
Pleasant	Langford	Kelso	Taylor	Kennedy
4400–4699 Lake	5600–6499 Lake	6500–6799 Lake	4700–5599 Lake	6800–6999 Lake

Study the locations of the addresses for five minutes. As you study, silently repeat the addresses to yourself. Then cover the boxes and try to answer the questions below, marking your answers on the following answer grid. You needn't time yourself as you are answering the questions during this first exercise. In the actual test, you will have five minutes to answer 88 questions. See the complete sample Memory for Addresses sections at the end of this chapter.

1. Langford

2. 4700–5599 Lake

3. 4700–5599 Fargo

4. Argo

5. 4400–4699 Lake

6. Pleasant

7. Kelso

8. Kennedy

9. 6500–6799 Lake

10. Marietta

11. 4400–4699 Lake

12. 6500–6799 East

13. Taylor

14. 6800–6999 Lake

ANSWER GRID

1. Ⓐ Ⓑ Ⓒ Ⓓ Ⓔ
2. Ⓐ Ⓑ Ⓒ Ⓓ Ⓔ
3. Ⓐ Ⓑ Ⓒ Ⓓ Ⓔ
4. Ⓐ Ⓑ Ⓒ Ⓓ Ⓔ
5. Ⓐ Ⓑ Ⓒ Ⓓ Ⓔ

6. Ⓐ Ⓑ Ⓒ Ⓓ Ⓔ
7. Ⓐ Ⓑ Ⓒ Ⓓ Ⓔ
8. Ⓐ Ⓑ Ⓒ Ⓓ Ⓔ
9. Ⓐ Ⓑ Ⓒ Ⓓ Ⓔ
10. Ⓐ Ⓑ Ⓒ Ⓓ Ⓔ

11. Ⓐ Ⓑ Ⓒ Ⓓ Ⓔ
12. Ⓐ Ⓑ Ⓒ Ⓓ Ⓔ
13. Ⓐ Ⓑ Ⓒ Ⓓ Ⓔ
14. Ⓐ Ⓑ Ⓒ Ⓓ Ⓔ

Now check your gridded answers against the boxes. How did you do? More important, how did you approach the task? If you have a photographic memory, you are probably lounging back in your chair saying, "So give me something *hard*." If you do not—and most of us do not—you may be feeling a little discouraged.

Chances are, you went at the task using rote memory, the kind of drilling in of facts and figures we all learned too well in school. And chances are you didn't do very well. Why? There are two reasons that kind of drilling doesn't work on this section of the exam:

- As it stands, the task is too complex to tackle all at once.
- It's nearly impossible to learn these names and numbers by rote because they're almost meaningless; they are not associated with anything memorable.

Your approach, then, needs to be modified.

HOW TO PREPARE

In attacking this portion of the exam, you must do two things:

1. **Simplify** the task as much as possible.

2. Make the unmemorable memorable by **associating** these abstract and unfamiliar names and numbers with something more concrete and familiar to you.

You can take two steps right off the bat to **simplify** the task:

1. **Discard one of the boxes.** That is, memorize only four boxes, rather than five. During the test, you will know that anything that isn't in one of the four boxes you've memorized is automatically in the fifth box.

2. **Start with the single names.** Unless you're one of those unusual people who finds numbers easier to deal with than words, start by looking at the single names and use them to decide which box to discard.

DEALING WITH SINGLE NAMES

You want to use the single names to help you decide which box to discard, and use your two tools: simplification and association.

Simplify

Look quickly over all the boxes, concentrating only on the single names and paying no attention to the street names with number ranges. This leaves you with a simplified set of boxes:

A	B	C	D	E
Lynn	Morris	Marietta	Argo	Hawthorne
Pleasant	Langford	Kelso	Taylor	Kennedy

Associate

Scan your simplified boxes quickly, using your life experiences to decide which names you will find easiest to remember. Here you can use one of the most important tools of memory: **association**. Unfamiliar names are easier to remember if you associate them with words or images already stored in your long-term memory—what memory experts call "linking." You can remember the unmemorable if you link it with something familiar and memorable.

Here's how it works: If I were a candidate taking the test, I would begin by picking boxes A, B, D, and E and leaving out Box C. Why?

Box A contains a name that is an actual word we use daily, "pleasant," so that automatically makes it easy to remember, and Lynn is a person's name. I can therefore tell myself "Lynn is **A** pleasant person." What about Box B? Most of us are acquainted with finicky Morris the cat from the commercials, and I can conjure up a person named Mr. Langford (I can pretend he was my high school shop teacher), and decide I just don't like him very much. So: "It would **B** nice if Morris scratched Langford." I would skip Box C, because I don't know anyone named Marietta (perhaps you do, so you would pick that box), and the word Kelso means nothing to me. On to Box D: My mom used Argo Starch when I was a child, and since a tailor works with clothing, perhaps "The tailor would be **D**elighted to starch my clothes with Argo." Don't worry that "Taylor" and "tailor" are spelled differently. In your memory, they sound the same. Next, Box E: Hawthorne is the name of a famous author; Kennedy is the name of a famous president: "If Hawthorne were alive today he might **E**ven write a biography of Kennedy."

Sound silly? Yes. But it works.

Another way to approach the problem—a crazier way that's actually more effective and more fun (it's important to have fun with this so as not to become hopelessly depressed)—is to **make up a story involving all four of the boxes,** taking the boxes in strict order so as to remember which names belong to which.

My story might go something like this: My friend **Lynn** is a very **pleasant** person (Box A), but I have never liked her husband—in fact, I've often wished I could rent **Morris** the cat and have him scratch **Langford**, tearing Langford's expensive suit (Box B). Of course then I would probably have to take the suit to a **tailor** for repair, and the tailor might just put too much **Argo** Starch in it, and then I'd be in trouble (Box D). I think instead I'll just stay home and read **Hawthorne**'s biography of **Kennedy**, and keep out of trouble (Box E).

Even sillier? Yes. Memorable? You bet. In fact, chances are you'll remember this story long after you fervently wish to forget it!

Keep in mind, though, that it's important to **keep the story moving across the boxes in strict order**. This is the only way to keep the right names in the right boxes—two names per story element.

A third alternative is to **make simple words from certain letters in the two single names, and then make up a story**. For example Lynn/Pleasant might become LiP, Morris/Langford might become MOLe, Argo/Taylor might become ART, and Hawthorne Kennedy might become HAWK: "On my lip is a mole artfully shaped like a hawk." It's an awful picture, but again, it's memorable.

So you have three possible ways to associate the names. Remember, you only have to work with four of the five boxes.

1. Make up sentences that associate each name with the letter of its box—A, B, C, D, or E.

2. Make up a story that involves all four of the boxes, moving across the boxes in strict order.

3. Make simple words from selected letters in the two single names in each box, then make up a story using these words.

Having associated the names with the boxes in a way that makes them memorable, you can breathe a little easier. This takes practice, of course, but there are lots of practice exercises in this book. As you work through these exercises, try the three kinds of associations listed above, and see which one works best for you. That way, you don't have to waste precious seconds on exam day deciding which strategy to use.

Any of these methods will serve you well on questions that contain a single name, without the numbers. Moving on to the numbers, however, your heart may sink again, and you may begin to wonder if perhaps accounting or tree surgery would be more up your alley.

DEALING WITH NUMBERED ADDRESSES

But wait. Even with the numbers portion of the problem, the tried and true tricks of **simplification** and **association** can pull you through.

Simplify

It is possible that on the exam you take there will be only five number spans—that is, that the number spans will repeat across the five boxes. That's the case with the sample test materials most recently sent out by the USPS, and it's how the sample boxes in this chapter have been constructed. If you look back at the boxes on the second page of this chapter, you'll see that, for instance, the number range 4700–5599 is used with all three street names—with Fargo in Box A, with East in Box E, and with Lake in Box D. The exam you take may repeat number ranges in the same way, though there is no guarantee that this will be the case. If you see this repetition, at first you may be a bit relieved, thinking this makes your task simpler. However, a closer look will show that the repetition makes the task even harder, because each number span is linked with three different names in three different locations. So it's really no help.

Now, look again. This time pay attention to the number spans themselves. Is it really necessary to memorize every single digit? No, because, if you look at each row of numbers separately, only the first two digits of each of the five number spans are distinctive. That's the case whether the number ranges are the same across the boxes or different. Either way, you don't have to memorize both numbers in a range, because another box begins where this box leaves off. For example, you don't need to know that the range that begins with 4700 Fargo in Box A ends with 5599, because Box C picks up at 5600 Fargo. Thus, you only need the first *two* digits of each number. They may be duplicated in the other rows, but right now we are looking at only a row at a time—anyway, you'll be making up stories soon, linking the numbers with the names in the boxes, so the duplication won't matter.

One last item: Although you need not memorize the ranges in their entirety, you must keep in your mind the fact that **there is a range**, and it is always the same: 00–99. That way, if you run onto a question that asks you to identify the box for 4800 Fargo, you will be able to deduce that this is in Box A, because it is **in the range of** 4700–5599. Keep in mind that the ranges run into each other—you might have to mentally check where the range ends. Since you aren't memorizing the second number in the range, determining that 4800 Fargo is in Box A might take checking your mental picture of Box C, where 5600 Fargo begins.

Now your simplified set of boxes looks like this:

A	B	C	D	E
47 Fargo	68 Fargo	56 Fargo	65 Fargo	44 Fargo
56 East	65 East	68 East	44 East	47 East
44 Lake	56 Lake	65 Lake	47 Lake	68 Lake

As you take the sample exams later in this chapter, you should practice "erasing" the last six digits mentally, because in the actual exam you will not be allowed to mark on anything except the answer grid.

Associate

Look again at the four boxes you chose to memorize. They have to be the same four boxes you chose before, or you'll simply complicate matters again—for example, I will have to look at boxes A, B, D, and E.

Memory experts advise that the best method for remembering numbers is to substitute words or letters for each number. **Set up your substitution system ahead of time,** so you'll have it all ready on exam day. The easiest method is to think up words that rhyme with the numbers 0 through 9. Then, during the exam, you can make up a little story to go with each set. An example of a number/word set might be:

0 = *oh, go, Joe, no*
1 = *bun, fun, gun, run*
2 = *boo, new, woo, shoe*
3 = *bee, key, me, knee*
4 = *door, more, bore* (or *boor*), *poor*

5 = *dive, live, hive, jive*

6 = *sticks, fix, kicks, tricks*

7 = *heaven, leaven, Kevin, raven*

8 = *hate, gate, bait, late*

9 = *mine, dine, sign, fine*

Another method is to associate each number with its first two letters: 0 = *ze*; 1 = *on*; 2 = *tw*, and so on. It has to be the first *two* letters, because some of the first letters are repeated: For example, *t* is the first letter of both *two* and *three*. This is fine, if it is easiest for you, but at some point you'll still have to substitute whole words for the letters. Be careful not to use any word that for personal reasons might remind you of any other number.

Having memorized your list (which may be different from mine, since we all have favorite words), you can substitute words for any number you wish. 42, for example, can become *poor shoe*; 35 *bee hive*; 91 *fine fun*, and so on.

Now **simplify** the boxes again, mentally deleting any repetition. All the boxes contain the same street names, in this case Fargo, East, and Lake. The order is the same–Fargo is always first and Lake always last—so you need not spend much time on these three street names. Instead, you can go straight to the numbers. So here's your simplified set of boxes.

A	B	C	D	E
47	68	ignore	65	44
56	65		44	47
44	56		47	68

Now you are ready to start making up stories using the words you associated with the numbers.

Previously, for the single names, you told your story horizontally across all the boxes, two elements to a box. For the numbers, however, you will work vertically, **concentrating on one box at a time**, making up a story to go with **each separate box**.

It is important to decide, **before you go into the test**, words that are going to be associated with the boxes A, B, C, D, and E. Use a category of words that is meaningful to you—a hobby, jobs you have held in the past, a special interest. The words should present a vivid, concrete, **visual image**. Here are some possibilities:

- For me, because I have several pets, it is easiest to use **animals**: A = anteater or antelope; B = buffalo or bat; C = cat or cockatoo; D = dog or dinosaur; E = elk or elephant.
- You might be a gourmet and prefer the names for **foods**: apple, broccoli, cantaloupe, dill, eggplant.
- **Cars** are a possibility: Aurora, Buick, Cadillac, Dodge, El Dorado (if you can easily visualize their shapes).
- Try **sports teams**: Astros, Buffalo Bills, Cardinals, Dodgers, Eagles (if you can easily visualize their uniforms).

The main thing is for the general category to be something you are interested in, so that you will find it easy to make up stories under the stress of the test situation.

Using animals, I might make up the following stories:

> An Anteater named **Poor** (4) **Kevin** (7) (47)
> took a **drive** (5) in the **sticks** (6) (56)
> in my **four** (4)-**door** (4). (44)

> The Buffalo **kicks** (6) the **gate** (8). (68)
> The buffalo **kicks** (6) the **hive** (5). (65)
> The buffalo takes a **dive** (5), just for **kicks** (6). (56)

(In this example I would leave out the poem for Cat or Cockatoo.)

> A Dog with a **stick** (6) **arrived** (5) (65)
> at my **poor** (4) **door** (4). (44)
> He thought he'd found the **door** (4) to **heaven** (7)! (47)

> An Elephant armed with a **forty-four** (44)
> shot a **poor** (4) **raven** (7). (47)
> What a **sick** (6) **fate** (8)! (68)

You already have the vertical order of the streets in mind: Fargo/East/Lake. This is easy to fix in your memory in seconds. Now remember: The first line of your poem is always associated with the street address on the first line of each box (in this case, Fargo), the second line with the second line in each box (East), and the third line with the third line in each box (Lake). So, suppose the question were 6800-6999 **Lake**. Lake is the **third street name** in each of the boxes, so you will automatically zero in on the **third line of each of your stories**: Is it D? No, because the third line of the Dog poem is "door to heaven" or 47. However the third line of the E poem is "sick fate" or 68. Ah ha! The correct box is E.

COMBINING NAMES AND NUMBERS

Now your mental set of boxes looks like this:

A = Anteater	B = Buffalo	C	D = Dog	E = Elephant
For names:				
My friend **Lynn** is a **pleasant** person	but I have never liked her husband **Langford**. I'd like to rent **Morris** the cat to scratch him.		But I'd probably have to take his suit to a **tailor**, who might put too much **Argo** starch in it.	I'd better just stay home and read **Hawthorne's** biography of **Kennedy**.
For numbers:				
An **A**nteater named **Poor Kevin** (47) ⠀⠀⠀⠀Fargo	The Buffalo **kicks** the **gate**! (68) ⠀⠀⠀⠀Fargo		A Dog with a **stick arrived** (65) ⠀⠀⠀⠀Fargo	An Elephant with a **forty-four** (44) ⠀⠀⠀⠀Fargo
took a **drive** in the **sticks** (56) ⠀⠀⠀⠀East	The Buffalo **kicks** the **hive**! (65) ⠀⠀⠀⠀East		at my **poor door.** (44) ⠀⠀⠀⠀East	shot a **poor raven.** (47) ⠀⠀⠀⠀East
in my **four-door** (44) ⠀⠀⠀⠀Lake	He takes a **dive**, just for **kicks**! (56) ⠀⠀⠀⠀Lake		He thought he'd found the **door** to heaven! (47) ⠀⠀⠀⠀Lake	What a **sick fate**! (68) ⠀⠀⠀⠀Lake

If you find it difficult to make up a story using one of the words you decided on before the test, you can always use another word, **as long as it rhymes with the number** so that you can remember it. For example, In Box D, I used the word *arrived*, even though it was not on my original list. The nice part about rhyming words with numbers is that you can find a substitute word, right on the spot, that makes more sense for your story.

TAKING THE TEST

Once you've set up your memorization system **in advance,** there are only a couple of other things to keep in mind as you take the actual exam.

Use the Practice Sessions

Before the exam begins, you will be given three practice sessions, during which you will be instructed in how to use the answer grid and other things you may need to know. You will be given a chance to do practice exercises to help familiarize you with the format of the questions. These practice exercises will be based on the same boxes as the ones on the actual test, but **the practice exercises don't count.**

In the past, some of the practice exercises have been set up so that the boxes are actually in front of you as you answer the practice questions. In addition, an extra minute or two has been given for memorization before one or more of the practice exercises. So you may have those few extra minutes to make up your stories and fix them in your mind. Well before the test, using the examples in this book, familiarize yourself with the directions for taking the test and with the answer grid, so that you can spend the entire pretest period on making up your stories, rather than answering the *practice* questions, which don't count. Use the practice questions *only* to test how well your memorization process is going; spend most of the time on the memorization itself.

Between the five minutes officially allotted to memorization and the extra minutes you gain from the practice exercises, you may actually have 11–14 minutes to work with the boxes before you have to answer the real questions, the ones that count. That makes the memorization task a lot easier than it looks at first glance.

Guessing and Timing

This part of the exam is scored by taking your right answer score and then subtracting one fourth of a point for each wrong answer. Thus, random guessing will not help your score. However, if you can eliminate one or more alternatives, it is to your advantage to guess.

For the actual scored part of the test, you will have five minutes to answer as many of the 88 questions as you can. You have to work as quickly and as accurately as you can, though you will not be expected to answer all the questions in the time allowed. If you wish, you may skip around.

Most people find the single names easier to remember. If you're one of them, you might want to go through the whole test and quickly answer all the single-name questions and then go back to the numbers. If you do skip around, though, **be careful not to lose your place on the answer grid.** It's best to always keep the index finger of your non-writing hand on the answer to the question you're working on at the moment. Losing your place can cost valuable seconds on this test.

How to Answer Memory For Addresses Questions

Remember, there are two things—and only two—that you need to do to succeed on the Memory for Addresses portion of the test:

1. Simplify

- Decide which four of the five boxes to memorize—choose the easiest four for you and discard the fifth.
- Mentally eliminate all elements in those boxes that you do not need to memorize—the first two digits of each address range are the only numbers you need be concerned with memorizing.

2. Associate

- Beginning with the single names (the ones without number ranges), make up a story that will carry you across all four boxes in strict order.
- Before the test, decide on the category of words to use for boxes A, B, C, D, and E. It can be animals, furniture, vegetables—anything you relate to that will plant a strong visual image in your mind.
- Turning to the number ranges and using your prememorized list of words that rhyme with numbers, make up a story that will carry you vertically down each box. With numbers you will be working with only one box at a time.
- Remember that any element you have not memorized will automatically go in the "discarded" box.

To do well on this portion of the test, you have to do the following **ahead of time:**

- **Devise your number/word scheme.** Find rhyming words to substitute for the numbers.
- **Decide what the boxes will be called.** Use animals (Antelope, Bat . . .), fruits (Apple, Broccoli . . .), or whatever works for you.
- **Practice making up stories.** Use the practice sections that follow and the sample exams in this book to polish your story-making skills.

As you practice, you will be amazed at how rapidly your skill for this part of the test improves. Two complete practice sections follow this section, starting on the next page. Before you take them, work out your system. What category of words will you use? What words will you rhyme with the numbers?

After you've set up your system, turn to the two practice sections. For each practice section, give yourself eight minutes to memorize the boxes. (The extra minutes represent the time you would be given to do the practice questions before the actual exam.) Then turn the page and take five minutes to answer the 88 questions. The answers come after each practice set. Good luck!

PART B: MEMORY FOR ADDRESSES

1.	Ⓐ	Ⓑ	Ⓒ	Ⓓ	Ⓔ	31.	Ⓐ	Ⓑ	Ⓒ	Ⓓ	Ⓔ	61.	Ⓐ	Ⓑ	Ⓒ	Ⓓ	Ⓔ
2.	Ⓐ	Ⓑ	Ⓒ	Ⓓ	Ⓔ	32.	Ⓐ	Ⓑ	Ⓒ	Ⓓ	Ⓔ	62.	Ⓐ	Ⓑ	Ⓒ	Ⓓ	Ⓔ
3.	Ⓐ	Ⓑ	Ⓒ	Ⓓ	Ⓔ	33.	Ⓐ	Ⓑ	Ⓒ	Ⓓ	Ⓔ	63.	Ⓐ	Ⓑ	Ⓒ	Ⓓ	Ⓔ
4.	Ⓐ	Ⓑ	Ⓒ	Ⓓ	Ⓔ	34.	Ⓐ	Ⓑ	Ⓒ	Ⓓ	Ⓔ	64.	Ⓐ	Ⓑ	Ⓒ	Ⓓ	Ⓔ
5.	Ⓐ	Ⓑ	Ⓒ	Ⓓ	Ⓔ	35.	Ⓐ	Ⓑ	Ⓒ	Ⓓ	Ⓔ	65.	Ⓐ	Ⓑ	Ⓒ	Ⓓ	Ⓔ
6.	Ⓐ	Ⓑ	Ⓒ	Ⓓ	Ⓔ	36.	Ⓐ	Ⓑ	Ⓒ	Ⓓ	Ⓔ	66.	Ⓐ	Ⓑ	Ⓒ	Ⓓ	Ⓔ
7.	Ⓐ	Ⓑ	Ⓒ	Ⓓ	Ⓔ	37.	Ⓐ	Ⓑ	Ⓒ	Ⓓ	Ⓔ	67.	Ⓐ	Ⓑ	Ⓒ	Ⓓ	Ⓔ
8.	Ⓐ	Ⓑ	Ⓒ	Ⓓ	Ⓔ	38.	Ⓐ	Ⓑ	Ⓒ	Ⓓ	Ⓔ	68.	Ⓐ	Ⓑ	Ⓒ	Ⓓ	Ⓔ
9.	Ⓐ	Ⓑ	Ⓒ	Ⓓ	Ⓔ	39.	Ⓐ	Ⓑ	Ⓒ	Ⓓ	Ⓔ	69.	Ⓐ	Ⓑ	Ⓒ	Ⓓ	Ⓔ
10.	Ⓐ	Ⓑ	Ⓒ	Ⓓ	Ⓔ	40.	Ⓐ	Ⓑ	Ⓒ	Ⓓ	Ⓔ	70.	Ⓐ	Ⓑ	Ⓒ	Ⓓ	Ⓔ
11.	Ⓐ	Ⓑ	Ⓒ	Ⓓ	Ⓔ	41.	Ⓐ	Ⓑ	Ⓒ	Ⓓ	Ⓔ	71.	Ⓐ	Ⓑ	Ⓒ	Ⓓ	Ⓔ
12.	Ⓐ	Ⓑ	Ⓒ	Ⓓ	Ⓔ	42.	Ⓐ	Ⓑ	Ⓒ	Ⓓ	Ⓔ	72.	Ⓐ	Ⓑ	Ⓒ	Ⓓ	Ⓔ
13.	Ⓐ	Ⓑ	Ⓒ	Ⓓ	Ⓔ	43.	Ⓐ	Ⓑ	Ⓒ	Ⓓ	Ⓔ	73.	Ⓐ	Ⓑ	Ⓒ	Ⓓ	Ⓔ
14.	Ⓐ	Ⓑ	Ⓒ	Ⓓ	Ⓔ	44.	Ⓐ	Ⓑ	Ⓒ	Ⓓ	Ⓔ	74.	Ⓐ	Ⓑ	Ⓒ	Ⓓ	Ⓔ
15.	Ⓐ	Ⓑ	Ⓒ	Ⓓ	Ⓔ	45.	Ⓐ	Ⓑ	Ⓒ	Ⓓ	Ⓔ	75.	Ⓐ	Ⓑ	Ⓒ	Ⓓ	Ⓔ
16.	Ⓐ	Ⓑ	Ⓒ	Ⓓ	Ⓔ	46.	Ⓐ	Ⓑ	Ⓒ	Ⓓ	Ⓔ	76.	Ⓐ	Ⓑ	Ⓒ	Ⓓ	Ⓔ
17.	Ⓐ	Ⓑ	Ⓒ	Ⓓ	Ⓔ	47.	Ⓐ	Ⓑ	Ⓒ	Ⓓ	Ⓔ	77.	Ⓐ	Ⓑ	Ⓒ	Ⓓ	Ⓔ
18.	Ⓐ	Ⓑ	Ⓒ	Ⓓ	Ⓔ	48.	Ⓐ	Ⓑ	Ⓒ	Ⓓ	Ⓔ	78.	Ⓐ	Ⓑ	Ⓒ	Ⓓ	Ⓔ
19.	Ⓐ	Ⓑ	Ⓒ	Ⓓ	Ⓔ	49.	Ⓐ	Ⓑ	Ⓒ	Ⓓ	Ⓔ	79.	Ⓐ	Ⓑ	Ⓒ	Ⓓ	Ⓔ
20.	Ⓐ	Ⓑ	Ⓒ	Ⓓ	Ⓔ	50.	Ⓐ	Ⓑ	Ⓒ	Ⓓ	Ⓔ	80.	Ⓐ	Ⓑ	Ⓒ	Ⓓ	Ⓔ
21.	Ⓐ	Ⓑ	Ⓒ	Ⓓ	Ⓔ	51.	Ⓐ	Ⓑ	Ⓒ	Ⓓ	Ⓔ	81.	Ⓐ	Ⓑ	Ⓒ	Ⓓ	Ⓔ
22.	Ⓐ	Ⓑ	Ⓒ	Ⓓ	Ⓔ	52.	Ⓐ	Ⓑ	Ⓒ	Ⓓ	Ⓔ	82.	Ⓐ	Ⓑ	Ⓒ	Ⓓ	Ⓔ
23.	Ⓐ	Ⓑ	Ⓒ	Ⓓ	Ⓔ	53.	Ⓐ	Ⓑ	Ⓒ	Ⓓ	Ⓔ	83.	Ⓐ	Ⓑ	Ⓒ	Ⓓ	Ⓔ
24.	Ⓐ	Ⓑ	Ⓒ	Ⓓ	Ⓔ	54.	Ⓐ	Ⓑ	Ⓒ	Ⓓ	Ⓔ	84.	Ⓐ	Ⓑ	Ⓒ	Ⓓ	Ⓔ
25.	Ⓐ	Ⓑ	Ⓒ	Ⓓ	Ⓔ	55.	Ⓐ	Ⓑ	Ⓒ	Ⓓ	Ⓔ	85.	Ⓐ	Ⓑ	Ⓒ	Ⓓ	Ⓔ
26.	Ⓐ	Ⓑ	Ⓒ	Ⓓ	Ⓔ	56.	Ⓐ	Ⓑ	Ⓒ	Ⓓ	Ⓔ	86.	Ⓐ	Ⓑ	Ⓒ	Ⓓ	Ⓔ
27.	Ⓐ	Ⓑ	Ⓒ	Ⓓ	Ⓔ	57.	Ⓐ	Ⓑ	Ⓒ	Ⓓ	Ⓔ	87.	Ⓐ	Ⓑ	Ⓒ	Ⓓ	Ⓔ
28.	Ⓐ	Ⓑ	Ⓒ	Ⓓ	Ⓔ	58.	Ⓐ	Ⓑ	Ⓒ	Ⓓ	Ⓔ	88.	Ⓐ	Ⓑ	Ⓒ	Ⓓ	Ⓔ
29.	Ⓐ	Ⓑ	Ⓒ	Ⓓ	Ⓔ	59.	Ⓐ	Ⓑ	Ⓒ	Ⓓ	Ⓔ						
30.	Ⓐ	Ⓑ	Ⓒ	Ⓓ	Ⓔ	60.	Ⓐ	Ⓑ	Ⓒ	Ⓓ	Ⓔ						

SAMPLE MEMORY FOR ADDRESSES SECTION 1

Below are five boxes labeled A, B, C, D, and E. Each box contains three sets of addresses (which include street names with number ranges) and two single names. Study the boxes for **ten minutes** and memorize the location (A, B, C, D, or E) of each of the numbered addresses and single names. Then answer the 88 questions on the next page by darkening the circle (A, B, C, D, or E) that corresponds to the box in which the address or name appears. You will have **five minutes** to answer the 88 questions.

A	B	C	D	E
4800–5099 Arbor	3300–3799 Arbor	4200–4799 Arbor	5100–5599 Arbor	3800–4199 Arbor
Bianca	Melrose	Chavez	Varner	Harlan
5100–5599 Fell	4200–4799 Fell	3300–3799 Fell	4800–5099 Fell	3800–4199 Fell
Springer	Benton	York	Dewey	Fairfield
3800–4199 Rhonda	5100–5599 Rhonda	3300–3799 Rhonda	4800–5099 Rhonda	4200–4799 Rhonda

1. Bianca
2. 3300–3799 Arbor
3. 5100–5599 Rhonda
4. 4800–5099 Fell
5. 3300–3799 Rhonda
6. Melrose
7. Varner
8. 4800–5099 Arbor
9. 4200–4799 Fell
10. Dewey
11. 3300–3799 Fell
12. 4800–5099 Rhonda
13. Fairfield
14. 3800–4199 Rhonda
15. 3800–4199 Arbor
16. York
17. Bianca
18. 3800–4199 Fell
19. 5100–5599 Fell
20. 3300–3799 Fell
21. 4200–4799 Rhonda
22. Springer
23. 5100–5599 Arbor
24. Springer
25. 4200–4799 Fell

26. 4200–4799 Arbor
27. Varner
28. 3800–4199 Fell
29. 4800–5099 Rhonda
30. 3800–4199 Arbor
31. Dewey
32. Harlan
33. 4800–5099 Fell
34. Bianca
35. 3300–3799 Rhonda
36. Melrose
37. 3800–4199 Arbor
38. 3800–4199 Rhonda
39. 4200–4799 Rhonda
40. 5100–5599 Fell
41. Fairfield
42. Springer
43. 4200–4799 Arbor
44. Benton
45. 5100–5599 Arbor
46. 5100–5599 Rhonda
47. 4200–4799 Arbor
48. Dewey
49. 3300–3799 Fell
50. Varner

51. Chavez

52. 4200–4799 Rhonda

53. 3300–3799 Arbor

54. Benton

55. 4400–4799 Fell

56. 3800–4199 Arbor

57. Springer

58. 5100–5599 Rhonda

59. York

60. 4200–4799 Rhonda

61. 4800–5099 Arbor

62. Dewey

63. 4800–5099 Rhonda

64. Chavez

65. 4800–5099 Fell

66. 3800–4199 Rhonda

67. Fairfield

68. 3300–3799 Arbor

69. 4200–4799 Arbor

70. Bianca

71. 3800–4199 Fell

72. 3300–3799 Rhonda

73. Benton

74. 5100–5599 Fell

75. Harlan

76. 3800–4199 Arbor

77. 3300–3799 Fell

78. Varner

79. 5100–5599 Rhonda

80. 4200–4799 Fell

81. Harlan

82. Melrose

83. 4800–5099 Arbor

84. Benton

85. Chavez

86. Springer

87. 5100–5599 Arbor

88. York

ANSWERS TO MEMORY FOR ADDRESSES SECTION 1

1. A	23. D	45. D	67. E
2. B	24. A	46. B	68. B
3. B	25. B	47. C	69. C
4. D	26. C	48. D	70. A
5. C	27. D	49. C	71. E
6. B	28. E	50. D	72. C
7. D	29. D	51. C	73. B
8. A	30. E	52. E	74. A
9. B	31. D	53. B	75. E
10. D	32. E	54. B	76. E
11. C	33. D	55. B	77. C
12. D	34. A	56. E	78. D
13. E	35. C	57. A	79. B
14. A	36. B	58. B	80. B
15. E	37. E	59. C	81. E
16. C	38. A	60. E	82. B
17. A	39. E	61. A	83. A
18. E	40. A	62. D	84. B
19. A	41. E	63. D	85. C
20. C	42. A	64. C	86. A
21. E	43. C	65. D	87. D
22. A	44. B	66. A	88. C

PART B: MEMORY FOR ADDRESSES

1.	Ⓐ Ⓑ Ⓒ Ⓓ Ⓔ	31.	Ⓐ Ⓑ Ⓒ Ⓓ Ⓔ	61.	Ⓐ Ⓑ Ⓒ Ⓓ Ⓔ
2.	Ⓐ Ⓑ Ⓒ Ⓓ Ⓔ	32.	Ⓐ Ⓑ Ⓒ Ⓓ Ⓔ	62.	Ⓐ Ⓑ Ⓒ Ⓓ Ⓔ
3.	Ⓐ Ⓑ Ⓒ Ⓓ Ⓔ	33.	Ⓐ Ⓑ Ⓒ Ⓓ Ⓔ	63.	Ⓐ Ⓑ Ⓒ Ⓓ Ⓔ
4.	Ⓐ Ⓑ Ⓒ Ⓓ Ⓔ	34.	Ⓐ Ⓑ Ⓒ Ⓓ Ⓔ	64.	Ⓐ Ⓑ Ⓒ Ⓓ Ⓔ
5.	Ⓐ Ⓑ Ⓒ Ⓓ Ⓔ	35.	Ⓐ Ⓑ Ⓒ Ⓓ Ⓔ	65.	Ⓐ Ⓑ Ⓒ Ⓓ Ⓔ
6.	Ⓐ Ⓑ Ⓒ Ⓓ Ⓔ	36.	Ⓐ Ⓑ Ⓒ Ⓓ Ⓔ	66.	Ⓐ Ⓑ Ⓒ Ⓓ Ⓔ
7.	Ⓐ Ⓑ Ⓒ Ⓓ Ⓔ	37.	Ⓐ Ⓑ Ⓒ Ⓓ Ⓔ	67.	Ⓐ Ⓑ Ⓒ Ⓓ Ⓔ
8.	Ⓐ Ⓑ Ⓒ Ⓓ Ⓔ	38.	Ⓐ Ⓑ Ⓒ Ⓓ Ⓔ	68.	Ⓐ Ⓑ Ⓒ Ⓓ Ⓔ
9.	Ⓐ Ⓑ Ⓒ Ⓓ Ⓔ	39.	Ⓐ Ⓑ Ⓒ Ⓓ Ⓔ	69.	Ⓐ Ⓑ Ⓒ Ⓓ Ⓔ
10.	Ⓐ Ⓑ Ⓒ Ⓓ Ⓔ	40.	Ⓐ Ⓑ Ⓒ Ⓓ Ⓔ	70.	Ⓐ Ⓑ Ⓒ Ⓓ Ⓔ
11.	Ⓐ Ⓑ Ⓒ Ⓓ Ⓔ	41.	Ⓐ Ⓑ Ⓒ Ⓓ Ⓔ	71.	Ⓐ Ⓑ Ⓒ Ⓓ Ⓔ
12.	Ⓐ Ⓑ Ⓒ Ⓓ Ⓔ	42.	Ⓐ Ⓑ Ⓒ Ⓓ Ⓔ	72.	Ⓐ Ⓑ Ⓒ Ⓓ Ⓔ
13.	Ⓐ Ⓑ Ⓒ Ⓓ Ⓔ	43.	Ⓐ Ⓑ Ⓒ Ⓓ Ⓔ	73.	Ⓐ Ⓑ Ⓒ Ⓓ Ⓔ
14.	Ⓐ Ⓑ Ⓒ Ⓓ Ⓔ	44.	Ⓐ Ⓑ Ⓒ Ⓓ Ⓔ	74.	Ⓐ Ⓑ Ⓒ Ⓓ Ⓔ
15.	Ⓐ Ⓑ Ⓒ Ⓓ Ⓔ	45.	Ⓐ Ⓑ Ⓒ Ⓓ Ⓔ	75.	Ⓐ Ⓑ Ⓒ Ⓓ Ⓔ
16.	Ⓐ Ⓑ Ⓒ Ⓓ Ⓔ	46.	Ⓐ Ⓑ Ⓒ Ⓓ Ⓔ	76.	Ⓐ Ⓑ Ⓒ Ⓓ Ⓔ
17.	Ⓐ Ⓑ Ⓒ Ⓓ Ⓔ	47.	Ⓐ Ⓑ Ⓒ Ⓓ Ⓔ	77.	Ⓐ Ⓑ Ⓒ Ⓓ Ⓔ
18.	Ⓐ Ⓑ Ⓒ Ⓓ Ⓔ	48.	Ⓐ Ⓑ Ⓒ Ⓓ Ⓔ	78.	Ⓐ Ⓑ Ⓒ Ⓓ Ⓔ
19.	Ⓐ Ⓑ Ⓒ Ⓓ Ⓔ	49.	Ⓐ Ⓑ Ⓒ Ⓓ Ⓔ	79.	Ⓐ Ⓑ Ⓒ Ⓓ Ⓔ
20.	Ⓐ Ⓑ Ⓒ Ⓓ Ⓔ	50.	Ⓐ Ⓑ Ⓒ Ⓓ Ⓔ	80.	Ⓐ Ⓑ Ⓒ Ⓓ Ⓔ
21.	Ⓐ Ⓑ Ⓒ Ⓓ Ⓔ	51.	Ⓐ Ⓑ Ⓒ Ⓓ Ⓔ	81.	Ⓐ Ⓑ Ⓒ Ⓓ Ⓔ
22.	Ⓐ Ⓑ Ⓒ Ⓓ Ⓔ	52.	Ⓐ Ⓑ Ⓒ Ⓓ Ⓔ	82.	Ⓐ Ⓑ Ⓒ Ⓓ Ⓔ
23.	Ⓐ Ⓑ Ⓒ Ⓓ Ⓔ	53.	Ⓐ Ⓑ Ⓒ Ⓓ Ⓔ	83.	Ⓐ Ⓑ Ⓒ Ⓓ Ⓔ
24.	Ⓐ Ⓑ Ⓒ Ⓓ Ⓔ	54.	Ⓐ Ⓑ Ⓒ Ⓓ Ⓔ	84.	Ⓐ Ⓑ Ⓒ Ⓓ Ⓔ
25.	Ⓐ Ⓑ Ⓒ Ⓓ Ⓔ	55.	Ⓐ Ⓑ Ⓒ Ⓓ Ⓔ	85.	Ⓐ Ⓑ Ⓒ Ⓓ Ⓔ
26.	Ⓐ Ⓑ Ⓒ Ⓓ Ⓔ	56.	Ⓐ Ⓑ Ⓒ Ⓓ Ⓔ	86.	Ⓐ Ⓑ Ⓒ Ⓓ Ⓔ
27.	Ⓐ Ⓑ Ⓒ Ⓓ Ⓔ	57.	Ⓐ Ⓑ Ⓒ Ⓓ Ⓔ	87.	Ⓐ Ⓑ Ⓒ Ⓓ Ⓔ
28.	Ⓐ Ⓑ Ⓒ Ⓓ Ⓔ	58.	Ⓐ Ⓑ Ⓒ Ⓓ Ⓔ	88.	Ⓐ Ⓑ Ⓒ Ⓓ Ⓔ
29.	Ⓐ Ⓑ Ⓒ Ⓓ Ⓔ	59.	Ⓐ Ⓑ Ⓒ Ⓓ Ⓔ		
30.	Ⓐ Ⓑ Ⓒ Ⓓ Ⓔ	60.	Ⓐ Ⓑ Ⓒ Ⓓ Ⓔ		

SAMPLE MEMORY FOR ADDRESSES SECTION 2

Below are five boxes labeled A, B, C, D, and E. Each box contains three sets of addresses (which include street names with number ranges) and two single names. Study the boxes for **ten minutes** and memorize the location (A, B, C, D, or E) of each of the numbered addresses and single names. Then answer the 88 questions on the next page by darkening the circle (A, B, C, D, or E) that corresponds to the box in which the address or name appears. You will have **five minutes** to answer the 88 questions.

A	B	C	D	E
5700–6299 River	4600–5199 River	6300–6999 River	5200–5699 River	7000–7499 River
Bates	Pryor	Seaver	Tompkins	Gross
3300–3899 Dodge	5200–5699 Dodge	3900–4599 Dodge	5700–6299 Dodge	4600–5199 Dodge
Miklow	Wang	Kurtz	Hanks	Xavier
1200–1799 Cotton	3300–3899 Cotton	2700–3299 Cotton	1800–2199 Cotton	2200–2699 Cotton

1. Wang
2. 6300–6999 River
3. 2200–2699 Cotton
4. Bates
5. 5700–6299 Dodge
6. 2700–3299 Cotton
7. 4600–5199 River
8. Tompkins
9. Miklow
10. 4600–5199 Dodge
11. 1200–1799 Cotton
12. Gross
13. 5200–5699 River
14. Kurtz
15. 3300–3699 Cotton
16. 3900–4599 Dodge
17. Pryor
18. 7000–7499 River
19. Hanks
20. 3300–3899 Dodge
21. Miklow
22. Seaver
23. 5200–5699 Dodge
24. 7000–7499 River
25. Tompkins

26. 1200–1799 Cotton
27. 5200–5699 River
28. Xavier
29. Kurtz
30. 5700–6299 Dodge
31. Bates
32. 2200–2699 Cotton
33. Wang
34. 6300–6999 River
35. 1800–2199 Cotton
36. Gross
37. 5700–6299 River
38. Seaver
39. 5700–6299 Dodge
40. 3300–3899 Cotton
41. Bates
42. Xavier
43. 5200–5699 River
44. 2700–3299 Cotton
45. Pryor
46. 3300–3899 Dodge
47. Kurtz
48. 4600–5199 River
49. 4600–5199 Dodge
50. Hanks

51. 2200–2699 Cotton

52. 5700–6299 River

53. 1800–2199 Cotton

54. Wang

55. 3900–4599 Dodge

56. 5700–6299 River

57. Tompkins

58. 4600–5199 Dodge

59. 2700–3299 Cotton

60. Miklow

61. 4600–5199 River

62. 3900–4599 Dodge

63. Pryor

64. Gross

65. 1800–2199 Cotton

66. 5700–6299 Dodge

67. 7000–7499 River

68. Seaver

69. 3300–3699 Dodge

70. 3300–3899 Cotton

71. Hanks

72. 6300–6999 River

73. Xavier

74. 1200–1799 Cotton

75. 5700–6299 Dodge

76. Wang

77. Kurtz

78. 7000–7499 River

79. 3300–3899 Cotton

80. Bates

81. Tompkins

82. 6300–6999 River

83. 3300–3899 Dodge

84. Gross

85. 5200–5699 Dodge

86. 2700–3299 Cotton

87. 5700–6299 River

88. Hanks

ANSWERS TO MEMORY FOR ADDRESSES SECTION 2

1. B	23. B	45. B	67. E
2. C	24. E	46. A	68. C
3. E	25. D	47. C	69. A
4. A	26. A	48. B	70. B
5. D	27. D	49. E	71. D
6. C	28. E	50. D	72. C
7. B	29. C	51. E	73. E
8. D	30. D	52. A	74. A
9. A	31. A	53. D	75. D
10. E	32. E	54. B	76. B
11. A	33. B	55. C	77. C
12. E	34. C	56. A	78. E
13. D	35. D	57. D	79. B
14. C	36. E	58. E	80. A
15. B	37. A	59. C	81. D
16. C	38. C	60. A	82. C
17. B	39. D	61. B	83. A
18. E	40. B	62. C	84. E
19. D	41. A	63. B	85. B
20. A	42. E	64. E	86. C
21. A	43. D	65. D	87. A
22. C	44. C	66. D	88. D

C·H·A·P·T·E·R

NUMBER SERIES QUESTIONS

8

CHAPTER SUMMARY

This chapter helps you deal with Part C of the postal exam, Number Series. If you become familiar with the most common patterns used, you can conquer this section of the exam.

I n many Postal Service jobs, employees must work with numbers, sometimes in complicated series. The ability to reason with numbers is necessary when dealing with addresses that involve complex numbers and ranges of numbers, and it is especially important for recognizing codes when sorting mail or operating sorting, routing, and marking machines. The Number Series portion of the postal exam is designed to test your aptitude for reasoning accurately and efficiently using numbers and for paying close attention to detail.

WHAT THE NUMBER SERIES SECTION IS LIKE

Part C of the postal exam contains 24 items, and you will have 20 minutes to answer as many as you can. You will want to try to answer all the questions in this section, even if you have to guess on some. Since only right answers count, guessing—even random guessing—cannot hurt you.

Each item in the Number Series portion of the exam includes:

- A problem consisting of a series of seven numbers that follow some definite order.
- Five options (A, B, C, D, E), each of which consists of two numbers. The correct answer is the two numbers that would come next in the series if the same order were followed.

The simplest possible Number Series question would thus go like this:

1. 1 2 3 4 5 6 7. . . . . **A)** 9 10   **B)** 7 8   **C)** 8 10   **D)** 8 9   **E)** 9 11

The series established in the problem is simply the numbers in order, 1–7. Obviously the next two numbers should be 8 and 9, answer **D**. Unfortunately, the problems you have to solve on the actual exam won't be quite so simple.

There are two basic types of series tested in this portion of the exam: simple and complex. Here's an outline of the types of series; they are treated in more detail in the next section, "How to Prepare."

SIMPLE SERIES

There are three basic subtypes of simple series:

- Simple addition or subtraction
- Alternating addition or subtraction
- Addition or subtraction with repetition

Simple Addition or Subtraction

In the simplest type of series, the same number is added to or subtracted from each number in the series to arrive at the next. For example:

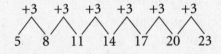

Alternating Addition or Subtraction

Rather than adding or subtracting the same number to or from each number in the series, **two different numbers** are added or subtracted alternately. For example:

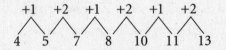

Addition or Subtraction with Repetition

This subtype is a variation of the alternating addition and subtraction subtype. A number is repeated (R) before adding or subtracting. For example:

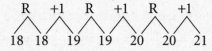

COMPLEX SERIES

Whereas the simple number series have only one pattern (sometimes with repetition), the complex number series will have two patterns. Here again, repetition might be thrown in.

The complex series consists of two basic types:

- Alternating repetition
- Alternating series

Alternating Repetition

In this type, a **random number** (RN) is introduced every second or third number into what is otherwise a simple addition or subtraction series. For example:

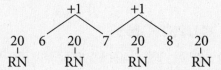

Alternating Patterns

Alternating patterns series are the most difficult. In this type, there are actually **two patterns**—even three, if you count repetition or random numbers. Every other number or every third number follows an entirely different pattern from the other numbers. For example:

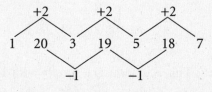

To make matters even more complicated, random numbers and alternating repetition may be introduced into this type, as well.

How to Prepare

The best preparation for Number Series questions is becoming familiar with the kinds of series you are likely to see on the exam. If you have a store of possible pattern types in your memory, you're more likely to recognize a given pattern at a glance, without having to spend a lot of time puzzling it out. And if you've practiced with the patterns, you're more likely to remember them. Below are sample problems representing all of the most common kinds of series. Use them to get familiar with the various types. Then use the sample test section at the end of this chapter for more practice with these types.

FIRST STEPS IN DEALING WITH NUMBER SERIES QUESTIONS

Your first step in tackling a Number Series question should be to glance at the series to get the lay of the land. First of all, look for repetition and random numbers. There's no point in trying to figure out what number to add to the first number to get the second number when the second number has simply been inserted at random. A quick glance at the series should show you whether numbers repeat or have been inserted at random.

Next, try to determine whether the series is a simple or a complex series. If the pattern shows itself on your first glance, you're probably dealing with a simple series.

It may be helpful to say the numbers aloud. Sometimes the ear can pick up what the eye cannot. Of course you should do this very softly, so as not to distract the other test-takers, and so they will not think you are muttering to yourself.

TYPES OF NUMBER SERIES QUESTIONS

If the pattern leaps out at you when you first look at a question, then the hard work is done. If it doesn't, try to figure out whether you're dealing with a simple or a complex series. Try your hand at the sample problems below, which are arranged from simplest to most complex. These will familiarize you with the most common kinds of patterns you can expect to see on the exam.

Simple Series

Start with a series with a clear pattern:

2. 3 6 9 12 15 18 21 . . . . **A)** 22 25   **B)** 24 27   **C)** 23 26   **D)** 28 30   **E)** 27 29

You probably found this one pretty easy. This is obviously a **simple addition series**. The numbers increase by 3. The only trick is making sure that you add correctly to get 24 27, answer **B**.

Here's another example that is probably obvious at a glance:

3. 37 35 33 31 29 27 25 . . . . **A)** 24 23   **B)** 23 20   **C)** 22 20   **D)** 23 21   **E)** 24 22

This series involves **simple subtraction**. The numbers decrease by 2. Therefore, the answer is **D**.

Now try one that's slightly more complex:

4. 1 2 4 5 7 8 10 . . . . **A)** 11 12   **B)** 12 14   **C)** 10 13   **D)** 12 13   **E)** 11 13

This series involves **alternating addition**. Two different numbers are added alternately: 1 is added to the first number, 2 to the second, 1 to the third, 2 to the fourth, and so on. Therefore, on your answer sheet you would darken circle **E**.

Here's a similar example:

5. 29 26 24 21 19 16 14 . . . . **A)** 11 9   **B)** 12 8   **C)** 12 9   **D)** 11 8   **E)** 10 9

This is an example of a series with **alternating subtraction**. The numbers decrease as follows: 3 is subtracted from the first number, 2 from the second, 3 from the third, 2 from the fourth, and so on. The answer is therefore **A**.

A slightly more complicated type involves addition along with simple repetition of numbers:

6. 20 20 21 21 22 22 23 . . . . **A)** 23 23   **B)** 23 24   **C)** 24 24   **D)** 22 23   **E)** 21 22

This series involves **addition with repetition**. Each number is repeated and then increased by 1. Note that, at the end of the series, 22 has already been repeated, but 23 has not. It would be easy to get confused if you answered too quickly. The correct answer repeats 23 and then adds 1 to get 24, answer **B**.

Then there's a variation on the same type:

7. 21 21 20 20 19 19 18 . . . . **A)** 18 18   **B)** 18 17   **C)** 17 18   **D)** 17 17   **E)** 18 19

This series uses **subtraction with repetition**. Each number in this series is repeated and then decreased by 1. Again, you have to be careful to note whether or not the last number has been repeated. It has not, so the answer is **B**.

Complex Series

If the pattern is not obvious at a glance, chances are you are dealing with a **complex series**. Here, saying the numbers aloud may be even more helpful than it was when dealing with the simple series.

Again, start out by **looking for repetition or random numbers**. When you can eliminate repeated or random numbers from the series, the patterns for the other numbers will emerge more clearly.

Once you've eliminated repeated and random numbers, the next step is to **look at every other number, then at every third number**.

For example, a problem might look like this:

8. 17 3 17 4 17 5 17 . . . . **A)** 6 17   **B)** 6 7   **C)** 17 6   **D)** 5 6   **E)** 17 7

By looking at every other number, you will see that the random number 17 has been inserted (**17** 3 **17** 4 **17** 5 **17**). The series otherwise simply increases by 1 (17 **3** 17 **4** 17 **5** 17). So you have **alternating repetition** in **two separate patterns**. Again, it's important to keep track of whether the random number has repeated at the end of the series. In this case, it has, so you should choose answer A. (A random number could also be inserted as every third number rather than every other number.)

A more complex problem of this type might be something like this:

9. 10 12 50 15 17 50 20 . . . . **A)** 50 21   **B)** 21 50   **C)** 50 22   **D)** 22 50   **E)** 22 24

In this case, by looking at every third number, you will see that the random number 50 has been introduced (10 12 **50** 15 17 **50** 20). Once you see that random number, it's easier to see that the series otherwise increases first by 2 (10 + 2 = 12), then by 3 (12 + 3 = 15), then by 2 (15 + 2 = 17), then by 3 (17 + 3 = 20). The number 50 is inserted before each addition of 3. So you actually have **alternating repetition** with an **alternating addition series**. The answer, then, is **D**. At the end of the series, 3 has just been added, so it's time to add 2 and then repeat 50.

A much more difficult case involves a series in which every other number or every third number follows an entirely different pattern from the other numbers—you have **two alternating patterns**. For example:

10. 1 20 3 19 5 18 7 . . . . **A)** 1 18   **B)** 19 9   **C)** 18 8   **D)** 17 9   **E)** 7 19

Here one of the two alternating patterns starts with 1 and **increases** by 2: **1** 20 **3** 19 **5** 18 **7**. The other pattern starts with 20 and **decreases** by 1: 1 **20** 3 **19** 5 **18** 7. The series ends with the "add 2" pattern, so it's time for the "subtract 1" pattern (17) and then the "add 2" pattern (9), so the answer is **D**.

An **alternating series** might also involve **repetition** of one of the numbers in the series:

11. 8 8 1 10 10 3 12 . . . . **A)** 13 13   **B)** 12 5   **C)** 12 4   **D)** 13 5   **E)** 4 12

One of the two alternating patterns starts with 8, which is repeated, and then the repeated number increases by 2 (8 + 2 = 10): **8 8** 1 **10 10** 3 12. The other pattern starts with 1 and increases by 2 (1 + 2 = 3): 8 8 **1** 10 10 **3** 12. When the series ends, it's time to repeat 12 and then switch to the "add 2" pattern. Therefore you should choose answer **B**.

An even more difficult example might involve **a random number introduced into two alternating patterns**:

12. 9 19 2 9 17 3 9 . . . . **A)** 15 4   **B)** 4 11   **C)** 9 19   **D)** 4 18   **E)** 15 10

Here you see the random number 9 introduced into two alternating patterns: **9** 19 2 **9** 17 3 **9**. (Beware: It can be particularly difficult to find a random number when it *begins* the series.) The first of the two alternating patterns starts with 19 and decreases by 2 (19 − 2 = 17): 9 **19** 2 9 **17** 3 9. The second of the two alternating patterns starts with 2 and increases by 1 (2 + 1 = 3): 9 19 **2** 9 17 **3** 9. The series ends with 9, so it's time to subtract 2 from 17 and then to add 1 to 3. Therefore you would darken circle A on your answer sheet.

STRATEGIES FOR NUMBER SERIES QUESTIONS

You'll go into Part C of the postal worker exam armed with your knowledge of the possible types of series and with the practice you'll accumulate as you work through this book. There are just a few additional strategies you need to know for test day.

Write in the Test Booklet

Take advantage of the fact that **you are allowed to write in the test booklet** for this section of the exam. Whether the series is simple or complex, you will start by looking for repetition. The moment you spot a repetition, **circle the repeating number or write it in the margin**.

Watch the Time

In Part C of the exam, you have 20 minutes to answer 24 questions—less than a minute per question. It's a good idea, when this section begins, to write down the starting time on your test booklet. Then add 20 minutes and write down the ending time. The examiner will not give you a signal when time is almost up, so you have to keep track of the time on your own. As you work, glance at the clock or at your watch periodically, and don't spend too much time on one question.

Easy Questions First

Some Number Series questions are much harder than others, but you don't get extra credit for the hard ones. All the questions count the same. So start by skimming for easy questions, and answer those first. Be sure, though, that when you skip a question you **make a mark beside it**, so that you will not forget it and can return to it easily. Make sure you skip on the answer grid, too.

When to Guess

Guessing on this portion of the exam—unlike on some other portions—will not hurt your score. Thus, this is the only section of the exam on which it is safe to guess at random. If you just can't see what's going on with a particular series, simply mark any answer and move on. Don't spend a lot of time on a question that stumps you.

Here's one reason you marked the ending time on your answer sheet: Save the last 30 seconds or so for marking answers on any questions you marked to come back to or that you haven't gotten to yet. If you see time is running out before you have hope of finishing, simply fill in any circle for each remaining question. **Don't leave any question blank on your answer grid.**

An additional hint: Some testing experts believe that if you must make random guesses, you should make them all the same—for example, all Cs. That way the law of averages will work for you.

How to Answer Number Series Questions

- **Write on your test booklet.** At the beginning of the test, write down the starting time and projected ending time. As you work, make note of the repetitions and patterns you discover.
- **Keep moving.** You have a little less than one minute for each question, but you'll be able to answer some questions in less time than that. Just don't spend two whole minutes on any one question. If you're stumped, mark an answer at random and move on.
- **Answer all the questions.** If time is nearly up and you have not answered all the questions, go through quickly and **guess**.
- **Start each problem by looking for repetition.**
- **Next, glance over the problem** to determine whether the series is simple or complex.
- **If the series is simple,** look for:
  simple addition or subtraction
  alternating addition or subtraction
  addition or subtraction with repetition
- **If the series is complex,** look for:
  alternating repetition
  alternating patterns
- **Remember that repeating random numbers may be introduced into any series.**

What follows is a sample test section, complete with 24 questions. Before you begin, set an alarm clock or stopwatch for 20 minutes. Try to spend a little less than one minute on each question. For this practice test, don't guess at random if you run out of time, though you should do so in the actual exam. When the 20 minutes are up, you can go back to the questions you couldn't answer and use them for additional practice. That way, you'll increase your skill at reasoning with numbers.

An answer key, with explanations of the types of series involved in each question, follows the test section. Be sure to study the explanations carefully; they'll give you additional reinforcement in working with Number Series questions. With practice and study, your ability to recognize these series can only get better.

PART C: NUMBER SERIES

	A	B	C	D	E
1.	Ⓐ	Ⓑ	Ⓒ	Ⓓ	Ⓔ
2.	Ⓐ	Ⓑ	Ⓒ	Ⓓ	Ⓔ
3.	Ⓐ	Ⓑ	Ⓒ	Ⓓ	Ⓔ
4.	Ⓐ	Ⓑ	Ⓒ	Ⓓ	Ⓔ
5.	Ⓐ	Ⓑ	Ⓒ	Ⓓ	Ⓔ
6.	Ⓐ	Ⓑ	Ⓒ	Ⓓ	Ⓔ
7.	Ⓐ	Ⓑ	Ⓒ	Ⓓ	Ⓔ
8.	Ⓐ	Ⓑ	Ⓒ	Ⓓ	Ⓔ

	A	B	C	D	E
9.	Ⓐ	Ⓑ	Ⓒ	Ⓓ	Ⓔ
10.	Ⓐ	Ⓑ	Ⓒ	Ⓓ	Ⓔ
11.	Ⓐ	Ⓑ	Ⓒ	Ⓓ	Ⓔ
12.	Ⓐ	Ⓑ	Ⓒ	Ⓓ	Ⓔ
13.	Ⓐ	Ⓑ	Ⓒ	Ⓓ	Ⓔ
14.	Ⓐ	Ⓑ	Ⓒ	Ⓓ	Ⓔ
15.	Ⓐ	Ⓑ	Ⓒ	Ⓓ	Ⓔ
16.	Ⓐ	Ⓑ	Ⓒ	Ⓓ	Ⓔ

	A	B	C	D	E
17.	Ⓐ	Ⓑ	Ⓒ	Ⓓ	Ⓔ
18.	Ⓐ	Ⓑ	Ⓒ	Ⓓ	Ⓔ
19.	Ⓐ	Ⓑ	Ⓒ	Ⓓ	Ⓔ
20.	Ⓐ	Ⓑ	Ⓒ	Ⓓ	Ⓔ
21.	Ⓐ	Ⓑ	Ⓒ	Ⓓ	Ⓔ
22.	Ⓐ	Ⓑ	Ⓒ	Ⓓ	Ⓔ
23.	Ⓐ	Ⓑ	Ⓒ	Ⓓ	Ⓔ
24.	Ⓐ	Ⓑ	Ⓒ	Ⓓ	Ⓔ

SAMPLE NUMBER SERIES SECTION

Below, on the left, you will see a series of numbers that follow some definite order. On the right are five sets of two numbers each, labeled A, B, C, D, and E. Look at the number series to find its pattern, and then darken the circle for the answer pair that would come next in the series, if the same pattern were followed. You have 20 minutes for this section.

1. 12 27 14 24 16 21 18 . . . . **A)** 20 22 **B)** 18 20 **C)** 20 24 **D)** 18 19 **E)** 19 21

2. 5 9 13 17 21 25 29 . . . . **A)** 37 33 **B)** 31 34 **C)** 25 21 **D)** 33 37 **E)** 30 33

3. 21 19 21 17 21 15 21 . . . . **A)** 13 21 **B)** 19 21 **C)** 13 11 **D)** 15 19 **E)** 21 19

4. 6 8 40 11 13 40 16 . . . . **A)** 19 40 **B)** 18 21 **C)** 18 40 **D)** 40 19 **E)** 19 21

5. 9 10 8 9 7 8 6 . . . . **A)** 4 5 **B)** 7 5 **C)** 4 2 **D)** 7 8 **E)** 7 6

6. 13 15 27 17 19 26 . . . . **A)** 28 30 **B)** 28 27 **C)** 21 25 **D)** 25 24 **E)** 21 23

7. 24 21 18 15 12 9 6 . . . . **A)** 3 1 **B)** 4 2 **C)** 3 0 **D)** 4 1 **E)** 3 6

8. 17 17 20 20 23 23 26 . . . . **A)** 26 29 **B)** 29 29 **C)** 29 32 **D)** 26 26 **E)** 26 28

9. 10 12 27 14 16 27 18 . . . . **A)** 20 22 **B)** 27 29 **C)** 27 20 **D)** 20 29 **E)** 20 27

10. 22 25 23 26 24 27 25 . . . . **A)** 27 24 **B)** 22 24 **C)** 28 30 **D)** 28 26 **E)** 28 25

11. 27 2 25 4 23 6 21 . . . . **A)** 8 10 **B)** 19 17 **C)** 23 4 **D)** 8 19 **E)** 15 8

12. 37 40 43 46 49 52 55 . . . . **A)** 58 61 **B)** 57 59 **C)** 58 60 **D)** 57 60 **E)** 59 62

13. 22 21 21 20 20 19 19 . . . . **A)** 18 17 **B)** 18 18 **C)** 19 18 **D)** 17 17 **E)** 20 21

14. 5 16 10 14 15 12 20 . . . . **A)** 25 30 **B)** 25 10 **C)** 10 8 **D)** 10 30 **E)** 10 25

15. 11 13 34 15 17 33 19 . . . . **A)** 21 23 **B)** 18 35 **C)** 21 32 **D)** 32 21 **E)** 32 31

16. 8 11 9 12 10 13 11. . . . . **A)** 13 10 **B)** 14 12 **C)** 9 7 **D)** 14 17 **E)** 9 12

17. 3 25 6 25 9 25 12. . . . . **A)** 15 18 **B)** 25 28 **C)** 25 15 **D)** 15 25 **E)** 3 25

18. 15 32 17 28 19 24 21. . . . . **A)** 23 25 **B)** 20 16 **C)** 23 20 **D)** 25 22 **E)** 20 23

19. 10 7 17 14 24 21 31. . . . . **A)** 28 38 **B)** 41 51 **C)** 28 25 **D)** 40 37 **E)** 41 38

20. 54 48 42 36 30 24 18. . . . . **A)** 12 6 **B)** 11 5 **C)** 16 10 **D)** 10 4 **E)** 12 18

21. 9 12 13 11 17 10 21. . . . . **A)** 20 14 **B)** 17 18 **C)** 20 19 **D)** 9 25 **E)** 25 29

22. 14 8 18 23 8 27 32. . . . . **A)** 8 41 **B)** 8 36 **C)** 36 41 **D)** 34 8 **E)** 37 8

23. 3 9 15 21 27 33 39. . . . . **A)** 46 52 **B)** 44 50 **C)** 43 49 **D)** 45 51 **E)** 47 53

24. 12 27 14 24 16 21 18. . . . . **A)** 23 10 **B)** 20 22 **C)** 18 20 **D)** 23 20 **E)** 18 15

ANSWERS TO NUMBER SERIES SECTION

1. **B.** This series has two alternating patterns. The first pattern begins with 12, and each number increases by 2 (12, 14, 16, 18). The alternate series begins with 27, and each number decreases by 3 (27, 24, 21).

2. **D.** In this simple addition series, each number increases by 4.

3. **A.** In this alternating repetition series, the random number 21 has been inserted as every other number in a series in which each number decreases by 2.

4. **C.** This is an alternating addition series with repetition of a random number. The random number 40 appears as every third number. The regular pattern, beginning with 6, is add 2 and then add 3, but 40 is inserted before each "add 3" step.

5. **B.** This is an alternating addition and subtraction series. The pattern is add 1, subtract 2.

6. **E.** There are two alternating patterns in this series, with the second pattern being inserted every third number. The first pattern, beginning with 13, adds 2 to each number to arrive at the next. The second pattern, beginning with 27, subtracts 1 from each number.

7. **C.** In this simple subtraction series, 3 is subtracted from each number to arrive at the next.

8. **A.** This is an addition series with repetition. Each number is repeated before adding 3.

9. **E.** This is a simple addition series with the random number 27 inserted as every third number. Otherwise, the pattern is to add 2 to each number to arrive at the next.

10. **D.** In this alternating addition and subtraction series, the pattern is add 3, then subtract 2, then add 3, and so on.

11. **D.** There are two alternating patterns in this series. Beginning with 27, the pattern is subtract 2 (27, 25, 23, 21); the alternating pattern, beginning with 2, is add 2 (2, 4, 6).

12. **A.** In this simple addition series, each number is increased by 3.

13. **B.** This is a simple subtraction series with repetition. Each number decreases by 1 and then repeats.

14. **E.** There are two alternating patterns in this series. The first pattern begins with 5 and increases by 5 (5, 10, 15, 20). The alternating pattern begins with 16 and decreases by 2 (16, 14, 12).

15. **C.** This is a series with two alternating patterns. The first pattern begins with 11, and the numbers increase by 2 (11, 13, 15, 17, 19). Every third number, beginning with 34, follows the alternate pattern of subtracting 1 (34, 33).

16. **B.** This is an alternating addition and subtraction series. Beginning with 8, the pattern is add 3, subtract 2.

17. **C.** This is a simple addition series with the random number 25 inserted as every other number. In the addition series, each number increases by 3.

18. **E.** Two patterns alternate here. The first pattern begins with 15, and each number increases by 2 (15, 17, 19, 21). The alternating pattern begins with 32, and each number decreases by 4 (32, 28, 24).

19. **A.** This series alternates subtracting 3 and adding 10.

20. **A.** This is a simple subtraction series. Each number decreases by 6.

21. **D.** There are two alternating patterns in this series. The first series begins with 9, and each number increases by 4 (9, 13, 17, 21). The other series begins with 12, and each number decreases by 1 (12, 11, 10).

22. B. This is an alternating addition series with the random number 8 inserted as every third number. The addition pattern is add 4, add 5. After each addition of 5, the number 8 is inserted.

23. D. This is a simple addition series. Each number increases by 6.

24. C. There are two alternating patterns in this series. The first series begins with 12 and increases by 2 (12, 14, 16, 18). The alternate series begins with 27 and decreases by 3 (27, 24, 21).

C·H·A·P·T·E·R 9

FOLLOWING ORAL DIRECTIONS

CHAPTER SUMMARY

Part D of the postal exam, Following Oral Directions, is pretty unusual, but it doesn't have to be all that hard. This chapter familiarizes you with the format so that you can keep your cool on exam day and work methodically through this section of the test.

The section of the postal exam on Following Oral Directions is designed to do just what its title suggests: test how well you follow directions. The tasks you will be asked to perform on this portion of the test probably will not correspond to anything you'll do on an actual postal service job, but it will test your ability to follow instructions to the letter, without having to have them repeated. The USPS wants to know how much time and effort it will take for a supervisor to train you for your job and for specific tasks that may come up within that job. If you do well on this portion of the test, you will stand a better chance of being hired. And after you are hired, if you have to be told only once how to do something, you will obviously be a better employee than if you have to keep asking, "How's that again?"

WHAT FOLLOWING ORAL DIRECTIONS IS LIKE

Part D of the postal exam consists of 20 to 25 questions and takes about 25 minutes to complete. You will be given both a worksheet and an answer grid. Each question will consist of a short set of verbal instructions, which will be read to you by an examiner, either in person or on tape. These instructions will require two main actions:

1. Performing the clerical task exactly as instructed

2. Marking your answer grid exactly as instructed

The worksheet will have 15 to 25 numbered lines, each with geometric shapes, numbers, letters, and/or blank lines to fill in. There may be more than one clerical task you have to do on your worksheet before you mark the answer grid.

The answer grid will also be numbered, with more numbers than there are questions. This is because you will not be marking your answer grid in any particular order and will probably be leaving some blank. This isn't like a typical standardized test, where you start with question 1 and then do 2 and then 3, and you, the test taker, get to decide whether or not to skip a question and a space on the answer grid. In Following Oral Directions, skipping around on the answer grid is built in. You might be told to mark number 24 on your answer grid, then number 13, then number 20, and then number 2. Between sets of instructions, the examiner will pause for a sufficient time for you to do what is asked **but will not repeat the instructions.** Thus, it's important for you to listen carefully.

At the beginning of Part D, you will be given general information about the purpose of the test. Then you will be allowed a practice session, during which the examiner will read aloud to you. During the actual exam, the instructions will be read aloud at a rate of approximately 80 words per minute, with pauses of approximately two seconds between each task.

The Tasks

The clerical tasks you have to perform may be simple and straightforward. The examiner might say something like this: "Look at Line 8, which has a number with a line beside it." (The examiner pauses briefly.) "On the line, write the letter A." (The examiner pauses for two seconds.) "Now, on your answer grid, find number 5 and darken the space for the letter you just wrote on the line." (The examiner pauses for five seconds.)

Or the task may be a bit more complicated, involving more than one step. The examiner might say, "Look at Line 12." (The examiner pauses briefly.) "There are two circles and two boxes of different sizes." (The examiner pauses again.) "If 4 is more than 2, and if 5 is less than 3, write A in the smaller circle." (The examiner pauses for two seconds.) "Otherwise, write C in the larger box." (Another pause.) "Now, on your answer grid, find number 14 and darken the space for the letter you just wrote on the line." In this case, if you were listening carefully, you perceived that you should *not* write A in the smaller circle, because while 4 is more than 2, 5 isn't less than 3. So you waited to find out what you should do instead, which was to write C in the larger box. And then, on your answer grid, you filled in space C next to number 14.

Sample Problem

The best way to do this sample problem—and the complete sample section at the end of this chapter—is to have a relative or friend carefully read the instructions aloud, pausing for the required length of time. This will give you the flavor of the actual test-taking situation. The second best way is to make a tape for yourself, in which you play the role of examiner, reading the instructions carefully and pausing for the required length of time. As a last resort, if neither of these options is possible right now, you may simply read the examiner instructions silently and only once, one step at a time, never referring back to the previous step. However, you should **definitely** arrange for someone to act as examiner when you do the practice section at the end of the chapter.

Here are two lines of your worksheet:

Line 2. 2   4   9   8   6
Line 3. ◯   ◯   ☐   ☐

Here's your answer grid:

ANSWER GRID

1.	Ⓐ	Ⓑ	Ⓒ	Ⓓ	Ⓔ	5.	Ⓐ	Ⓑ	Ⓒ	Ⓓ	Ⓔ	9.	Ⓐ	Ⓑ	Ⓒ Ⓓ Ⓔ
2.	Ⓐ	Ⓑ	Ⓒ	Ⓓ	Ⓔ	6.	Ⓐ	Ⓑ	Ⓒ	Ⓓ	Ⓔ	10.	Ⓐ	Ⓑ	Ⓒ Ⓓ Ⓔ
3.	Ⓐ	Ⓑ	Ⓒ	Ⓓ	Ⓔ	7.	Ⓐ	Ⓑ	Ⓒ	Ⓓ	Ⓔ				
4.	Ⓐ	Ⓑ	Ⓒ	Ⓓ	Ⓔ	8.	Ⓐ	Ⓑ	Ⓒ	Ⓓ	Ⓔ				

And here's what you should have your helper read to you:

You should follow the instructions that I shall read to you. I cannot repeat them.

Look at Line 2 on your worksheet. (**Pause slightly.**) There are five numbers on the line, all of which are even numbers except one. Draw a circle around the odd number. (**Pause two seconds.**) Now, on your answer grid, find the number you just circled (**pause two seconds**) and darken the space for A as in apple.

Look at Line 3. (**Pause slightly.**) You will see two circles and two squares. If M comes before Q, and if 14 comes before 12, write the letter B as in baker in the second circle. (**Pause slightly.**) Otherwise, write the letter C as in cat in the first square. (**Pause two seconds.**) Now, on your answer grid, find number 7. (**Pause two seconds.**) Darken the space for the letter you just wrote in the circle or square. (**Pause five seconds.**)

If this were a real exam, the examiner would continue reading more instructions after the five-second pause.

How did you do? Your worksheet should look like this:

Line 2 2   4   ⑨   8   6

Line 3 ◯   ◯   ▢C   ▢

Your answer grid should look like this:

ANSWER GRID

1. Ⓐ Ⓑ Ⓒ Ⓓ Ⓔ   5. Ⓐ Ⓑ Ⓒ Ⓓ Ⓔ   9. ⒶＡ Ⓑ Ⓒ Ⓓ Ⓔ
2. Ⓐ Ⓑ Ⓒ Ⓓ Ⓔ   6. Ⓐ Ⓑ Ⓒ Ⓓ Ⓔ   10. Ⓐ Ⓑ Ⓒ Ⓓ Ⓔ
3. Ⓐ Ⓑ Ⓒ Ⓓ Ⓔ   7. Ⓐ Ⓑ ⒸＣ Ⓓ Ⓔ
4. Ⓐ Ⓑ Ⓒ Ⓓ Ⓔ   8. Ⓐ Ⓑ Ⓒ Ⓓ Ⓔ

If you missed an answer, look closely to see where you went wrong. There are lots of ways to make a wrong turn in following the instructions, all of which you can avoid simply by concentrating and using your hands and pencil to help you keep track of where you are. Let's look at what can go wrong:

- You can lose your place right at the start if you don't keep track of which line of the worksheet you're supposed to be on. The instructions might have you skip around on the worksheet. At the very first sentence, "Look at Line __," **place your pencil at the beginning of the line.**

- You could mark the correct letter (first A, then C) on the answer grid but not in the correct number. For the instructions on Line 2, you might have marked number 1 on the answer grid, thinking, "This is question 1," or you might have marked number 2 on the answer grid to match the line you were told to look at initially. You can avoid this problem by **doing exactly what the examiner tells you on the worksheet.** That way, when the examiner said, "Now, on your answer grid, find the number you just circled," you could look back at your worksheet to find out which number to find on the answer grid.

- In a two- or three-step problem like the one you had to do with Line 3, it's easy to hear the first step and then stop listening. In that case, you would have heard, "If M comes before Q," and then stopped listening or let your attention wander. You would have jumped the gun and written a B in the second circle. Instead, you needed to hear the second step, "if 14 comes before 12" to know that you should write a C in the first square. **Listen carefully for "if" instructions; they often involve more than one step.**

- You can lose your place on the answer grid. Then the examiner may start reading the next question while you are still searching. Once again, use your pencil. The instant the examiner tells you to find a given number on the answer grid, **put a finger of your nonwriting hand on the relevant Line on the worksheet and move your pencil to the given number on the answer grid.**

Don't despair if one or more of these things happened to you in this brief sample. Although this part of the exam is not difficult, it does require total concentration, which is a skill. Practice, along with careful preparation, will help you concentrate better.

How to Prepare

This portion of the exam is not difficult, and the time limits involved are reasonable. However, three things are of crucial importance, and you should practice them in preparing for the exam:

1. You must concentrate totally, allowing no distractions to enter your mind.

2. You must listen to *all* the instructions and never skip a step. Remember, some instructions will involve more than one step.

3. You must not become flustered—and you won't, if you practice beforehand.

As with the other sections of the exam, the best way to prepare for the Following Oral Directions portion is to **practice**. There's a sample test section at the end of this chapter, in addition to the complete tests in Chapters 7 and 12. Again, it is important, when taking the practice exam, to find a relative or friend who will carefully read the instructions to you, pausing in the appropriate places.

Taking the Test

Listen to the Instructions

In the other sections of the exam, listening to instructions is important. In the Following Oral Directions portion, it is absolutely crucial. In fact, it is the whole point of the test. So at the beginning, be very careful to **pay close attention to the examiner's directions.** Before the actual test, you will be given a short practice session designed to let you get used to the examiner's voice. If you have any trouble hearing or understanding the speaker, **be sure to say so.** In order to do well on this part of the exam, you must be able to concentrate, and any distraction—especially not being able to hear clearly—can hurt you. So ask the examiner to speak more loudly or, if you will be following taped instructions, ask that the volume be turned up. It is okay to ask to be moved closer to the examiner or to the speaker. It's your score that is at stake, and it's your right to work under the best conditions possible.

Tips on Following Oral Directions

When the actual examination begins, remember:

- **Always work from left to right unless you are specifically instructed to do otherwise.** If the examiner says, "Look at the first box," this means the first box starting from the left. Of course, the examiner may occasionally say, "Look at the second box from the right," and, in that case, you must do as instructed. But generally you will work from left to right.

- The moment the examiner tells you to look at a certain line on your worksheet, **look immediately at that line and place your pencil on it.** Do not wait for the next task in the set of instructions before doing this. This is very important, so that you will not to lose your place and become frantic.

- On the other hand, when the examiner gives the second task in the set, **do not rush** to accomplish it. Listen carefully to this first step, but remember that the task may involve more than one step. Be alert for the word *if* and especially for the combination *if . . . and* or *if . . . or.* These are your clues that you are going to be asked to make a choice, and you cannot begin work on the task until you hear what the choice is. Examples might include:

    "If 4 is more than 3, *and* C comes before A . . ." In this case, the entire statement must be true.

    "If 4 is more than 3, *or* C comes before A . . ." In this case, only part of the statement must be true.

    There is a crucial distinction between the two instructions. That's why you must listen to the **complete** set of instructions before proceeding. Moving before the examiner is finished with this particular task can result in a wrong answer.

- At the end of the exam, only the answer grid will be scored, so if it is helpful, you may make notes on the worksheet. For example, if the instructions call for a series of numbers, you might want to jot down those numbers on your worksheet. Just be sure, after you are finished with that particular task, to draw a line through your worksheet notes, so you won't become confused.

- For the final set of instructions, you will be asked to mark your answer grid, and you will be given a bit more time, about 5 seconds, to do this. This is a step that requires special concentration for two reasons:

    - **You will NOT be marking your answer sheet in order.** After working on Line 8, for example, you may be asked to mark number 15 on your answer grid. Usually, if not always, the line you have just finished working on and the number on your answer grid will be different.

    - There should be only one circle darkened on each answer used; however, **you will not be using all the numbers on the answer grid.** So in this sense, the Following Oral Directions portion of the exam will be unlike any test you have ever taken!

    For these two reasons, at this step, it will be easy to lose your place. So, again, remember, the cardinal rule: **concentrate.** Do not assume anything; listen carefully.

What To Do If You Make a Mistake

If you discover you've made a mistake, don't become frantic and decide to change careers. Remember, your two biggest enemies are distraction and losing your cool. If you discover you have made a mistake—for example, if you start to darken a circle on the answer sheet and are horrified to discover one is already darkened for that number—simply leave the answer grid the way it is and tune into the examiner's instructions again. Neither erase your original answer nor search for a new place on the answer grid to mark, unless one becomes obvious in that split second. If you do either of these things, you will miss the next set of instructions, and then you will become truly upset. It's natural to miss an answer now and then. **Just resume your concentration and move on.**

This section of the exam is scored right answers only—no penalty for wrong answers—so guessing won't hurt you. However, guessing early in the exam can mean that you mark a number on your answer grid that you'll need later for a question you're sure of, so you should only guess if you have a pretty good idea of the answer. If you've completely lost track of what you're doing, don't mark a circle at random. Let that question go, and focus on the next one.

How To Answer Following Oral Instructions Questions

- **Speak up.** During the practice session before the actual test, if you have any trouble hearing or understanding the examiner or taped instructions, ask to have the instructions read louder or to be moved closer to the examiner.
- **You will not be marking your answer grid in any particular order**; there will be lots of skipping around, and you won't use all the answers.
- **Pay close attention to everything the examiner says.** Concentrate, concentrate, concentrate. The examiner will not repeat instructions.
- **Do what the examiner tells you.** Don't be tempted to skip marking on the worksheet because the worksheet doesn't count. Your markings on the worksheet will ensure that you can darken the proper circle on your answer grid.
- **Listen carefully for two-step instructions.** Wait for all steps to be read to you. Be especially alert for the words *if . . . and* and for the words *if . . . or.*
- **You may mark on your worksheet.** Take advantage of this, but be sure to cross out your notations at the end of **each** problem, so you won't get confused.
- **If you make a mistake, don't get flustered.** Simply forget it and **resume concentration** on the examiner's instructions.

What follows is a sample test section: first the answer grid, then the worksheet, and then the examiner instructions. After the examiner instructions comes the answer key. Have a friend or relative read the examiner instructions to you. If you do not wish to be tied to someone else's schedule, you may have another person tape the instructions, reading carefully and pausing the required amount of time between each task. As a last resort, if there is no one else to help you, you may tape the instructions yourself. However, if you must do this, you should let some time elapse, preferably a day or two, before taking the sample test. This will prevent any memory you may have of the tasks from muddying the waters.

As you take this sample test section, remember the tips you've just read. Above all, keep your cool and don't get flustered.

PART D: FOLLOWING ORAL DIRECTIONS

1.	Ⓐ	Ⓑ	Ⓒ	Ⓓ	Ⓔ		18.	Ⓐ	Ⓑ	Ⓒ	Ⓓ	Ⓔ		35.	Ⓐ	Ⓑ	Ⓒ	Ⓓ	Ⓔ
2.	Ⓐ	Ⓑ	Ⓒ	Ⓓ	Ⓔ		19.	Ⓐ	Ⓑ	Ⓒ	Ⓓ	Ⓔ		36.	Ⓐ	Ⓑ	Ⓒ	Ⓓ	Ⓔ
3.	Ⓐ	Ⓑ	Ⓒ	Ⓓ	Ⓔ		20.	Ⓐ	Ⓑ	Ⓒ	Ⓓ	Ⓔ		37.	Ⓐ	Ⓑ	Ⓒ	Ⓓ	Ⓔ
4.	Ⓐ	Ⓑ	Ⓒ	Ⓓ	Ⓔ		21.	Ⓐ	Ⓑ	Ⓒ	Ⓓ	Ⓔ		38.	Ⓐ	Ⓑ	Ⓒ	Ⓓ	Ⓔ
5.	Ⓐ	Ⓑ	Ⓒ	Ⓓ	Ⓔ		22.	Ⓐ	Ⓑ	Ⓒ	Ⓓ	Ⓔ		39.	Ⓐ	Ⓑ	Ⓒ	Ⓓ	Ⓔ
6.	Ⓐ	Ⓑ	Ⓒ	Ⓓ	Ⓔ		23.	Ⓐ	Ⓑ	Ⓒ	Ⓓ	Ⓔ		40.	Ⓐ	Ⓑ	Ⓒ	Ⓓ	Ⓔ
7.	Ⓐ	Ⓑ	Ⓒ	Ⓓ	Ⓔ		24.	Ⓐ	Ⓑ	Ⓒ	Ⓓ	Ⓔ		41.	Ⓐ	Ⓑ	Ⓒ	Ⓓ	Ⓔ
8.	Ⓐ	Ⓑ	Ⓒ	Ⓓ	Ⓔ		25.	Ⓐ	Ⓑ	Ⓒ	Ⓓ	Ⓔ		42.	Ⓐ	Ⓑ	Ⓒ	Ⓓ	Ⓔ
9.	Ⓐ	Ⓑ	Ⓒ	Ⓓ	Ⓔ		26.	Ⓐ	Ⓑ	Ⓒ	Ⓓ	Ⓔ		43.	Ⓐ	Ⓑ	Ⓒ	Ⓓ	Ⓔ
10.	Ⓐ	Ⓑ	Ⓒ	Ⓓ	Ⓔ		27.	Ⓐ	Ⓑ	Ⓒ	Ⓓ	Ⓔ		44.	Ⓐ	Ⓑ	Ⓒ	Ⓓ	Ⓔ
11.	Ⓐ	Ⓑ	Ⓒ	Ⓓ	Ⓔ		28.	Ⓐ	Ⓑ	Ⓒ	Ⓓ	Ⓔ		45.	Ⓐ	Ⓑ	Ⓒ	Ⓓ	Ⓔ
12.	Ⓐ	Ⓑ	Ⓒ	Ⓓ	Ⓔ		29.	Ⓐ	Ⓑ	Ⓒ	Ⓓ	Ⓔ		46.	Ⓐ	Ⓑ	Ⓒ	Ⓓ	Ⓔ
13.	Ⓐ	Ⓑ	Ⓒ	Ⓓ	Ⓔ		30.	Ⓐ	Ⓑ	Ⓒ	Ⓓ	Ⓔ		47.	Ⓐ	Ⓑ	Ⓒ	Ⓓ	Ⓔ
14.	Ⓐ	Ⓑ	Ⓒ	Ⓓ	Ⓔ		31.	Ⓐ	Ⓑ	Ⓒ	Ⓓ	Ⓔ		48.	Ⓐ	Ⓑ	Ⓒ	Ⓓ	Ⓔ
15.	Ⓐ	Ⓑ	Ⓒ	Ⓓ	Ⓔ		32.	Ⓐ	Ⓑ	Ⓒ	Ⓓ	Ⓔ		49.	Ⓐ	Ⓑ	Ⓒ	Ⓓ	Ⓔ
16.	Ⓐ	Ⓑ	Ⓒ	Ⓓ	Ⓔ		33.	Ⓐ	Ⓑ	Ⓒ	Ⓓ	Ⓔ		50.	Ⓐ	Ⓑ	Ⓒ	Ⓓ	Ⓔ
17.	Ⓐ	Ⓑ	Ⓒ	Ⓓ	Ⓔ		34.	Ⓐ	Ⓑ	Ⓒ	Ⓓ	Ⓔ							

SAMPLE FOLLOWING ORAL DIRECTIONS SECTION

Listen closely to the instructions the examiner gives you. The examiner will refer you to the following lines. Write whatever the examiner tells you on the lines, and then fill in the answer grid as the examiner directs you. The examiner will not repeat the instructions.

Line 1.   42   44   46   48   50

Line 2.   collie   akita   bassett   elkhound   dachsund

Line 3.   D____   E____   A____   B____   C____

Line 4.   B   D   C   E   A

Line 5.   23____   31____   40____   15____   49____

Line 6.   camel   deer   apple   buffalo   elephant

Line 7.   43____   27____   35____   39____

Line 8.   14   15   16   17   __

Line 9.   _aboon   _adger   _uffalo   _eaver   __

Line 10.   3   11   9   6   7

Line 11.   29-E   34-C   D-A   8-E   C-D

Line 12.   A   25   4

Line 13.   B   D   C   E   A

Line 14.   41   42   45   43   44

Line 15.   B-E   A-C   D-B   D   E-A

Line 16.   1@   2$ 3%   4&   5#

Line 17.   15____   6____   23____   30____   14____

Line 18.   ☐12☐   ⃝14⃝   ☐7☐   ☐21☐   ⃝11⃝

Line 19.   Yellow   Carrot   Backyard   Monday   Greyhound

Line 20.   42   43   44   45   ___

EXAMINER INSTRUCTIONS

Follow closely the instructions I am about to read to you. I cannot repeat the instructions.

Look at Line 1. (**Pause slightly.**) Circle the fourth number in the line. (**Pause two seconds.**) Now, on your answer grid, find the number you just circled and darken space C as in cat for that number. (**Pause five seconds.**)

Look at Line 2. (**Pause slightly.**) There are five words. Underline the fourth word in the line. (**Pause two seconds.**) Now, on your answer grid, find number 23 (**pause two seconds**) and darken the space that is the first letter of the word you underlined. (**Pause five seconds.**)

Look at Line 3. (**Pause slightly.**) There are five letters, each followed by a line. Find the third letter in the line (**pause slightly**) and write the number 44 on the line next to it. (**Pause two seconds.**) Now, on your answer grid, darken the space for the number-letter combination you just wrote. (**Pause five seconds.**)

Look at Line 4. (**Pause slightly.**) If March comes before April, underline the first letter in the row. (**Pause slightly.**) However, if January comes after February, circle the last letter in the row. (**Pause two seconds.**) Now, on your answer grid, find number 13 (**pause two seconds**) and darken the space for the letter you just underlined or circled. (**Pause five seconds.**)

Look at Line 5. (**Pause slightly.**) There are five numbers, each followed by a line. Next to the even number, write the letter D as in dog. (**Pause two seconds.**) Now, on your answer grid, darken the space for the number-letter combination you just wrote. (**Pause five seconds.**)

Look at Line 6. (**Pause slightly.**) There are five words. Draw a line under the word that is the name of a fruit. (**Pause two seconds.**) Now, on your answer grid, find number 16 (**pause two seconds**) and darken the space that is the first letter of the word you just underlined. (**Pause five seconds.**)

Look at Line 7. (**Pause slightly.**) There are two boxes and two circles of different sizes, each containing a number followed by a blank. (**Pause slightly.**) If four is larger than ten, write the letter E as in easy next to the number in the small box. (**Pause slightly.**) Otherwise, write the letter C as in cat next to the number in the large circle. (**Pause two seconds.**) Now, on your answer grid, darken the space for the number-letter combination in the box or circle in which you just wrote. (**Pause five seconds.**)

Look at Line 8. (**Pause slightly.**) There are four numbers followed by a blank. On the blank, write the next number in order. (**Pause two seconds.**) Now, on your answer grid, find the number you just wrote and darken space E as in easy. (**Pause five seconds.**)

Look at Line 9. (**Pause slightly.**) There are four words, each word missing the first letter. When the same letter is added to each word, each word is the name of an animal. (**Pause two seconds.**) On the line that follows the four words, write the missing letter. (**Pause two seconds.**) Now, on your answer grid, find number 1 (**pause two seconds**) and darken the space for the letter you just wrote. (**Pause five seconds.**)

Look at Line 5 again. (**Pause two seconds.**) Draw a circle around the highest number on the line. (**Pause two seconds.**) Now, on your answer grid, find the number you just circled and darken space B as in baker. (**Pause five seconds.**)

Look at Line 10. (**Pause two seconds.**) There are five numbers. Circle the highest number. (**Pause two seconds.**) Now, on your answer grid, find the number you just circled and darken space A as in apple. (**Pause five seconds.**)

Look at Line 11. (**Pause slightly.**) There are two letter pairs and three number-letter pairs. Draw a line under the third number-letter pair in the line. (**Pause two seconds.**) Now, on your answer grid, darken the space for the number-letter pair you just underlined. (**Pause five seconds.**)

Look at Line 12. (**Pause slightly.**) If the triangle contains a number, draw a line under that number. (**Pause slightly.**) However, if the circle contains a number, draw a line under that number. (**Pause two seconds.**) Now, on your answer grid, find the number you just underlined and darken space D as in dog. (**Pause five seconds.**)

Look at Line 13. (**Pause slightly.**) Circle the third letter in the line. (**Pause two seconds.**) Now, on your answer grid, find number 42 (**pause two seconds**) and darken the space for the letter you just circled. (**Pause five seconds.**)

Look at Line 14. (**Pause slightly.**) There are five numbers in order, except one is in the wrong place. Draw a line under the number that is out of order. (**Pause two seconds.**) Now, on your answer grid, find the number you underlined and darken space E as in easy. (**Pause five seconds.**)

Look at Line 15. (**Pause slightly.**) There are four pairs of letters and one single letter. Write the number 17 to the right of the single letter. (**Pause two seconds.**) Now, on your answer grid, darken the number-letter combination you just wrote. (**Pause five seconds.**)

Look at Line 16. (**Pause slightly.**) There is a numbered list of symbols. Circle the dollar sign and the number next to it. (**Pause two seconds.**) Now, on your answer grid, find the number you just circled and darken space C as in cat. (**Pause five seconds.**)

Look at Line 7 again. (**Pause two seconds.**) Draw a line under the lowest number that is in a box. (**Pause two seconds.**) Write the letter A as in apple on the line next to the number you just underlined. (**Pause two seconds.**)

Now, on your answer grid, find the number you just underlined, and darken the space for the letter you just wrote. (**Pause five seconds.**)

Look at Line 17. (**Pause two seconds.**) There are five numbers, each of which is followed by a blank. On the blank next to the first number in the line, write the letter B as in baker. (**Pause two seconds.**) Now, on your answer grid, darken the space for the number-letter combination you just wrote. (**Pause five seconds.**)

Look at Line 18. (**Pause slightly.**) There are five numbers in circles and squares. Draw an X through the highest number that is in a circle. (**Pause two seconds.**) Now, on your answer grid, find the number you just drew an X through and darken space E as in easy. (**Pause five seconds.**)

Look at Line 19. (**Pause slightly.**) Draw a circle around the fourth word in the row. (**Pause two seconds.**) On your answer grid, find number 20. (**Pause two seconds.**) If the word you circled is the name of a vegetable, darken space A as in apple for that number. (**Pause slightly.**) However, if the word you circled is the name of a day of the week, darken space C as in cat. (**Pause five seconds.**)

Look at Line 11 again. (**Pause two seconds.**) There are two letter pairs and three number-letter pairs. Draw a circle around the number-letter pair that contains the highest number. (**Pause two seconds.**) Now, on your answer grid, darken the space for the number-letter combination you just circled. (**Pause five seconds.**)

Look at Line 20. (**Pause two seconds.**) There are four numbers in order followed by a blank. Write the next number in order on the blank. (**Pause two seconds.**) Now, on your answer grid, find the number you just wrote and darken space D as in dog. (**Pause five seconds.**)

Look at Line 17 again. (**Pause two seconds.**) Draw a circle around the highest number in the line. (**Pause two seconds.**) Now, on your answer grid, find the number you just circled and darken space D as in dog. (**Pause five seconds.**)

Look at Line 10 again. (**Pause two seconds.**) Draw a line under the even number. (**Pause two seconds.**) Now, on your answer grid, find the number you just underlined and darken space E as in easy for that number. (**Pause five seconds.**)

ANSWERS TO FOLLOWING ORAL DIRECTIONS SECTION

You should have filled in answers for only about half of the numbers on your answer grid. Where no letter is indicated next to a number below, the corresponding number on your answer grid should also be blank.

1. B		26.	
2. C		27.	
3.		28.	
4.		29.	
5.		30. D	
6. E		31.	
7.		32.	
8. E		33.	
9.		34. C	
10.		35. C	
11. A		36.	
12.		37.	
13. B		38.	
14. E		39. A	
15. B		40. D	
16. A		41.	
17. D		42. C	
18. E		43.	
19.		44. A	
20. C		45. E	
21.		46. D	
22.		47.	
23. E		48. C	
24.		49. B	
25. D		50.	

POSTAL EXAM 2

10

CHAPTER SUMMARY

This is the second of two practice exams in this book based on USPS Test 470. After working through the instructional material in the previous chapters, take this test to see how much your score has improved since you took the first exam.

ike the practice exam in Chapter 7, the exam that follows is based on information provided by the USPS about Test 470, the exam given to applicants for many entry-level jobs. You should take this test only after reading the preceding chapters on the various sections of the exam and working through the practice materials there.

Before you start this test, get prepared to simulate the actual test-taking experience as much as possible. First and foremost, have a stopwatch or alarm clock handy so that you can time yourself on each portion of the exam:

- **Part A: Address Checking.** Six minutes for 95 questions.
- **Part B: Memory for Addresses.** Ten minutes for memorization, and then five minutes for 88 questions.
- **Part C: Number Series.** Twenty minutes for 24 questions.

- **Part D: Following Oral Directions.** As long as it takes your examiner to read the questions with the appropriate pauses (about twenty minutes); 25 questions.

The other thing you need to have is a friend or relative to read you the instructions for Part D: Following Oral Directions. It's best if your reader can be right there reading to you while you take the exam, but, if that's not possible, you can have your reader tape the instructions for you. **Under no circumstances should you read the directions yourself.** That would not be an accurate representation of what the real test will be like.

The only other things you need before you begin the test are a nice quiet place to work, some number 2 pencils, and enough time to complete the test at one sitting—about an hour and ten minutes, with a couple minutes' break between each section.

The answer sheet you should use for answering the questions is on the following page. Then comes the exam itself, and after that is the answer key. The answer key is followed by a section on how to score your exam.

PART A: ADDRESS CHECKING

1. Ⓐ Ⓓ	20. Ⓐ Ⓓ	39. Ⓐ Ⓓ	58. Ⓐ Ⓓ	77. Ⓐ Ⓓ
2. Ⓐ Ⓓ	21. Ⓐ Ⓓ	40. Ⓐ Ⓓ	59. Ⓐ Ⓓ	78. Ⓐ Ⓓ
3. Ⓐ Ⓓ	22. Ⓐ Ⓓ	41. Ⓐ Ⓓ	60. Ⓐ Ⓓ	79. Ⓐ Ⓓ
4. Ⓐ Ⓓ	23. Ⓐ Ⓓ	42. Ⓐ Ⓓ	61. Ⓐ Ⓓ	80. Ⓐ Ⓓ
5. Ⓐ Ⓓ	24. Ⓐ Ⓓ	43. Ⓐ Ⓓ	62. Ⓐ Ⓓ	81. Ⓐ Ⓓ
6. Ⓐ Ⓓ	25. Ⓐ Ⓓ	44. Ⓐ Ⓓ	63. Ⓐ Ⓓ	82. Ⓐ Ⓓ
7. Ⓐ Ⓓ	26. Ⓐ Ⓓ	45. Ⓐ Ⓓ	64. Ⓐ Ⓓ	83. Ⓐ Ⓓ
8. Ⓐ Ⓓ	27. Ⓐ Ⓓ	46. Ⓐ Ⓓ	65. Ⓐ Ⓓ	84. Ⓐ Ⓓ
9. Ⓐ Ⓓ	28. Ⓐ Ⓓ	47. Ⓐ Ⓓ	66. Ⓐ Ⓓ	85. Ⓐ Ⓓ
10. Ⓐ Ⓓ	29. Ⓐ Ⓓ	48. Ⓐ Ⓓ	67. Ⓐ Ⓓ	86. Ⓐ Ⓓ
11. Ⓐ Ⓓ	30. Ⓐ Ⓓ	49. Ⓐ Ⓓ	68. Ⓐ Ⓓ	87. Ⓐ Ⓓ
12. Ⓐ Ⓓ	31. Ⓐ Ⓓ	50. Ⓐ Ⓓ	69. Ⓐ Ⓓ	88. Ⓐ Ⓓ
13. Ⓐ Ⓓ	32. Ⓐ Ⓓ	51. Ⓐ Ⓓ	70. Ⓐ Ⓓ	89. Ⓐ Ⓓ
14. Ⓐ Ⓓ	33. Ⓐ Ⓓ	52. Ⓐ Ⓓ	71. Ⓐ Ⓓ	90. Ⓐ Ⓓ
15. Ⓐ Ⓓ	34. Ⓐ Ⓓ	53. Ⓐ Ⓓ	72. Ⓐ Ⓓ	91. Ⓐ Ⓓ
16. Ⓐ Ⓓ	35. Ⓐ Ⓓ	54. Ⓐ Ⓓ	73. Ⓐ Ⓓ	92. Ⓐ Ⓓ
17. Ⓐ Ⓓ	36. Ⓐ Ⓓ	55. Ⓐ Ⓓ	74. Ⓐ Ⓓ	93. Ⓐ Ⓓ
18. Ⓐ Ⓓ	37. Ⓐ Ⓓ	56. Ⓐ Ⓓ	75. Ⓐ Ⓓ	94. Ⓐ Ⓓ
19. Ⓐ Ⓓ	38. Ⓐ Ⓓ	57. Ⓐ Ⓓ	76. Ⓐ Ⓓ	95. Ⓐ Ⓓ

PART B: MEMORY FOR ADDRESSES

1. Ⓐ Ⓑ Ⓒ Ⓓ Ⓔ	25. Ⓐ Ⓑ Ⓒ Ⓓ Ⓔ	49. Ⓐ Ⓑ Ⓒ Ⓓ Ⓔ
2. Ⓐ Ⓑ Ⓒ Ⓓ Ⓔ	26. Ⓐ Ⓑ Ⓒ Ⓓ Ⓔ	50. Ⓐ Ⓑ Ⓒ Ⓓ Ⓔ
3. Ⓐ Ⓑ Ⓒ Ⓓ Ⓔ	27. Ⓐ Ⓑ Ⓒ Ⓓ Ⓔ	51. Ⓐ Ⓑ Ⓒ Ⓓ Ⓔ
4. Ⓐ Ⓑ Ⓒ Ⓓ Ⓔ	28. Ⓐ Ⓑ Ⓒ Ⓓ Ⓔ	52. Ⓐ Ⓑ Ⓒ Ⓓ Ⓔ
5. Ⓐ Ⓑ Ⓒ Ⓓ Ⓔ	29. Ⓐ Ⓑ Ⓒ Ⓓ Ⓔ	53. Ⓐ Ⓑ Ⓒ Ⓓ Ⓔ
6. Ⓐ Ⓑ Ⓒ Ⓓ Ⓔ	30. Ⓐ Ⓑ Ⓒ Ⓓ Ⓔ	54. Ⓐ Ⓑ Ⓒ Ⓓ Ⓔ
7. Ⓐ Ⓑ Ⓒ Ⓓ Ⓔ	31. Ⓐ Ⓑ Ⓒ Ⓓ Ⓔ	55. Ⓐ Ⓑ Ⓒ Ⓓ Ⓔ
8. Ⓐ Ⓑ Ⓒ Ⓓ Ⓔ	32. Ⓐ Ⓑ Ⓒ Ⓓ Ⓔ	56. Ⓐ Ⓑ Ⓒ Ⓓ Ⓔ
9. Ⓐ Ⓑ Ⓒ Ⓓ Ⓔ	33. Ⓐ Ⓑ Ⓒ Ⓓ Ⓔ	57. Ⓐ Ⓑ Ⓒ Ⓓ Ⓔ
10. Ⓐ Ⓑ Ⓒ Ⓓ Ⓔ	34. Ⓐ Ⓑ Ⓒ Ⓓ Ⓔ	58. Ⓐ Ⓑ Ⓒ Ⓓ Ⓔ
11. Ⓐ Ⓑ Ⓒ Ⓓ Ⓔ	35. Ⓐ Ⓑ Ⓒ Ⓓ Ⓔ	59. Ⓐ Ⓑ Ⓒ Ⓓ Ⓔ
12. Ⓐ Ⓑ Ⓒ Ⓓ Ⓔ	36. Ⓐ Ⓑ Ⓒ Ⓓ Ⓔ	60. Ⓐ Ⓑ Ⓒ Ⓓ Ⓔ
13. Ⓐ Ⓑ Ⓒ Ⓓ Ⓔ	37. Ⓐ Ⓑ Ⓒ Ⓓ Ⓔ	61. Ⓐ Ⓑ Ⓒ Ⓓ Ⓔ
14. Ⓐ Ⓑ Ⓒ Ⓓ Ⓔ	38. Ⓐ Ⓑ Ⓒ Ⓓ Ⓔ	62. Ⓐ Ⓑ Ⓒ Ⓓ Ⓔ
15. Ⓐ Ⓑ Ⓒ Ⓓ Ⓔ	39. Ⓐ Ⓑ Ⓒ Ⓓ Ⓔ	63. Ⓐ Ⓑ Ⓒ Ⓓ Ⓔ
16. Ⓐ Ⓑ Ⓒ Ⓓ Ⓔ	40. Ⓐ Ⓑ Ⓒ Ⓓ Ⓔ	64. Ⓐ Ⓑ Ⓒ Ⓓ Ⓔ
17. Ⓐ Ⓑ Ⓒ Ⓓ Ⓔ	41. Ⓐ Ⓑ Ⓒ Ⓓ Ⓔ	65. Ⓐ Ⓑ Ⓒ Ⓓ Ⓔ
18. Ⓐ Ⓑ Ⓒ Ⓓ Ⓔ	42. Ⓐ Ⓑ Ⓒ Ⓓ Ⓔ	66. Ⓐ Ⓑ Ⓒ Ⓓ Ⓔ
19. Ⓐ Ⓑ Ⓒ Ⓓ Ⓔ	43. Ⓐ Ⓑ Ⓒ Ⓓ Ⓔ	67. Ⓐ Ⓑ Ⓒ Ⓓ Ⓔ
20. Ⓐ Ⓑ Ⓒ Ⓓ Ⓔ	44. Ⓐ Ⓑ Ⓒ Ⓓ Ⓔ	68. Ⓐ Ⓑ Ⓒ Ⓓ Ⓔ
21. Ⓐ Ⓑ Ⓒ Ⓓ Ⓔ	45. Ⓐ Ⓑ Ⓒ Ⓓ Ⓔ	69. Ⓐ Ⓑ Ⓒ Ⓓ Ⓔ
22. Ⓐ Ⓑ Ⓒ Ⓓ Ⓔ	46. Ⓐ Ⓑ Ⓒ Ⓓ Ⓔ	70. Ⓐ Ⓑ Ⓒ Ⓓ Ⓔ
23. Ⓐ Ⓑ Ⓒ Ⓓ Ⓔ	47. Ⓐ Ⓑ Ⓒ Ⓓ Ⓔ	71. Ⓐ Ⓑ Ⓒ Ⓓ Ⓔ
24. Ⓐ Ⓑ Ⓒ Ⓓ Ⓔ	48. Ⓐ Ⓑ Ⓒ Ⓓ Ⓔ	72. Ⓐ Ⓑ Ⓒ Ⓓ Ⓔ

PART B: MEMORY FOR ADDRESSES CONT.

73.	Ⓐ Ⓑ Ⓒ Ⓓ Ⓔ	79.	Ⓐ Ⓑ Ⓒ Ⓓ Ⓔ	85.	Ⓐ Ⓑ Ⓒ Ⓓ Ⓔ
74.	Ⓐ Ⓑ Ⓒ Ⓓ Ⓔ	80.	Ⓐ Ⓑ Ⓒ Ⓓ Ⓔ	86.	Ⓐ Ⓑ Ⓒ Ⓓ Ⓔ
75.	Ⓐ Ⓑ Ⓒ Ⓓ Ⓔ	81.	Ⓐ Ⓑ Ⓒ Ⓓ Ⓔ	87.	Ⓐ Ⓑ Ⓒ Ⓓ Ⓔ
76.	Ⓐ Ⓑ Ⓒ Ⓓ Ⓔ	82.	Ⓐ Ⓑ Ⓒ Ⓓ Ⓔ	88.	Ⓐ Ⓑ Ⓒ Ⓓ Ⓔ
77.	Ⓐ Ⓑ Ⓒ Ⓓ Ⓔ	83.	Ⓐ Ⓑ Ⓒ Ⓓ Ⓔ		
78.	Ⓐ Ⓑ Ⓒ Ⓓ Ⓔ	84.	Ⓐ Ⓑ Ⓒ Ⓓ Ⓔ		

PART C: NUMBER SERIES

1.	Ⓐ Ⓑ Ⓒ Ⓓ Ⓔ	9.	Ⓐ Ⓑ Ⓒ Ⓓ Ⓔ	17.	Ⓐ Ⓑ Ⓒ Ⓓ Ⓔ
2.	Ⓐ Ⓑ Ⓒ Ⓓ Ⓔ	10.	Ⓐ Ⓑ Ⓒ Ⓓ Ⓔ	18.	Ⓐ Ⓑ Ⓒ Ⓓ Ⓔ
3.	Ⓐ Ⓑ Ⓒ Ⓓ Ⓔ	11.	Ⓐ Ⓑ Ⓒ Ⓓ Ⓔ	19.	Ⓐ Ⓑ Ⓒ Ⓓ Ⓔ
4.	Ⓐ Ⓑ Ⓒ Ⓓ Ⓔ	12.	Ⓐ Ⓑ Ⓒ Ⓓ Ⓔ	20.	Ⓐ Ⓑ Ⓒ Ⓓ Ⓔ
5.	Ⓐ Ⓑ Ⓒ Ⓓ Ⓔ	13.	Ⓐ Ⓑ Ⓒ Ⓓ Ⓔ	21.	Ⓐ Ⓑ Ⓒ Ⓓ Ⓔ
6.	Ⓐ Ⓑ Ⓒ Ⓓ Ⓔ	14.	Ⓐ Ⓑ Ⓒ Ⓓ Ⓔ	22.	Ⓐ Ⓑ Ⓒ Ⓓ Ⓔ
7.	Ⓐ Ⓑ Ⓒ Ⓓ Ⓔ	15.	Ⓐ Ⓑ Ⓒ Ⓓ Ⓔ	23.	Ⓐ Ⓑ Ⓒ Ⓓ Ⓔ
8.	Ⓐ Ⓑ Ⓒ Ⓓ Ⓔ	16.	Ⓐ Ⓑ Ⓒ Ⓓ Ⓔ	24.	Ⓐ Ⓑ Ⓒ Ⓓ Ⓔ

PART D: FOLLOWING ORAL DIRECTIONS

1.	Ⓐ Ⓑ Ⓒ Ⓓ Ⓔ	18.	Ⓐ Ⓑ Ⓒ Ⓓ Ⓔ	35.	Ⓐ Ⓑ Ⓒ Ⓓ Ⓔ
2.	Ⓐ Ⓑ Ⓒ Ⓓ Ⓔ	19.	Ⓐ Ⓑ Ⓒ Ⓓ Ⓔ	36.	Ⓐ Ⓑ Ⓒ Ⓓ Ⓔ
3.	Ⓐ Ⓑ Ⓒ Ⓓ Ⓔ	20.	Ⓐ Ⓑ Ⓒ Ⓓ Ⓔ	37.	Ⓐ Ⓑ Ⓒ Ⓓ Ⓔ
4.	Ⓐ Ⓑ Ⓒ Ⓓ Ⓔ	21.	Ⓐ Ⓑ Ⓒ Ⓓ Ⓔ	38.	Ⓐ Ⓑ Ⓒ Ⓓ Ⓔ
5.	Ⓐ Ⓑ Ⓒ Ⓓ Ⓔ	22.	Ⓐ Ⓑ Ⓒ Ⓓ Ⓔ	39.	Ⓐ Ⓑ Ⓒ Ⓓ Ⓔ
6.	Ⓐ Ⓑ Ⓒ Ⓓ Ⓔ	23.	Ⓐ Ⓑ Ⓒ Ⓓ Ⓔ	40.	Ⓐ Ⓑ Ⓒ Ⓓ Ⓔ
7.	Ⓐ Ⓑ Ⓒ Ⓓ Ⓔ	24.	Ⓐ Ⓑ Ⓒ Ⓓ Ⓔ	41.	Ⓐ Ⓑ Ⓒ Ⓓ Ⓔ
8.	Ⓐ Ⓑ Ⓒ Ⓓ Ⓔ	25.	Ⓐ Ⓑ Ⓒ Ⓓ Ⓔ	42.	Ⓐ Ⓑ Ⓒ Ⓓ Ⓔ
9.	Ⓐ Ⓑ Ⓒ Ⓓ Ⓔ	26.	Ⓐ Ⓑ Ⓒ Ⓓ Ⓔ	43.	Ⓐ Ⓑ Ⓒ Ⓓ Ⓔ
10.	Ⓐ Ⓑ Ⓒ Ⓓ Ⓔ	27.	Ⓐ Ⓑ Ⓒ Ⓓ Ⓔ	44.	Ⓐ Ⓑ Ⓒ Ⓓ Ⓔ
11.	Ⓐ Ⓑ Ⓒ Ⓓ Ⓔ	28.	Ⓐ Ⓑ Ⓒ Ⓓ Ⓔ	45.	Ⓐ Ⓑ Ⓒ Ⓓ Ⓔ
12.	Ⓐ Ⓑ Ⓒ Ⓓ Ⓔ	29.	Ⓐ Ⓑ Ⓒ Ⓓ Ⓔ	46.	Ⓐ Ⓑ Ⓒ Ⓓ Ⓔ
13.	Ⓐ Ⓑ Ⓒ Ⓓ Ⓔ	30.	Ⓐ Ⓑ Ⓒ Ⓓ Ⓔ	47.	Ⓐ Ⓑ Ⓒ Ⓓ Ⓔ
14.	Ⓐ Ⓑ Ⓒ Ⓓ Ⓔ	31.	Ⓐ Ⓑ Ⓒ Ⓓ Ⓔ	48.	Ⓐ Ⓑ Ⓒ Ⓓ Ⓔ
15.	Ⓐ Ⓑ Ⓒ Ⓓ Ⓔ	32.	Ⓐ Ⓑ Ⓒ Ⓓ Ⓔ	49.	Ⓐ Ⓑ Ⓒ Ⓓ Ⓔ
16.	Ⓐ Ⓑ Ⓒ Ⓓ Ⓔ	33.	Ⓐ Ⓑ Ⓒ Ⓓ Ⓔ	50.	Ⓐ Ⓑ Ⓒ Ⓓ Ⓔ
17.	Ⓐ Ⓑ Ⓒ Ⓓ Ⓔ	34.	Ⓐ Ⓑ Ⓒ Ⓓ Ⓔ		

POSTAL EXAM 2

PART A: ADDRESS CHECKING

Below are 95 pairs of addresses. Look at each pair and decide if the two addresses are alike or different in any way. If they are exactly ALIKE, darken circle A on your answer sheet; if they are DIFFERENT, darken circle D. You will have six minutes to answer the 95 questions.

1.	2109 Gunther Ave	2190 Gunther Ave
2.	Quincy IL 62301	Quincy IL 62301
3.	1073 S Lowell St	1075 S Lowell St
4.	5104 Kitty Lee Rd	5104 Kitty Dee Rd
5.	Lincoln NE 68506	Lincoln ME 68506
6.	3434 Walden Rd	3434 Walden Rd
7.	4110 Dakota Tr	4110 Lakota Tr
8.	7510 W Benton Dr	7510 W Benton Dr
9.	1112 N Amhurst St	1112 N Amherst St
10.	Newfield NY 14867	Newfield NY 18467
11.	Denver CO 80211	Denver CO 80211
12.	1201 Myrtle Ave	1201 Myrtle St
13.	1712 Briar Ridge Dr	1712 Briar Bridge Dr
14.	Del Mar CA 92014	Del Mar CA 92014
15.	4006 Cottage Grove Ave	4006 Cottage Grove Ave
16.	1040 Newton Rd	1040 Newtown Rd
17.	Des Moines IA 50311	Des Moines IN 50311
18.	Zanesville OH 43701	Zanesville OH 43107
19.	2450 Bittersweet Ct	2450 Bittersweet Ct
20.	3115 Fairview Av	5113 Fairview Av

21. 4435 Naples Av SW   4435 Naples Av SE

22. Eagle Butte SD 57625   Eagle Butte SD 57625

23. 1582 Ginseng Tr   1582 Ginsing Tr

24. South Haven MI 49090   South Heaven MI 49090

25. 1418 Eastview Dr   1814 Eastview Dr

26. 1389 Covered Bridge Rd   1389 Covered Bridge Rd

27. Plainfield IN 46168   Planefield IN 46168

28. 2517 Holiday Rd   2517 Holiday Dr

29. 5721 Haywood Av   5721 Haywood Av

30. Cherokee NC 28719   Cherokee SC 28719

31. 5306 Georgia Av NW   5306 Georgia Av NW

32. 8117 E Burlington St   8117 E Burlington St

33. Washington DC 20015   Washington DC 20815

34. Signal Mountain TN 37377   Signal Mountain TN 37337

35. 2132 Post Rd N   2132 Post Rd N

36. 4239 S Van Buren St   4236 S Van Buren St

37. Madison WI 53713   Madison WA 53713

38. 2255 Balsam Ct   2255 Balsam Dr

39. 3189 Woodside Rd   3189 Woodside Rd

40. Portland OR 97223   Portland OR 97223

41. 2449 Shady Glen Ct   2449 Shady Glen Ct

42. 3115 Emerald St   3115 Emerald Ct

43. 4365 Country Ln   4365 Country Ln

44. Minneapolis MN 55403   Minneapolis MN 54503

45. 1707 Carriage Hill St   1707 Carriage Hill St

46. Chevy Chase MD 20815   Chevy Case MD 20815

47. 2801 Highway 6 E   2081 Highway 6 E

48. 1133 Apple Way   1133 Apple Way

49. Spokane WA 99204   Spokane WA 99204

50. 1211 Bella Vista Pl   1112 Bella Vista Pl

51. 1902 Boston Way   1902 Beston Way

52. 1108 Clements St   1108 Clemens St

53. Newark NJ 07102   Newark NY 07102

54. Stanford CA 94305   Stanford CA 94305

55. 2318 Ridgeland Hwy   2318 Ridgeland Way

56. 1318 N Linn St   1318 S Linn St

57. 1613 Dubuque St NE   1613 Dubuque St NE

58. Little Rock AR 72201   Little Rock AZ 72201

59. 2430 Muscatine Av   2430 Muscatine Av

60. 7711 Kirkwood Pl   7711 Kirkwood Pl

61. 2519 Aster Av   2519 Oster Av

62. Dallas TX 75275   Dallas TX 75375

63. Baton Rouge LA 70813   Batan Rouge LA 70813

64. 1309 E Church St   1309 E Church St

65. 2117 Ferson Av   1217 Ferson Av

66. Huntington NY 11743   Huntington NY 11743

67. 1609 Westwinds Dr   1609 Westwinds Rd

68. Tuscaloosa AL 35487   Tuscaloosa AL 35478

69. 1845 Cross Park Wy   1845 Cross Park Wy

70. 1515 Summary Tr   1515 Summary Dr

71.	2331 Hutchinson Dr	2331 Hutchinson Dr
72.	Moscow ID 83843	Moscow IA 83843
73.	1518 Bowery St	1518 Bovery St
74.	1339 Teeters Ct	1339 Teeters Ct
75.	Louisville KY 40292	Louisville KS 40292
76.	Coral Gables FL 33124	Coral Gable FL 33124
77.	1203 S Lowell St	1203 S Lowell St
78.	3217 Friendship Rd	3217 Friendship Rd
79.	Oxford MS 38677	Oxford MS 38877
80.	3314 Riverside Dr SE	3314 Riverside Dr SE
81.	4037 W Overlook Dr	4307 W Overlook Dr
82.	Kansas City MO 64110	Kansas City MS 64110
83.	4204 Anderson Av SE	4204 Andersen Av SE
84.	1807 S Gilbert Dr	1807 S Gilbert Dr
85.	Albuquerque NM 87131	Albuquerque NM 77131
86.	Chapel Hill NC 27599	Chapel Hill NC 27599
87.	1728 Gleason Av	1728 Cleason Av
88.	1540 S Summit St	1540 N Summit St
89.	2228 Richards Dr	2228 Richards Rd
90.	Grand Forks ND 58202	Grand Forks ND 58202
91.	1906 Rochester Ct	1908 Rochester Ct
92.	1212 Village Rd	1212 Village Rd
93.	1815 DeForest St	1815 DeForest St
94.	11 Arbor Hill Ct	111 Arbor Hill Ct
95.	Norman OK 73019	Norman OK 73019

PART B: MEMORY FOR ADDRESSES

Below are five boxes labeled A, B, C, D, and E. Each box contains three sets of addresses (which include street names with number ranges) and 2 single names. Study the boxes for **ten minutes** and memorize the location (A, B, C, D, or E) of each of the numbered addresses and single names. Then answer the 88 questions on the next page by darkening the circle (A, B, C, D, or E) that corresponds to the box in which the address or name appears. You will have **five minutes** to answer the 88 questions.

A	B	C	D	E
2300–2899 Benton	3500–4099 Benton	1700–2299 Benton	2900–3499 Benton	4100–4699 Benton
Robinson	Walton	Jacobs	Ewald	Kelly
4400–4799 Dilly	5200–5599 Dilly	4800–5199 Dilly	4000–4399 Dilly	5600–5999 Dilly
Weinsek	Merck	O'Connell	Gore	Appleby
1200–1899 Tulane	3300–3899 Tulane	1900–2599 Tulane	2600–3299 Tulane	3900–4599 Tulane

1. Walton

2. 4000–4399 Dilly

3. Jacobs

4. Weinsek

5. 4400–4799 Dilly

6. 1700–2299 Benton

7. Merck

8. Kelly

9. 4000–4399 Dilly

10. 1900–2599 Tulane

11. Walton

12. 4100–4699 Benton

13. Merck

14. Gore

15. Jacobs

16. 2300–2899 Benton

17. 4800–5199 Dilly

18. Weinsek

19. Merck

20. 2900–3499 Benton

21. 5200–5599 Dilly

22. Appleby

23. 1200–1899 Tulane

24. O'Connell

25. 1700–2299 Benton

26. Walton

27. Appleby

28. Ewald

29. 5600–5999 Dilly

30. 3500–4099 Benton

31. Robinson

32. 1900–2599 Tulane

33. 2300–2899 Benton

34. Ewald

35. Kelly

36. 5200–5599 Dilly

37. O'Connell

38. 2600–3299 Tulane

39. 4100–4699 Benton

40. Weinsek

41. 5200–5599 Dilly

42. 2600–3299 Tulane

43. 1700–2299 Benton

44. Kelly

45. 1200–1899 Tulane

46. 2900–3499 Benton

47. 3300–3899 Tulane

48. Merck

49. O'Connell

50. 5600–5999 Dilly

51. 4400–4799 Dilly

52. 3900–4599 Tulane

53. Gore

54. 3500–4099 Benton

55. Jacobs

56. 2900–3499 Benton

57. 1200–1899 Tulane

58. 4800–5199 Dilly

59. Appleby

60. 3300–3899 Tulane

61. 2900–3499 Benton

62. Jacobs

63. Ewald

64. Gore

65. 5600–5999 Dilly

66. 2600–3299 Tulane

67. Weinsek

68. 3500–4099 Benton

69. 1900–2599 Tulane

70. Robinson

71. 4000–4399 Dilly

72. Kelly

73. 3500–4099 Benton

74. 1700–2299 Benton

75. Walton

76. 2600–3299 Tulane

77. Robinson

78. 4000–4399 Dilly

79. 3900–4599 Tulane

80. 4800–5199 Dilly

81. Robinson

82. 3300–3899 Tulane

83. 4100–4699 Benton

84. Gore

85. 4800–5199 Dilly

86. 3900–4099 Tulane

87. 2300–2899 Benton

88. 5200–5599 Dilly

PART C: NUMBER SERIES

Below, on the left, you will see a series of seven numbers that follow some definite order. On the right are five sets of two numbers each, labeled A, B, C, D, and E. Look at the number series to find its pattern, and then darken the circle for the answer pair that would come next in the series if the same pattern were followed. You will have 20 minutes to answer as many of the 24 questions as you can.

1. 21 9 21 11 21 13 21 . . . . **A)** 21 15   **B)** 9 22   **C)** 15 21   **D)** 5 21   **E)** 22 15

2. 32 29 26 23 20 17 14 . . . . **A)** 11 8   **B)** 12 8   **C)** 11 7   **D)** 32 29   **E)** 10 9

3. 2 44 4 41 6 38 8 . . . . **A)** 10 12   **B)** 35 32   **C)** 34 9   **D)** 35 10   **E)** 10 52

4. 3 4 7 8 11 12 15 . . . . **A)** 16 17   **B)** 16 19   **C)** 18 19   **D)** 18 21   **E)** 17 19

5. 17 17 28 28 39 39 50 . . . . **A)** 60 71   **B)** 50 61   **C)** 50 71   **D)** 61 72   **E)** 50 62

6. 7 12 9 14 11 16 13 . . . . **A)** 16 13   **B)** 18 15   **C)** 10 15   **D)** 18 23   **E)** 10 7

7. 2 5 28 8 11 20 14 . . . . **A)** 12 4   **B)** 12 17   **C)** 18 12   **D)** 17 6   **E)** 17 12

8. 4 9 11 16 18 23 25 . . . . **A)** 27 29   **B)** 30 35   **C)** 30 32   **D)** 27 32   **E)** 27 30

9. 6 10 14 18 22 26 30 . . . . **A)** 36 40   **B)** 33 37   **C)** 38 42   **D)** 32 34   **E)** 34 38

10. 17 14 14 11 11 8 8 . . . . **A)** 8 5   **B)** 5 2   **C)** 8 2   **D)** 5 5   **E)** 5 8

11. 13 29 15 26 17 23 19 . . . . **A)** 21 23   **B)** 20 21   **C)** 20 17   **D)** 25 27   **E)** 22 20

12. 16 26 56 36 46 68 56 . . . . **A)** 80 66   **B)** 64 82   **C)** 66 80   **D)** 78 68   **E)** 66 82

13. 7 9 66 12 14 66 17 . . . . **A)** 19 66   **B)** 66 19   **C)** 19 22   **D)** 20 66   **E)** 66 20

14. 34 30 26 22 18 14 10 . . . . **A)** 8 6   **B)** 6 4   **C)** 14 18   **D)** 6 2   **E)** 4 0

15. 3 5 35 10 12 35 17 . . . . **A)** 22 35   **B)** 35 19   **C)** 19 35   **D)** 19 24   **E)** 22 24

16. 36 31 29 24 22 17 15 . . . . **A)** 13 11   **B)** 10 5   **C)** 13 8   **D)** 12 7   **E)** 10 8

17. 42 40 38 35 33 31 28 . . . . **A)** 25 22   **B)** 26 23   **C)** 26 24   **D)** 25 23   **E)** 26 22

18. 29 27 28 26 27 25 26 . . . . **A)** 28 26   **B)** 24 22   **C)** 28 27   **D)** 24 25   **E)** 24 26

19. 11 14 14 17 17 20 20 . . . . **A)** 23 23   **B)** 23 26   **C)** 21 24   **D)** 24 24   **E)** 24 27

20. 17 32 19 29 21 26 23 . . . . **A)** 25 25   **B)** 20 22   **C)** 23 25   **D)** 25 22   **E)** 27 32

21. 53 53 40 40 27 27 14 . . . . **A)** 1 14   **B)** 14 11   **C)** 14 14   **D)** 14 3   **E)** 14 1

22. 7 10 8 11 9 12 10 . . . . **A)** 8 11   **B)** 13 11   **C)** 13 15   **D)** 11 13   **E)** 12 9

23. 10 34 12 31 14 28 16 . . . . **A)** 25 18   **B)** 30 13   **C)** 19 26   **D)** 18 20   **E)** 25 22

24. 44 41 38 35 32 29 26 . . . . **A)** 24 21   **B)** 22 19   **C)** 23 19   **D)** 29 32   **E)** 23 20

PART D: FOLLOWING ORAL DIRECTIONS

Listen closely to the instructions the examiner gives you. The examiner will refer you to the following lines. Write whatever the examiner tells you on the lines, and then fill in the answer grid as the examiner directs you. The examiner will not repeat the instructions.

Line 1.   12_____   25_____   17_____   32_____   6_____

Line 2.   A_____

Line 3.   cat   bed   eat   dog   ask

Line 4.   47 (square)   44 (triangle)   41 (circle)

Line 5.   G   H   I   J   D

Line 6.   1 (square)   7 (square)   13 (square)   6 (circle)   11 (square)

Line 7.   10 − 3 =

Line 8.   D   E_____   C   A   B

Line 9.   32_____   15_____   45_____   12_____   27_____

Line 10.   C   _____   E   F   G

Line 11.   1   2   3   4   _____

Line 12.   C-D   E-A   D-B   B-11   C-E

Line 13.   B   D   E   D   B

Line 14.   12   23   15   7   20

Line 15.   D   B   A   C   E

Line 16.   12-7   4-15   19-C   16-3   7-11

Line 17.   4   13   E   5   27

Line 18.   8____

Line 19.   5   6   7   2   8

Line 20.   [11]   (4)   [9]   (13)   [18]

Line 21.   b_t   c_t   r_t   ____

Line 22.   (9___)   [12___]   (4___)   [22___]

Line 23.   A   D   E   B   C

Line 24. $10 + 6 =$

EXAMINER INSTRUCTIONS

Look at Line 1. (**Pause slightly.**) There are five numbers, each with a blank line beside it. Next to the fourth number in the line, write the letter A as in apple. (**Pause 2 seconds.**) Now, on your answer grid, darken the space for the number-letter combination you just created. (**Pause five seconds.**)

Look at Line 2. (**Pause slightly.**) There is a letter with a line beside it. On the line, write the number 13. (**Pause two seconds.**) Now, on your answer grid, darken the space for the number-letter combination you just wrote. (**Pause five seconds.**)

Look at Line 3. (**Pause slightly.**) There are five words. Underline the fourth word in the line. (**Pause two seconds.**) Now, on your answer grid, find number 18 and darken the space that is the first letter of the word you just underlined. (**Pause five seconds.**)

Look at Line 4. (**Pause slightly.**) There are three shapes with numbers in them. Find the triangle and draw an X through it. (**Pause two seconds.**) Now, on your answer grid, find the number you just drew an X through and darken space E as in elephant. (**Pause five seconds.**)

Look at Line 5. (**Pause slightly.**) There are five letters in alphabetical order, except one letter is out of order. (**Pause slightly.**) Circle the letter that does not belong. (**Pause two seconds.**) Now, on your answer grid, find number 47 and darken the space for the letter you just circled. (**Pause five seconds.**)

Look at Line 6. (**Pause slightly.**) There are four numbers in squares and one in a circle. Draw a line under the number that is in a circle. (**Pause two seconds.**) Now, on your answer grid, find the number you just underlined and darken space A as in apple. (**Pause five seconds.**)

Look at Line 7. (**Pause slightly.**) Subtract the two numbers and write the answer after the equal sign. (**Pause two seconds.**) Now, on your answer grid, find the number you just wrote and darken space C as in cat. (**Pause five seconds.**)

Look at Line 8. (**Pause slightly.**) There are five letters, one of which is followed by a blank. Write the number 14 in the blank. (**Pause two seconds.**) On your answer grid, darken the number-letter combination you created. (**Pause five seconds.**)

Look at Line 9. (**Pause slightly.**) Draw a circle around the *lowest* number. (**Pause two seconds.**) Now, on your answer grid, find the number which you just circled and darken space C as in cat for that number. (**Pause five seconds.**)

Look at Line 10. (**Pause slightly.**) There is a series of letters in alphabetical order with a blank where one letter is missing. (**Pause slightly.**) Write the missing letter in the blank. (**Pause two seconds.**) On your answer grid, find number 40 and darken the space for the letter you just wrote. (**Pause five seconds.**)

Look at Line 11. (**Pause slightly.**) There are four numbers followed by a line. On the line, write the number that would come next in order. (**Pause two seconds.**) Now, look on your answer grid, find the number you just wrote and darken space B as in boy. (**Pause five seconds.**)

Look at Line 12. (**Pause slightly.**) There are four pairs of letters and one number-letter pair. Circle the number-letter pair. (**Pause two seconds.**) On your answer grid, find the number-letter pair you just circled and darken that space. (**Pause five seconds.**)

Look at Line 13. (**Pause slightly.**) Draw a line under the letter that is *not* repeated on the line. (**Pause two seconds.**) Now, on your answer grid, find number 34 (**pause two seconds**) and darken the space for the letter under which you just drew the line. (**Pause five seconds.**)

Look at Line 14. (**Pause slightly.**) There are five numbers. Draw a line under the *highest* number. (**Pause two seconds.**) Now, on your answer grid, find the number you just underlined and darken space A as in apple. (**Pause five seconds.**)

Look at Line 15. (**Pause slightly.**) There are five letters. Draw a line under the second letter. (**Pause two seconds.**) Now, on your answer grid, find number 1 (**pause two seconds**) and darken the space for the letter under which you drew a line. (**Pause five seconds.**)

Look at Line 16. (**Pause slightly.**) There are four number pairs and one number-letter pair. (**Pause slightly.**) Draw a line under the number-letter pair. (**Pause two seconds.**) On your answer grid, darken the space for the number-letter combination you just underlined. (**Pause five seconds.**)

Look at Line 9 again. (**Pause two seconds.**) Find the *highest* number and write the letter B as in boy on the blank line to the right of it. (**Pause two seconds.**) On your answer grid, darken the space for the number-letter combination you just wrote. (**Pause five seconds.**)

Look at Line 17. (**Pause two seconds.**) There are four numbers and one letter. Draw a circle around the letter. (**Pause two seconds.**) Now, look on your answer grid, find number 27 and darken the space for the letter you just circled. (**Pause five seconds.**)

Look at Line 18. (**Pause slightly.**) There is a number with a line beside it. On the line, write the letter B as in boy. (**Pause two seconds.**) Now, on your answer grid, darken the space for the number-letter combination you just created. (**Pause five seconds.**)

Look at Line 19. (**Pause slightly.**) There are five numbers, one of which is out of order. (**Pause two seconds.**) Circle the number that does not belong in the sequence. (**Pause two seconds.**) Now, on your answer grid, find the number you just circled and darken space D as in dog. (**Pause five seconds.**)

Look at Line 20. (**Pause slightly.**) There are five numbers in circles and squares. Draw a circle around the *lowest* number that is in a square. (**Pause three seconds.**) On your answer grid, find the number you just circled and darken space C as in cat. (**Pause five seconds.**)

Look at Line 21. (**Pause slightly.**) There are 3 three-letter words, each missing the second letter. When the same letter is added, each word is the name of a small animal or rodent. (**Pause slightly.**) On the line that follows the three words, write the missing letter. (**Pause two seconds.**) Now, on your answer grid, find number 10 and darken the space for the letter you just wrote. (**Pause five seconds.**)

Look at Line 22. (**Pause slightly.**) There are two circles and two boxes of different sizes with numbers in them. (**Pause slightly.**) If Thursday comes before Wednesday and Monday is the first day of the week, write D as in dog in the smaller square. (**Pause slightly.**) Otherwise write E as in elephant in the smaller circle. (**Pause two seconds.**) Now, on your answer grid, darken the space for the number-letter combination you just created. (**Pause five seconds.**)

Look at the letters in Line 23. (**Pause slightly.**) If 7 is less than 9 and 12 is more than 5, underline the last letter. (**Pause two seconds.**) Otherwise, draw a circle around the third letter. (**Pause slightly.**) Now, on your answer grid, find number 21 and darken the space you just underlined or circled. (**Pause five seconds.**)

Look at Line 24. (**Pause slightly.**) Add the two numbers together and write the answer after the equal sign. (**Pause two seconds.**) Now, on your answer grid, find the number you just wrote and darken space D as in dog. (**Pause 5 seconds**).

ANSWERS

PART A: ADDRESS CHECKING

1. D	25. D	49. A	73. D
2. A	26. A	50. D	74. A
3. D	27. D	51. D	75. D
4. D	28. D	52. D	76. D
5. D	29. A	53. D	77. A
6. A	30. D	54. A	78. A
7. D	31. A	55. D	79. D
8. A	32. A	56. D	80. A
9. D	33. D	57. A	81. D
10. D	34. D	58. D	82. D
11. A	35. A	59. A	83. D
12. D	36. D	60. A	84. A
13. D	37. D	61. D	85. D
14. A	38. D	62. D	86. A
15. A	39. A	63. D	87. D
16. D	40. A	64. A	88. D
17. D	41. A	65. D	89. D
18. D	42. D	66. A	90. A
19. A	43. A	67. D	91. D
20. D	44. D	68. D	92. A
21. D	45. A	69. A	93. A
22. A	46. D	70. D	94. D
23. D	47. D	71. A	95. A
24. D	48. A	72. D	

PART B: MEMORY FOR ADDRESSES

1. B	23. A	45. A	67. A
2. D	24. C	46. D	68. B
3. C	25. C	47. B	69. C
4. A	26. B	48. B	70. A
5. A	27. E	49. C	71. D
6. C	28. D	50. E	72. E
7. B	29. E	51. A	73. B
8. E	30. B	52. E	74. C
9. D	31. A	53. D	75. B
10. C	32. C	54. B	76. D
11. B	33. A	55. C	77. A
12. E	34. D	56. D	78. D
13. B	35. E	57. A	79. E
14. D	36. B	58. C	80. C
15. C	37. C	59. E	81. A
16. A	38. D	60. B	82. B
17. C	39. E	61. D	83. E
18. A	40. A	62. C	84. D
19. B	41. B	63. D	85. C
20. D	42. D	64. D	86. E
21. B	43. C	65. E	87. A
22. E	44. E	66. D	88. B

PART C: NUMBER SERIES

1. **C.** In this series, the random number 21 is interpolated every other number into an otherwise simple addition series that increases by 2, beginning with the number 9.

2. **A.** In this simple subtraction series, the numbers decrease by 3.

3. **D.** Here are two alternating patterns, one addition and one subtraction. The first starts with 2 and increases by 2; the second starts with 44 and decreases by 3.

4. **B.** This alternating addition series first adds 1, then 3, then 1, then 3, and so on.

5. **B.** In this simple addition with repetition series, each number in the series repeats itself, and then increases by 11 to arrive at the next number.

6. **B.** This is an alternating addition and subtraction series, in which the addition of 5 is alternated with the subtraction of 3.

7. **E.** Two patterns alternate here, with every third number following the alternate pattern. In the main series, beginning with 2, 3 is added to each number to arrive at the next. In the alternating series, beginning with 28, 8 is subtracted from each number to arrive at the next.

8. **C.** This is an alternating addition series that adds 5, then 2, then 5, and so on.

9. **E.** This simple addition series adds 4 to each number to arrive at the next.

10. **D.** In this simple subtraction with repetition series, each number is repeated, then 3 is subtracted to give the next number, which is then repeated, and so on.

11. **B.** Here there are two alternating patterns, with every other number following a different pattern. The first pattern begins with 13 and adds 2 to each

number to arrive at the next; the alternating pattern begins with 29 and subtracts 3 each time.

12. **C.** Here every third number follows a different pattern from the main series. In the main series, beginning with 16, 10 is added to each number to arrive at the next. In the alternating series, beginning with 56, 12 is added to each number to arrive at the next.

13. **A.** This is an alternating addition series with repetition, in which a random number, 66, is interpolated as every third number. The regular series adds 2, then 3, then 2, and so on, with 66 repeated after each "add 2" step.

14. **D.** This is a simple subtraction series, in which 4 is subtracted from each number to arrive at the next.

15. **C.** This is an alternating addition series, with a random number, 35, interpolated as every third number. The pattern of addition is to add 2, add 5, add 2, and so on. The number 35 comes after each "add 2" step.

16. **E.** This is an alternating subtraction series, which subtracts 5, then 2, then 5, and so on.

17. **C.** This is an alternating subtraction series in which 2 is subtracted twice, then 3 is subtracted once, then 2 is subtracted twice, and so on.

18. **D.** In this alternating addition and subtraction series, 2 is subtracted, then 1 is added, and so on.

19. **A.** This is a simple addition series with repetition. It adds 3 to each number to arrive at the next, which is repeated before 3 is added again.

20. **C.** Here are two alternating patterns. The first begins with 17 and adds 2; the second begins with 32 and subtracts 3.

21. E. In this series, each number is repeated, then 13 is subtracted to arrive at the next number.

22. B. This is an alternating addition and subtraction series. The pattern is add 3, subtract 2, add 3, and so on.

23. A. Two patterns alternate here. The first pattern begins with 10 and adds 2 to each number to arrive at the next; the alternating pattern begins with 34 and subtracts 3 each time.

24. E. This is a simple subtraction series, in which 3 is subtracted from each number to arrive at the next.

PART D: FOLLOWING ORAL DIRECTIONS

You should have filled in only the numbers listed below with the answers indicated. The rest of the numbers on your answer grid should be blank. However, filling in a number that should have been blank does not count, as only questions you got right are scored.

1. B	**9.** C	**18.** D	**40.** D
2. D	**10.** A	**19.** C	**44.** E
4. E	**11.** B	**21.** C	**45.** B
5. B	**12.** C	**23.** A	**47.** D
6. A	**13.** A	**27.** E	
7. C	**14.** E	**32.** A	
8. B	**16.** D	**34.** E	

SCORING

As with the first exam in this book, first you must determine your raw score on the exam. Then you can convert your raw score to a score on a scale of 1 to 100 to see how your score will look to the USPS.

YOUR RAW SCORE

Parts A and B of the postal exam are scored in a way that makes random guessing work against you: A fraction of your wrong answer score is subtracted from your right answer score. Parts C and D are scored by counting right answers only. So here's how to determine your raw score for each part.

Part A: Address Checking

First, count the questions you got right. Then, count the number of questions you got wrong. Subtract your wrong answers from your right answers to get your raw score. Questions you didn't answer don't count either way.

1. Number of questions right: _____

2. Number of questions wrong: _____

3. Subtract number 2 from number 1:   _____

The result of number 3 above is your raw score on Part A.

Part B: Memory for Addresses

Count the questions you got right. Then, count the number of questions you got wrong and divide by four. Subtract the results of the division from the number you got right to get your raw score. Questions you didn't answer don't count either way.

4. Number of questions right: _____

5. Number of questions wrong: _____

6. Divide number 5 by 4:   _____

7. Subtract number 6 from number 4:   _____

The result of number 7 above is your raw score on Part B.

Part C: Number Series and Part D: Following Oral Directions

Your raw scores on Part C and Part D are simply the number of questions you got right. Nothing is subtracted for wrong answers or questions you left blank.

8. Number of questions right on Part C: _____

9. Number of questions right on Part D: _____

Total Raw Score

For your total raw score, add together the four numbers in blanks 3, 7, 8, and 9 above.

10. Total raw score: _____

SCALED SCORE

Now that you have your raw score, use the table below to convert it to an approximate score on a scale of 1 to 100.

RAW SCORE TO SCALED SCORE CONVERSION	
Raw Score	**Scaled Score**
220 or above	100
200–219	95–99
180–199	90–94
160–179	85–89
140–159	80–84
120–139	75–79
100–119	70–74
below 100	below 70

Chances are you've seen some improvement—maybe a lot of improvement—since you took the first exam in this book. If you're still weak in some areas, review the relevant chapters and try doing the practice exercises again after letting some time elapse.

POSTAL EXAM 3

11

CHAPTER SUMMARY

This is the third practice exam in this book based on USPS Test 470. This test provides more practice to help you get ready for the Postal Worker Exam.

 ere's a third practice Postal Worker Exam for you to use to hone your skills. Don't take this exam until you've worked through the chapters on the various sections of the exam.

Before you start this test, get prepared to simulate the actual test-taking experience as much as possible. Get out your stopwatch or alarm clock so that you can time yourself on each portion of the exam:

- **Part A: Address Checking.** Six minutes for 95 questions.
- **Part B: Memory for Addresses.** Ten minutes for memorization, and then five minutes for 88 questions.
- **Part C: Number Series.** Twenty minutes for 24 questions.
- **Part D: Following Oral Directions.** As long as it takes your examiner to read the questions with the appropriate pauses (about 20 minutes); 25 questions.

The other thing you need to have is a friend or relative to read you the instructions for Part D: Following Oral Directions. You can have your reader tape the instructions for you if that's more convenient. **But you should not read the directions yourself.** That would not be an accurate representation of what the real test will be like.

The only other things you need before you begin the test are a nice quiet place to work, some number 2 pencils, and enough time to complete the test at one sitting—about an hour and ten minutes, with a couple minutes' break between each section.

The answer sheet you should use for answering the questions is on the following page. Then comes the exam itself, and after that is the answer key. The answer key is followed by a section on how to score your exam.

PART A: ADDRESS CHECKING

1. (A) (D)	20. (A) (D)	39. (A) (D)	58. (A) (D)	77. (A) (D)
2. (A) (D)	21. (A) (D)	40. (A) (D)	59. (A) (D)	78. (A) (D)
3. (A) (D)	22. (A) (D)	41. (A) (D)	60. (A) (D)	79. (A) (D)
4. (A) (D)	23. (A) (D)	42. (A) (D)	61. (A) (D)	80. (A) (D)
5. (A) (D)	24. (A) (D)	43. (A) (D)	62. (A) (D)	81. (A) (D)
6. (A) (D)	25. (A) (D)	44. (A) (D)	63. (A) (D)	82. (A) (D)
7. (A) (D)	26. (A) (D)	45. (A) (D)	64. (A) (D)	83. (A) (D)
8. (A) (D)	27. (A) (D)	46. (A) (D)	65. (A) (D)	84. (A) (D)
9. (A) (D)	28. (A) (D)	47. (A) (D)	66. (A) (D)	85. (A) (D)
10. (A) (D)	29. (A) (D)	48. (A) (D)	67. (A) (D)	86. (A) (D)
11. (A) (D)	30. (A) (D)	49. (A) (D)	68. (A) (D)	87. (A) (D)
12. (A) (D)	31. (A) (D)	50. (A) (D)	69. (A) (D)	88. (A) (D)
13. (A) (D)	32. (A) (D)	51. (A) (D)	70. (A) (D)	89. (A) (D)
14. (A) (D)	33. (A) (D)	52. (A) (D)	71. (A) (D)	90. (A) (D)
15. (A) (D)	34. (A) (D)	53. (A) (D)	72. (A) (D)	91. (A) (D)
16. (A) (D)	35. (A) (D)	54. (A) (D)	73. (A) (D)	92. (A) (D)
17. (A) (D)	36. (A) (D)	55. (A) (D)	74. (A) (D)	93. (A) (D)
18. (A) (D)	37. (A) (D)	56. (A) (D)	75. (A) (D)	94. (A) (D)
19. (A) (D)	38. (A) (D)	57. (A) (D)	76. (A) (D)	95. (A) (D)

PART B: MEMORY FOR ADDRESSES

1. (A) (B) (C) (D) (E)	25. (A) (B) (C) (D) (E)	49. (A) (B) (C) (D) (E)
2. (A) (B) (C) (D) (E)	26. (A) (B) (C) (D) (E)	50. (A) (B) (C) (D) (E)
3. (A) (B) (C) (D) (E)	27. (A) (B) (C) (D) (E)	51. (A) (B) (C) (D) (E)
4. (A) (B) (C) (D) (E)	28. (A) (B) (C) (D) (E)	52. (A) (B) (C) (D) (E)
5. (A) (B) (C) (D) (E)	29. (A) (B) (C) (D) (E)	53. (A) (B) (C) (D) (E)
6. (A) (B) (C) (D) (E)	30. (A) (B) (C) (D) (E)	54. (A) (B) (C) (D) (E)
7. (A) (B) (C) (D) (E)	31. (A) (B) (C) (D) (E)	55. (A) (B) (C) (D) (E)
8. (A) (B) (C) (D) (E)	32. (A) (B) (C) (D) (E)	56. (A) (B) (C) (D) (E)
9. (A) (B) (C) (D) (E)	33. (A) (B) (C) (D) (E)	57. (A) (B) (C) (D) (E)
10. (A) (B) (C) (D) (E)	34. (A) (B) (C) (D) (E)	58. (A) (B) (C) (D) (E)
11. (A) (B) (C) (D) (E)	35. (A) (B) (C) (D) (E)	59. (A) (B) (C) (D) (E)
12. (A) (B) (C) (D) (E)	36. (A) (B) (C) (D) (E)	60. (A) (B) (C) (D) (E)
13. (A) (B) (C) (D) (E)	37. (A) (B) (C) (D) (E)	61. (A) (B) (C) (D) (E)
14. (A) (B) (C) (D) (E)	38. (A) (B) (C) (D) (E)	62. (A) (B) (C) (D) (E)
15. (A) (B) (C) (D) (E)	39. (A) (B) (C) (D) (E)	63. (A) (B) (C) (D) (E)
16. (A) (B) (C) (D) (E)	40. (A) (B) (C) (D) (E)	64. (A) (B) (C) (D) (E)
17. (A) (B) (C) (D) (E)	41. (A) (B) (C) (D) (E)	65. (A) (B) (C) (D) (E)
18. (A) (B) (C) (D) (E)	42. (A) (B) (C) (D) (E)	66. (A) (B) (C) (D) (E)
19. (A) (B) (C) (D) (E)	43. (A) (B) (C) (D) (E)	67. (A) (B) (C) (D) (E)
20. (A) (B) (C) (D) (E)	44. (A) (B) (C) (D) (E)	68. (A) (B) (C) (D) (E)
21. (A) (B) (C) (D) (E)	45. (A) (B) (C) (D) (E)	69. (A) (B) (C) (D) (E)
22. (A) (B) (C) (D) (E)	46. (A) (B) (C) (D) (E)	70. (A) (B) (C) (D) (E)
23. (A) (B) (C) (D) (E)	47. (A) (B) (C) (D) (E)	71. (A) (B) (C) (D) (E)
24. (A) (B) (C) (D) (E)	48. (A) (B) (C) (D) (E)	72. (A) (B) (C) (D) (E)

PART B: MEMORY FOR ADDRESSES CONT.

73. Ⓐ Ⓑ Ⓒ Ⓓ Ⓔ   79. Ⓐ Ⓑ Ⓒ Ⓓ Ⓔ   85. Ⓐ Ⓑ Ⓒ Ⓓ Ⓔ
74. Ⓐ Ⓑ Ⓒ Ⓓ Ⓔ   80. Ⓐ Ⓑ Ⓒ Ⓓ Ⓔ   86. Ⓐ Ⓑ Ⓒ Ⓓ Ⓔ
75. Ⓐ Ⓑ Ⓒ Ⓓ Ⓔ   81. Ⓐ Ⓑ Ⓒ Ⓓ Ⓔ   87. Ⓐ Ⓑ Ⓒ Ⓓ Ⓔ
76. Ⓐ Ⓑ Ⓒ Ⓓ Ⓔ   82. Ⓐ Ⓑ Ⓒ Ⓓ Ⓔ   88. Ⓐ Ⓑ Ⓒ Ⓓ Ⓔ
77. Ⓐ Ⓑ Ⓒ Ⓓ Ⓔ   83. Ⓐ Ⓑ Ⓒ Ⓓ Ⓔ
78. Ⓐ Ⓑ Ⓒ Ⓓ Ⓔ   84. Ⓐ Ⓑ Ⓒ Ⓓ Ⓔ

PART C: NUMBER SERIES

1. Ⓐ Ⓑ Ⓒ Ⓓ Ⓔ   9. Ⓐ Ⓑ Ⓒ Ⓓ Ⓔ   17. Ⓐ Ⓑ Ⓒ Ⓓ Ⓔ
2. Ⓐ Ⓑ Ⓒ Ⓓ Ⓔ   10. Ⓐ Ⓑ Ⓒ Ⓓ Ⓔ   18. Ⓐ Ⓑ Ⓒ Ⓓ Ⓔ
3. Ⓐ Ⓑ Ⓒ Ⓓ Ⓔ   11. Ⓐ Ⓑ Ⓒ Ⓓ Ⓔ   19. Ⓐ Ⓑ Ⓒ Ⓓ Ⓔ
4. Ⓐ Ⓑ Ⓒ Ⓓ Ⓔ   12. Ⓐ Ⓑ Ⓒ Ⓓ Ⓔ   20. Ⓐ Ⓑ Ⓒ Ⓓ Ⓔ
5. Ⓐ Ⓑ Ⓒ Ⓓ Ⓔ   13. Ⓐ Ⓑ Ⓒ Ⓓ Ⓔ   21. Ⓐ Ⓑ Ⓒ Ⓓ Ⓔ
6. Ⓐ Ⓑ Ⓒ Ⓓ Ⓔ   14. Ⓐ Ⓑ Ⓒ Ⓓ Ⓔ   22. Ⓐ Ⓑ Ⓒ Ⓓ Ⓔ
7. Ⓐ Ⓑ Ⓒ Ⓓ Ⓔ   15. Ⓐ Ⓑ Ⓒ Ⓓ Ⓔ   23. Ⓐ Ⓑ Ⓒ Ⓓ Ⓔ
8. Ⓐ Ⓑ Ⓒ Ⓓ Ⓔ   16. Ⓐ Ⓑ Ⓒ Ⓓ Ⓔ   24. Ⓐ Ⓑ Ⓒ Ⓓ Ⓔ

PART D: FOLLOWING ORAL DIRECTIONS

1. Ⓐ Ⓑ Ⓒ Ⓓ Ⓔ   18. Ⓐ Ⓑ Ⓒ Ⓓ Ⓔ   35. Ⓐ Ⓑ Ⓒ Ⓓ Ⓔ
2. Ⓐ Ⓑ Ⓒ Ⓓ Ⓔ   19. Ⓐ Ⓑ Ⓒ Ⓓ Ⓔ   36. Ⓐ Ⓑ Ⓒ Ⓓ Ⓔ
3. Ⓐ Ⓑ Ⓒ Ⓓ Ⓔ   20. Ⓐ Ⓑ Ⓒ Ⓓ Ⓔ   37. Ⓐ Ⓑ Ⓒ Ⓓ Ⓔ
4. Ⓐ Ⓑ Ⓒ Ⓓ Ⓔ   21. Ⓐ Ⓑ Ⓒ Ⓓ Ⓔ   38. Ⓐ Ⓑ Ⓒ Ⓓ Ⓔ
5. Ⓐ Ⓑ Ⓒ Ⓓ Ⓔ   22. Ⓐ Ⓑ Ⓒ Ⓓ Ⓔ   39. Ⓐ Ⓑ Ⓒ Ⓓ Ⓔ
6. Ⓐ Ⓑ Ⓒ Ⓓ Ⓔ   23. Ⓐ Ⓑ Ⓒ Ⓓ Ⓔ   40. Ⓐ Ⓑ Ⓒ Ⓓ Ⓔ
7. Ⓐ Ⓑ Ⓒ Ⓓ Ⓔ   24. Ⓐ Ⓑ Ⓒ Ⓓ Ⓔ   41. Ⓐ Ⓑ Ⓒ Ⓓ Ⓔ
8. Ⓐ Ⓑ Ⓒ Ⓓ Ⓔ   25. Ⓐ Ⓑ Ⓒ Ⓓ Ⓔ   42. Ⓐ Ⓑ Ⓒ Ⓓ Ⓔ
9. Ⓐ Ⓑ Ⓒ Ⓓ Ⓔ   26. Ⓐ Ⓑ Ⓒ Ⓓ Ⓔ   43. Ⓐ Ⓑ Ⓒ Ⓓ Ⓔ
10. Ⓐ Ⓑ Ⓒ Ⓓ Ⓔ   27. Ⓐ Ⓑ Ⓒ Ⓓ Ⓔ   44. Ⓐ Ⓑ Ⓒ Ⓓ Ⓔ
11. Ⓐ Ⓑ Ⓒ Ⓓ Ⓔ   28. Ⓐ Ⓑ Ⓒ Ⓓ Ⓔ   45. Ⓐ Ⓑ Ⓒ Ⓓ Ⓔ
12. Ⓐ Ⓑ Ⓒ Ⓓ Ⓔ   29. Ⓐ Ⓑ Ⓒ Ⓓ Ⓔ   46. Ⓐ Ⓑ Ⓒ Ⓓ Ⓔ
13. Ⓐ Ⓑ Ⓒ Ⓓ Ⓔ   30. Ⓐ Ⓑ Ⓒ Ⓓ Ⓔ   47. Ⓐ Ⓑ Ⓒ Ⓓ Ⓔ
14. Ⓐ Ⓑ Ⓒ Ⓓ Ⓔ   31. Ⓐ Ⓑ Ⓒ Ⓓ Ⓔ   48. Ⓐ Ⓑ Ⓒ Ⓓ Ⓔ
15. Ⓐ Ⓑ Ⓒ Ⓓ Ⓔ   32. Ⓐ Ⓑ Ⓒ Ⓓ Ⓔ   49. Ⓐ Ⓑ Ⓒ Ⓓ Ⓔ
16. Ⓐ Ⓑ Ⓒ Ⓓ Ⓔ   33. Ⓐ Ⓑ Ⓒ Ⓓ Ⓔ   50. Ⓐ Ⓑ Ⓒ Ⓓ Ⓔ
17. Ⓐ Ⓑ Ⓒ Ⓓ Ⓔ   34. Ⓐ Ⓑ Ⓒ Ⓓ Ⓔ

POSTAL EXAM 3

PART A: ADDRESS CHECKING

Below are 95 pairs of addresses. Look at each pair and decide if the two addresses are alike or different in any way. If they are exactly ALIKE, darken circle A on your answer sheet; if they are DIFFERENT, darken circle D. You will have six minutes to answer the 95 questions.

1.	9227 Desmond St	9277 Desmond St
2.	Philadelphia PA 19106	Philadelphia PA 19106
3.	2163 Narragansett Ave	2163 Narragansett Ave
4.	4923 Primrose Ln	4933 Primrose Ln
5.	1217 Nonesuch Rd	1217 Nonesuch Dr
6.	Wainscott NY 11975	Wainscott NY 19975
7.	5519 Ludlow Terr	5519 Ladlow Terr
8.	2334 Canal Rd	2334 Canal Rd
9.	Crown Point IN 46307	Crown Point IN 46307
10.	Jerusalem, Israel 91007	Jerusalem, Isreal 91007
11.	2314 Constitution Dr	2314 Constitution Dr
12.	3345 Gorham Rd	3354 Gorham Rd
13.	5656 Old Blue Point Dr	5656 Blue Point Dr
14.	Minneapolis MN 55401	Minneapolis NM 55401
15.	8943 Walnut Bl	8943 Walnut Bl
16.	3546 Bedell St	3546 Beddel St
17.	Columbus OH 43215	Columbus OH 43215
18.	8872 Depot Dr	8872 Depot Dr
19.	Boise ID 83725	Boise ID 83275
20.	1492 Bridgeton Rd	1492 Brideton Rd

21.	1957 Orchard Dr	1957 Orchard Dr
22.	3434 Greenleaf St	4343 Greenleaf St
23.	St. Louis MO 63108	St. Louis MI 63108
24.	Chicago IL 60605	Chicago IL 60605
25.	6872 S Summit St	6872 S Summit St
26.	1415 Clifford Ln	1514 Clifford Ln
27.	4950 Hunts Hill Rd	4950 Hunts Hill Rd
28.	Towson MD 21204	Towson ME 21204
29.	8779 Greenbriar Wy	8779 Greenbriar Wy
30.	1842 Cousins Av	1482 Cousins Av
31.	9818 Spring Dr	9818 Spring Rd
32.	Waltham MA 02154	Waltham MA 02145
33.	1717 Bridle Path Av	1717 Bridle Path Av
34.	Washington DC 20003	Washington DC 20003
35.	Inglewood CA 90312	Englewood CA 90312
36.	4858 Cumberland Bl	4858 Cumberlend Bl
37.	6669 Winslow Pl	6669 Winslow Pl
38.	7117 Whitney Av	7171 Whitney Av
39.	Richmond VA 23220	Richmond VR 23220
40.	1111 Merrill Rd	1111 Merill Rd
41.	2179 Caleb St	2179 Caleb St
42.	8743 Roberts Tr	8743 Roberts Tr
43.	Logan UT 84322	Logan UT 84822
44.	3356 Andrews Av	3356 Andrews Av
45.	6112 Munjoy St	6122 Munjoy St

46.	9784 Starboard Dr	9784 Sarboard Dr
47.	Fords NJ 08863	Fords NY 08863
48.	7846 Birchwood Pl	7846 Birchwood Pl
49.	5533 Shore Rd	5533 Shore Rd
50.	5858 Bonnybrier St	5858 Bonnybriar St
51.	Houghton MI 49931	Houghton MI 49931
52.	Gettysburg PA 17325	Gettysberg PA 17325
53.	1243 Heather Ln	1243 Heather Ln
54.	4517 Barstow Rd	4715 Barstow Rd
55.	9813 Heather Pl	9813 Feather Pl
56.	Aurora CO 80012	Aurora CO 80012
57.	8856 Kennedy Pk	8856 Kennedy Pl
58.	1868 Bradley Rd	1686 Bradley Rd
59.	Athens GA 30602	Athens GA 30602
60.	3536 Valley Dr	3536 Valley Dr
61.	1776 Fairfield Rd	1766 Fairfield Rd
62.	6001 Woodland Dr	6001 Woodland Dr
63.	Seattle WA 98134	Seattle WA 89134
64.	El Paso TX 79968	El Paso TS 79968
65.	1011 Dartmouth Pl	1110 Dartmouth Pl
66.	4316 Longfellow St	4316 Langfellow St
67.	7619 Osborne Av	7619 Osborne Av
68.	2020 Brackett Pl	2020 Blackett Pl
69.	Terre Haute IN 47809	Terre Haute IN 47809
70.	2756 Rosemont Bl	2756 Rosemont Bl

71.	3942 Wildwood Cr	3924 Wildwood Cr
72.	2619 Val Halla Rd	2619 Val Halla Rd
73.	7854 Ashmont St	7654 Ashmont St
74.	Edmonton Alberta T5J 0X6	Edmonton Alberta TJ5 0X6
75.	1292 Hastings Ln	1292 Hastings Ln
76.	3314 Bryant St	3413 Bryant St
77.	4774 Roosevelt Tr	4774 Roosevelt Tr
78.	Portland OR 97205	Portland OR 97205
79.	2784 Fleetwood Av	2874 Fleetwood Av
80.	1609 Ocean Bl	1609 Ocean Pl
81.	5418 Pleasant Dr	5418 Pleasant Dr
82.	1211 Wainwright Cr	1211 Wainright Cr
83.	Key West FL 33041	Key West FL 33014
84.	4241 Applegate St	4241 Applegate St
85.	1909 Seashore Av	1909 Seeshore Av
86.	Lincoln NE 68588	Lincoln NB 68588
87.	5712 Carson Pl	5712 Garson Pl
88.	3817 Litchfield Rd	3817 Litchfield Rd
89.	3555 Boundary Rd	3555 Boundary Rd
90.	Raleigh NC 27601	Raleigh NC 26701
91.	1515 Rockland Av	1515 Rochland Av
92.	3319 Middle Rd	3913 Middle Rd
93.	2514 Crystal Tr	2514 Crystal Tr
94.	Iowa City IA 52242	Iowa City IA 52442
95.	7856 Tamerlane Av	7856 Tamerlane Av

PART B: MEMORY FOR ADDRESSES

Below are five boxes labeled A, B, C, D, and E. Each box contains three sets of addresses (which include street names with number ranges) and two single names. Study the boxes for **ten minutes** and memorize the location (A, B, C, D, or E) of each of the numbered addresses and single names. Then answer the 88 questions on the next page by darkening the circle (A, B, C, D, or E) that corresponds to the box in which the address or name appears. You will have **five minutes** to answer the 88 questions.

A	B	C	D	E
4700–5599 Spring	3800–4699 Spring	5600–6499 Spring	2900–3799 Spring	6500–7399 Spring
Powers	Mathews	Vance	Goodman	Neal
2300–2999 Cliff	5200–5899 Cliff	3000–3899 Cliff	4500–5199 Cliff	3900–4499 Cliff
Roberts	West	London	Hardwick	Quinn
3700–4499 Grant	5300–6099 Grant	2900–3699 Grant	4500–5299 Grant	6100–6899 Grant

1. 5300–6099 Grant
2. 3000–3899 Cliff
3. Neal
4. 4700–5599 Spring
5. 4500–5299 Grant
6. London
7. 2900–3799 Spring
8. Quinn
9. 3700–4499 Grant
10. 5200–5899 Cliff
11. 6500–7399 Spring
12. West
13. 2300–2999 Cliff
14. 2900–3699 Grant
15. Powers
16. Goodman
17. 5600–6499 Spring
18. 6100–6899 Grant
19. 3800–4699 Spring
20. 4500–5299 Grant
21. Roberts
22. 2300–2999 Cliff
23. 2900–3699 Grant
24. 6500–7399 Spring
25. 4500–5199 Cliff

26. Mathews
27. Vance
28. 3800–4699 Spring
29. 3700–4499 Grant
30. 3900–4499 Cliff
31. Hardwick
32. 5200–5899 Cliff
33. 6100–6899 Grant
34. Goodman
35. 4700–5599 Spring
36. Vance
37. 5300–6099 Grant
38. 3900–4499 Cliff
39. London
40. 2900–3799 Spring
41. Powers
42. 3000–3899 Cliff
43. West
44. 4500–5299 Grant
45. 6500–7399 Spring
46. Roberts
47. 5600–6499 Spring
48. 5200–5899 Cliff
49. Neal
50. 3700–4499 Grant

51. Mathews

52. 5600–6499 Spring

53. 4500–5199 Cliff

54. Quinn

55. 5300–6099 Grant

56. Roberts

57. Hardwick

58. 3900–4499 Cliff

59. 2900–3699 Grant

60. Neal

61. 4700–5599 Spring

62. 3000–3899 Cliff

63. 6100–6899 Grant

64. Goodman

65. 2300–2999 Cliff

66. 3800–4699 Spring

67. 4500–5199 Cliff

68. Quinn

69. Roberts

70. Vance

71. 2900–3799 Spring

72. 3700–4499 Grant

73. 5200–5899 Cliff

74. Neal

75. 2900–3699 Grant

76. 3900–3799 Spring

77. Mathews

78. 2300–2999 Cliff

79. 6100–6899 Grant

80. London

81. West

82. 4500–5199 Cliff

83. 5600–6499 Spring

84. Powers

85. 5300–6099 Grant

86. Hardwick

87. 6500–7399 Spring

88. 3000–3899 Cliff

PART C: NUMBER SERIES

Below, on the left, you will see a series of seven numbers that follow some definite order. On the right are five sets of two numbers each, labeled A, B, C, D, and E. Look at the number series to find its pattern, and then darken the circle for the answer pair that would come next in the series if the same pattern were followed. You will have 20 minutes to answer as many of the 24 questions as you can.

1. 32 31 32 29 32 27 32 . . . . **A)** 25 32   **B)** 31 32   **C)** 29 32   **D)** 25 30   **E)** 29 30

2. 24 29 26 31 28 33 30 . . . . **A)** 33 28   **B)** 35 32   **C)** 32 35   **D)** 33 35   **E)** 33 38

3. 11 15 19 23 27 31 35 . . . . **A)** 38 41   **B)** 40 45   **C)** 33 37   **D)** 39 43   **E)** 37 41

4. 4 17 7 13 10 11 13 . . . . **A)** 13 10   **B)** 7 16   **C)** 17 7   **D)** 10 11   **E)** 10 7

5. 14 15 13 14 12 13 11 . . . . **A)** 9 10   **B)** 13 12   **C)** 10 12   **D)** 12 14   **E)** 12 10

6. 17 19 33 21 23 32 25 . . . . **A)** 24 34   **B)** 27 29   **C)** 27 31   **D)** 26 24   **E)** 31 27

7. 22 19 19 16 16 13 13 . . . . **A)** 10 7   **B)** 13 10   **C)** 12 12   **D)** 10 10   **E)** 16 16

8. 5 33 8 12 33 15 19 . . . . **A)** 33 22   **B)** 33 36   **C)** 22 26   **D)** 23 33   **E)** 23 26

9. 59 53 47 41 35 29 23 . . . . **A)** 16 10   **B)** 21 15   **C)** 15 9   **D)** 23 17   **E)** 17 11

10. 7 29 10 27 13 25 16 . . . . **A)** 19 22   **B)** 14 17   **C)** 23 19   **D)** 17 23   **E)** 20 27

11. 42 9 39 11 36 13 33 . . . . **A)** 15 35   **B)** 35 32   **C)** 16 31   **D)** 15 30   **E)** 12 39

12. 14 17 16 19 18 21 20 . . . . **A)** 21 18   **B)** 24 17   **C)** 17 18   **D)** 24 27   **E)** 23 22

13. 53 51 51 49 49 47 47 . . . . **A)** 45 43   **B)** 45 45   **C)** 49 49   **D)** 43 43   **E)** 49 51

14. 79 76 73 70 67 64 61 . . . . **A)** 58 55   **B)** 60 58   **C)** 56 53   **D)** 65 68   **E)** 58 53

15. 12 17 14 19 16 21 18 . . . . **A)** 21 16   **B)** 15 20   **C)** 23 20   **D)** 22 17   **E)** 17 24

16. 87 82 80 75 73 68 66 . . . . **A)** 64 59   **B)** 65 63   **C)** 60 55   **D)** 57 52   **E)** 61 59

17. 14 35 18 35 22 35 26 . . . . **A)** 30 34   **B)** 35 22   **C)** 35 30   **D)** 24 35   **E)** 35 28

18. 68 65 62 60 57 54 52 . . . . **A)** 50 47   **B)** 50 48   **C)** 49 47   **D)** 49 46   **E)** 47 44

19. 27 22 29 24 31 26 33 . . . . **A)** 28 35   **B)** 40 35   **C)** 38 31   **D)** 26 31   **E)** 38 35

20. 12 54 19 50 26 46 33 . . . . **A)** 40 36   **B)** 42 40   **C)** 53 29   **D)** 42 24   **E)** 46 26

21. 33 17 36 15 39 13 42 . . . . **A)** 45 48   **B)** 11 9   **C)** 40 16   **D)** 11 45   **E)** 10 44

22. 54 56 51 53 48 50 45 . . . . **A)** 40 42   **B)** 47 42   **C)** 43 48   **D)** 47 45   **E)** 50 45

23. 7 16 25 34 43 52 61 . . . . **A)** 69 78   **B)** 67 76   **C)** 72 81   **D)** 70 77   **E)** 70 79

24. 32 38 44 50 56 62 68 . . . . **A)** 70 76   **B)** 76 82   **C)** 74 80   **D)** 72 78   **E)** 80 86

PART D: FOLLOWING ORAL DIRECTIONS

Listen closely to the instructions the examiner gives you. The examiner will refer you to the following lines. Write whatever the examiner tells you on the lines, and then fill in the answer grid as the examiner directs you. The examiner will not repeat the instructions.

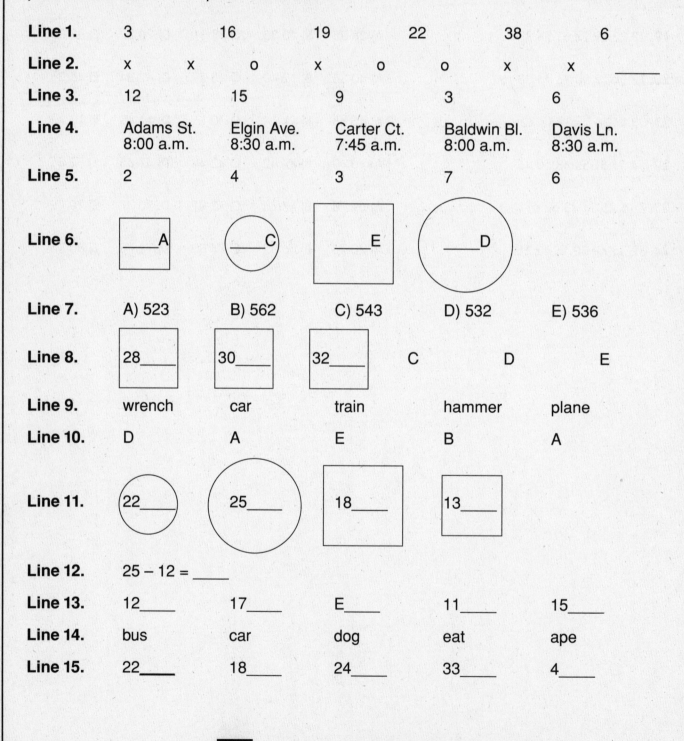

Line 1.   3   16   19   22   38   6

Line 2.   x   x   o   x   o   o   x   x   _____

Line 3.   12   15   9   3   6

Line 4.   Adams St.   Elgin Ave.   Carter Ct.   Baldwin Bl.   Davis Ln.
                8:00 a.m.   8:30 a.m.   7:45 a.m.   8:00 a.m.   8:30 a.m.

Line 5.   2   4   3   7   6

Line 6.   [____A]   (____C)   [____E]   (____D)

Line 7.   A) 523   B) 562   C) 543   D) 532   E) 536

Line 8.   [28____]   [30____]   [32____]   C   D   E

Line 9.   wrench   car   train   hammer   plane

Line 10.   D   A   E   B   A

Line 11.   (22____)   (25____)   [18____]   [13____]

Line 12.   25 − 12 = ____

Line 13.   12____   17____   E____   11____   15____

Line 14.   bus   car   dog   eat   ape

Line 15.   22____   18____   24____   33____   4____

Line 16.	18	19	20	21	____
Line 17.	A-E	C	D-A	B-C	D-E
Line 18.	10 + 11 = ____				
Line 19.	umbrella	carrot	wall	orange	waltz
Line 20.	10	11	12	18	13

EXAMINER INSTRUCTIONS

Look at Line 1. (**Pause slightly.**) Underline the number in the series that is greater than 15 and is an odd number. (**Pause two seconds.**) Now, on your answer grid, find the number you just underlined and darken space C as in cat. (**Pause five seconds.**)

Look at Line 2. (**Pause slightly.**) Count the number of *X*s in the line and write the number at the end of the line. (**Pause two seconds.**) Now, on your answer grid, find the number you wrote and darken space A as in apple. (**Pause five seconds.**)

Look at Line 3. (**Pause slightly.**) Circle the largest number on the line. (**Pause two seconds**) Now, on your answer grid, find the number you just circled and darken space D as in dog. (**Pause five seconds.**)

Look at Line 4. (**Pause slightly.**) It shows five postal substations and the times they open on weekdays. Locate the station that opens the earliest and circle the first letter of the substation name. (**Pause two seconds.**) Now, on your answer grid, find number 38 and darken the space for the letter you just circled. (**Pause five seconds.**)

Look at Line 5. (**Pause slightly.**) If the third number in the line is greater than the first number, go to number 27 on your answer grid and darken space B as in baker. (**Pause five seconds.**) However, if the third number is greater than the last number, go to line 39 on your answer grid and darken space D as in dog. (**Pause five seconds.**)

Look at Line 6. (**Pause slightly.**) There are two circles and two squares with letters in them. Next to the letter in the largest circle, write the number 49. (**Pause two seconds.**) Now, on your answer grid, darken the number-letter combination you just created. (**Pause five seconds.**)

Look at Line 7. (**Pause slightly.**) There are five numbers. Find the number that is lowest and circle the letter that precedes it. (**Pause two seconds.**) Now, on your answer grid, find number 35 and darken the letter you just circled. (**Pause five seconds.**)

Look at the boxes and letters in Line 8. (**Pause slightly.**) Write the first letter in the first box. (**Pause two seconds.**) Write the second letter in the third box. (**Pause two seconds.**) Write the third letter in the second box. (**Pause two seconds.**) Now, on your answer grid, darken the space for the number-letter combination in the first box. (**Pause five seconds.**) Next, darken the space for the number-letter combination in the second box. (**Pause five seconds.**) Finally, darken the space for the number-letter combination in the third box. (**Pause five seconds.**)

Look at Line 3 again. (**Pause two seconds.**) There are five numbers. Underline the smallest number. (**Pause two seconds.**) Now, on your answer grid, find the number you just underlined and darken space E as in elephant. (**Pause five seconds.**)

Look at Line 9. (**Pause two seconds.**) Circle the third word in the line. (**Pause two seconds.**) If the word you circled is the name of a tool, go to number 17 on your answer grid and darken space B as in baker. (**Pause two seconds.**) However, if the word you circled is a form of transportation, go to line 9 on your answer grid and darken space A as in apple. (**Pause five seconds.**)

Look at Line 10. (**Pause slightly.**) Circle the fourth letter in the line. (**Pause two seconds.**) Now, on your answer grid, go to number 41 and darken the space for the letter you just circled. (**Pause five seconds.**)

Look at Line 11. (**Pause slightly.**) There are circles and squares containing numbers. If November comes before June, write the letter C as in cat next to the number in the small square. (**Pause two seconds.**) If July comes before October, write the letter A as in apple in the large circle. (**Pause two seconds.**) Now, on your answer grid, fill in the number-letter combination you just created. (**Pause five seconds.**)

Look at Line 12. (**Pause slightly.**) Subtract the two numbers and write the answer after the equals sign. (**Pause two seconds.**) Now, on your answer grid, find the number you just wrote and darken space E as in elephant. (**Pause five seconds.**)

Look at Line 13. (**Pause slightly.**) There are four numbers and one letter. Circle the letter. (**Pause two seconds.**) Now, on your answer grid, go to number 43 and darken the letter you just circled. (**Pause five seconds.**)

Look at Line 14. (**Pause slightly.**) There are five words. Find the second word in the line, and circle the first letter of that word. (**Pause two seconds.**) Now, on your answer grid, find number 6 and darken the space for the letter you just circled. (**Pause five seconds.**)

Look at Line 15. (**Pause slightly.**) There are five numbers followed by lines. On the line next to the odd number, write the letter A as in apple. (**Pause two seconds.**) Now, on your answer grid, darken the space for the number-letter combination you just created. (**Pause five seconds.**)

Look at Line 16. (**Pause slightly.**) There are four numbers followed by a blank line. On the blank line, write the next number in order. (**Pause two seconds.**) Now, on your answer grid, find the number you just wrote and darken space B as in baker. (**Pause five seconds.**)

Look at Line 5 again. (**Pause two seconds.**) If the fourth number is equal to the sum of the first and third numbers, go to number 1 on your answer grid and darken space A as in apple. (**Pause five seconds.**) However, if the fourth number is equal to the sum of the second and third numbers, go to number 2 on your answer grid and darken space D as in dog. (**Pause five seconds.**)

Look at Line 17. (**Pause two seconds.**) There are four pairs of letters and one single letter. Write the number 4 next to the single letter. (**Pause two seconds.**) Now, on your answer grid, darken the space for the number-letter combination you just created. (**Pause five seconds.**)

Look at Line 13 again. (**Pause two seconds.**) Find the largest number and write the letter C as in cat next to it. (**Pause two seconds.**) Now, on your answer grid, darken the space for the number-letter combination you just created. (**Pause five seconds.**)

Look at Line 18. (**Pause two seconds.**) Add the two numbers together and write the answer after the equal sign. (**Pause two seconds.**) Now, on your answer grid, find the number you just wrote and darken space A as in apple. (**Pause five seconds.**)

Look at Line 19. (**Pause slightly.**) Draw a circle around the second word in the row. (**Pause two seconds.**) If the word you circled is the name of a fruit, go to number 18 on your answer grid and darken space C as in cat. (**Pause two seconds.**) However, if the word you circled is the name of a vegetable, go to line 44 on your answer grid and darken space D as in dog. (**Pause five seconds.**)

Look at Line 4 again. (**Pause two seconds.**) If the Adams Street and Baldwin Boulevard substations open at the same time, find number 37 on your answer grid and darken space B as in baker. (**Pause five seconds.**) However, if the Adams Street and Elgin Avenue substations open at the same time, find number 37 on your answer grid and darken space E as in elephant. (**Pause five seconds.**)

Look at Line 20. (**Pause two seconds.**) There are five numbers, one of which is out of order. (**Pause two seconds.**) Circle the number that does not belong in the sequence. (**Pause two seconds.**) Now, on your answer grid, find the number you just circled and darken space D as in dog. (**Pause five seconds.**)

ANSWERS

PART A: ADDRESS CHECKING

1. D	25. A	49. A	73. D
2. A	26. D	50. D	74. D
3. A	27. A	51. A	75. A
4. D	28. D	52. D	76. D
5. D	29. A	53. A	77. A
6. D	30. D	54. D	78. A
7. D	31. D	55. D	79. D
8. A	32. D	56. A	80. D
9. A	33. A	57. D	81. A
10. D	34. A	58. D	82. D
11. A	35. D	59. A	83. D
12. D	36. D	60. A	84. A
13. D	37. A	61. D	85. D
14. D	38. D	62. A	86. D
15. A	39. D	63. D	87. D
16. D	40. D	64. D	88. A
17. A	41. A	65. D	89. A
18. A	42. A	66. D	90. D
19. D	43. D	67. A	91. D
20. D	44. A	68. D	92. D
21. A	45. D	69. A	93. A
22. D	46. D	70. A	94. D
23. D	47. D	71. D	95. A
24. A	48. A	72. A	

PART B: MEMORY FOR ADDRESSES

1. B	23. C	45. E	67. D
2. C	24. E	46. A	68. E
3. E	25. D	47. C	69. A
4. A	26. B	48. B	70. C
5. D	27. C	49. E	71. D
6. C	28. B	50. A	72. A
7. D	29. A	51. B	73. B
8. E	30. E	52. C	74. E
9. A	31. D	53. D	75. C
10. B	32. B	54. E	76. D
11. E	33. E	55. B	77. B
12. B	34. D	56. A	78. A
13. A	35. A	57. D	79. E
14. C	36. C	58. E	80. C
15. A	37. B	59. C	81. B
16. D	38. E	60. E	82. D
17. C	39. C	61. A	83. C
18. E	40. D	62. C	84. A
19. B	41. A	63. E	85. B
20. D	42. C	64. D	86. D
21. A	43. B	65. A	87. E
22. A	44. D	66. B	88. C

PART C: NUMBER SERIES

1. **A.** This is an alternating repetition series. The number 32 alternates with a series, beginning with 31, in which each number decreases by 2.

2. **B.** This series alternates the addition of 5 with the subtraction of 3.

3. **D.** This is an addition series. Beginning with 11, each number increases by 4.

4. **B.** This is two alternating series. The first begins with 4 and increases by 3; the other begins with 17 and decreases by 4.

5. **E.** This is an alternating addition and subtraction series. The pattern is add 1, subtract 2.

6. **C.** This is an alternating series. The pattern beginning with 17 is to add 2. The pattern beginning with 33 is to subtract 1.

7. **D.** This series is subtraction with repetition. Beginning with 22, 3 is subtracted. That number is repeated, and then 3 is subtracted.

8. **A.** This is an alternating series with repetition. The pattern, beginning with 5, is add 3, then add 4, but 33 is inserted before each "add 3" step.

9. **E.** This is a simple subtraction series. Each number is 6 less than the previous number.

10. **C.** This is an alternating series. The first series begins with 7 and the numbers increase by 3 (7, 10, 13, 16); the alternate series begins with 29 and the numbers decrease by 2 (29, 27, 25).

11. **D.** This is an alternating series. Beginning with 42, the pattern is subtract 3 (42, 39, 36, 33); the alternating pattern, beginning with 9, is add 2 (9, 11, 13).

12. **E.** This series alternates the addition of 3 and the subtraction of 1.

13. **B.** This is a subtraction series with repetition. Beginning with 53, each number decreases by 2 and is repeated.

14. **A.** This series subtracts 3 from each number.

15. **C.** This is an alternating addition and subtraction series. Beginning with 12, the pattern is add 5, and then subtract 3.

16. **E.** This series alternates subtracting 5 and then subtracting 2.

17. **C.** This is an addition series with repetition. The series begins with 14 and each number increases by 4. The number 35 repeats between the numbers in the series.

18. **D.** This is a subtraction series: subtract 3, subtract 3, subtract 2, and then repeat.

19. **A.** This series alternates subtracting 5 and adding 7.

20. **B.** This is two alternating series. The first begins with 12 and adds 7; the second begins with 54 and subtracts 4.

21. **D.** This is an alternating series. The first series begins with 33 and each number increases by 3 (33, 36, 39, 42); the alternate series begins with 17 and each number decreases by 2 (17, 15, 13).

22. **B.** This series alternates adding 2, and then subtracting 5.

23. **E.** This is an addition series. Each number increases by 9.

24. **C.** This series begins with 32 and adds 6 to each number.

PART D: FOLLOWING ORAL DIRECTIONS

You should have filled in only the numbers listed below with the answers indicated. The rest of the numbers on your answer grid should be blank. However, filling in a number that should have been blank does not count, as only questions you got right are scored.

2. D	**15.** D	**27.** B	**38.** C
3. E	**17.** C	**28.** C	**41.** B
4. C	**18.** D	**30.** E	**43.** E
5. A	**19.** C	**32.** D	**44.** D
6. C	**21.** A	**33.** A	**49.** D
9. A	**22.** B	**35.** A	
13. E	**25.** A	**37.** B	

SCORING

As with the other exams in this book, first you must determine your raw score on the exam. Then you can convert your raw score to a score on a scale of 1 to 100 to see how your score will look to the USPS.

YOUR RAW SCORE

Parts A and B of the postal worker exam are scored in a way that makes random guessing work against you: A fraction of your wrong answer score is subtracted from your right answer score. Parts C and D are scored by counting right answers only. So here's how to determine your raw score for each part.

Part A: Address Checking

First, count the questions you got right. Then, count the number of questions you got wrong. Subtract your wrong answers from your right answers to get your raw score. Questions you didn't answer don't count either way.

1. Number of questions right: _____

2. Number of questions wrong: _____

3. Subtract number 2 from number 1: _____

The result of number 3 above is your raw score on Part A.

Part B: Memory for Addresses

Count the questions you got right. Then, count the number of questions you got wrong and divide by four. Subtract the results of the division from the number you got right to get your raw score. Questions you didn't answer don't count either way.

4. Number of questions right: _____

5. Number of questions wrong: _____

6. Divide number 5 by 4: _____

7. Subtract number 6 from number 4: _____

The result of number 7 above is your raw score on Part B.

Part C: Number Series and Part D: Following Oral Directions

Your raw scores on Part C and Part D are simply the number of questions you got right. Nothing is subtracted for wrong answers or questions you left blank.

8. Number of questions right on Part C: _____

9. Number of questions right on Part D: _____

Total Raw Score

For your total raw score, add together the four numbers in blanks 3, 7, 8, and 9 above.

10. Total raw score: _____

SCALED SCORE

Now that you have your raw score, use the table below to convert it to an approximate score on a scale of 1 to 100.

RAW SCORE TO SCALED SCORE CONVERSION	
Raw Score	**Scaled Score**
220 or above	100
200–219	95–99
180–199	90–94
160–179	85–89
140–159	80–84
120–139	75–79
100–119	70–74
below 100	below 70

Chances are you've seen some improvement—maybe a lot of improvement—since you took the first exam in this book. If you're still weak in some areas, review the relevant chapters and try doing the practice exercises again after letting some time elapse.

C·H·A·P·T·E·R

CAREER OPPORTUNITIES AT FEDEX AND UPS

There are plenty of opportunities for those interested in the shipping industry, and not just with the USPS. This chapter explores entry-level opportunities at Federal Express and the United Parcel Service and includes a list of hiring contacts at major cities throughout the country.

The U.S. Postal Service isn't the only organization in America that provides mail and package delivery services. It has numerous rivals in the profit-making companies large and small that perform similar functions—and employ people in similar types of jobs. So in addition to exploring employment with the Post Office, you may want to look into these companies to see if any of them offers the right opportunity for you. While there are many American companies involved in some facet of package delivery, the giants of the industry—and largest employers—are Federal Express and United Parcel Service.

FEDERAL EXPRESS

Federal Express Corporation (FedEx) is the world's largest express transportation company, providing fast and reliable services for documents, packages and freight. Headquartered in Memphis, Tennessee, FedEx delivers some 2.5 million items in over 200 countries every working day.

FedEx was founded by Frederick W. Smith, now the chairman, president, and CEO, who first came up with the idea for the company while an undergraduate at Yale University in the late 1960's. (The story goes that Smith described his concept for a reliable overnight delivery service in a term paper that received a grade of "C.") Undaunted, Smith found investors willing to finance his vision and FedEX began operations in April 1973. Today, the company has the world's largest fleet of air cargo delivery planes and is a world leader in the package delivery market, with 1996 revenues of $10.3 billion (up 9 percent over 1995).

FedEx continues to exhibit steady growth, introducing new services and expanding into new markets. Fiscal 1996 marked FedEx's third consecutive year of record earnings. It was also a year of significant developments that, in the words of Fred Smith, "strengthened our competitive advantage and extended our unique, global network." In the U.S., FedEx has recently expanded its integrated air/ground express network, created two new operations regions (Mid-Atlantic and Southwestern) to help the company keep pace with the growth of its domestic business, and announced plans to build a 400,000-square-foot technology complex near its Memphis global headquarters. In its important international operations, which now account for about 12 percent of FedEx's business and are growing by 25 percent a year, efforts have included extending the fast-growing Asia-Pacific operation, adding its own direct flights into China, and creating a Latin America and Caribbean division.

Federal Express: Company Profile

Began Operations: 1973
Headquarters:

Worldwide:	2005 Corporate Avenue
	Memphis, TN, 38132
	901-369-3600
Regional:	Asia: Hong Kong
	Europe: Brussels, Belgium
	Latin America: Miami, Florida

U.S. Hubs and Major Sorting Facilities:
Anchorage, Chicago,
Indianapolis, Los Angeles,
Memphis, Newark, Oakland

1996 Revenues:	$10.3 billion
Number of Employees Worldwide:	122,000
Number of Countries Served:	211
Number of Service Centers:	About 1,800
Size of Aircraft Fleet:	Over 550
Size of Vehicle Fleet:	About 37,000
Average Daily Package Volume:	2.5 million

THE EMPLOYMENT PICTURE

FedEx employs more than 122,000 people around the world to drive its fleet of 37,000 trucks, fly its 550 aircraft, and staff its 1,800 service centers. The number of employees has been growing steadily for the past 10 years, having almost quadrupled from 1986's 32,000.

Traditionally, FedEx has been considered a company with a congenial corporate culture and high employee morale, fostered by founder Fred Smith's "people first" philosophy. Smith has instituted what are hailed as progressive personnel practices—employees even get to evaluate their managers anonymously each year—and the company is perceived as offering good career opportunities. In 1993, however, seeds of discord were sown in this harmonious environment when FedEx pilots voted to unionize. Since then, unions have campaigned to organize other FedEx employees, a move the company has fought. And FedEx's management recently wrangled with its pilots while negotiating its first-ever union contract.

Despite this situation, in the last few years FedEx has been listed again and again as a desirable employer. It showed up in *America's Fastest Growing Employers* (1992), *The Best Companies for Minorities* (1993), *The Job Seeker's Guide to Socially Responsible Companies* (1995), and *The Almanac of American Employers, 1994-5*, which lists 500 of the country's largest, most successful, and fastest-growing employers. FedEx ranked among the top 10 of *The 100 Best Companies to Work for in America* (1993), which gave the company high marks for job security, openness and fairness, pay and benefits, opportunities, pride in work and company, and camaraderie and friendliness. The authors note that FedEx's biggest plus is that "you probably won't get zapped," and considers its biggest minus that "you may not be an overnight success."

There are four major entry-level positions at Federal Express. Each job requires that the applicant be at least 18 years old, have a high school diploma or General Equivalency Diploma (GED), and be able to successfully complete basic and recurrent training.

- *Service Agent.* Works at FedEx customer locations and assists customers with shipping needs. Requires the ability to operate a CRT, lift 75 pounds, and maneuver packages of any weight above 75 pounds with the appropriate equipment and/or assistance of another person. Must have good human relations and communication skills.
- *Customer Representative.* Works at FedEx call centers where customers call for assistance and information by phone. Must be able to type 25 words per minute and have strong telephone and written communication skills. Has to be available to work variable shifts and weekends/holidays.

- *Courier.* Picks up and delivers packages. Must be 21 years of age and licensed for the type of vehicle assigned. Requires the ability to lift 75 pounds and maneuver packages of any weight above 75 pounds with the appropriate equipment and/or assistance of another person. Needs good human relations and verbal communication skills. Neat appearance is required because of the contact with customers. And you'd better like to drive–the distance driven per day by FedEx employees in the U.S. is more than 2.5 million miles.
- *Handler.* Sorts packages at FedEx sorting facilities. Must be able to lift 75 pounds and maneuver packages of any weight above 75 pounds with the appropriate equipment and/or assistance of another person.

Federal Express believes in promoting from within the ranks whenever possible. In fact, one source estimates that 85 percent of non-entry-level positions are filled from inside the company. Available positions are listed for internal candidates each week through a booklet distributed to managers and through electronic mail. An employee who is interested in a position and meets the established criteria may apply for an interview. Only when no internal candidate is found to fill a position does the company conduct an external search.

Employee benefits at FedEx include tuition reimbursement, a pension plan, profit sharing and life insurance. Employees receive eight paid holidays, and two weeks of vacation after one year and three weeks after five years. FedEx has been a leader in encouraging flextime, and offers an extensive in-house training program to help employees achieve their potential. *The Almanac of American Employers, 1994-5* considers FedEx a "hot spot" for advancement for women and minorities.

For More Information

If you want to learn more about Federal Express, you can send for the FedEx Student Information Pack, which contains extensive information about the company, including an annual report. To obtain one, call (901) 395-4555. To get information about college recruiting or internships, call (901) 922-7213.

You can also go on-line to discover a lot about the company on the FedEx World Wide Website (http://www.fedex.com). Look under "What's New at FedEx" and "About FedEx" for the latest press releases, corporate information, and more. You may also be able to find the information by doing a key word search using Yahoo, Infoseek, or another World Wide Web search engine. Trade publications are another good source of information about FedEx.

For information on employment with Federal Express at their Tennessee headquarters, call the company's employment hotline at (901) 797-6830. For information on employment with FedEx in other areas, turn to the section on Applying to Work for FedEx and UPS at the rear of this chapter

UNITED PARCEL SERVICE

The United Parcel Service of America, Inc. is the world's largest package distribution company and the third largest private company in the U.S. Easily identified by the familiar chocolate-brown color of their trucks and uniforms, UPS employees transport more than 3.1 billion parcels and documents annually. The company serves more than 200 countries and territories—and every address in the U.S.

The giant UPS grew from the tiny American Messenger Company, a telephone message service founded by two Seattle teenagers in 1907. By 1915, the company had not only begun to establish itself in the package distribution business by delivering parcels for local department stores, but had already chosen the signature brown paint still used on its delivery vehicles. Steadily expanding its package delivery service across the continent, UPS covered all of the U.S. mainland by 1975 and entered the European market the following year.

Continually looking for opportunities to expand in the global marketplace, UPS now has a presence in over 200 countries, up from 41 in 1988. The company recently established its first joint venture in China, and plans to invest $400 million over the next several years to develop a regional hub network based in Taiwan. To enhance its domestic operations, in 1990 UPS bought a stake (now up to 14.8 percent) in Mail Boxes Etc., the leading neighborhood mailing and business service center franchise.

UPS has several features unusual for a large American employer. For one thing, there's its ownership structure. Most UPS stock is held by top and middle managers, who have usually climbed the career ladder within the company from entry-level jobs as delivery drivers and package sorters. This arrangement owes its existence to the belief of one of the founders that a company should be "owned by its managers and managed by its owners."

The company is also noted for its philanthropy. In 1992, grants given by the corporation and the UPS Foundation topped $19 million. UPS has supported efforts to stock soup kitchens, contributed to scholarship funds that assist minorities, collected relief supplies for Bosnian refugee schoolchildren, and helped adult literacy programs. The company matches employee gifts to higher education institutions and other organizations, sponsors scholarship programs for employees' children, and supports an employee volunteer program.

> **UPS: Company Profile**
>
> Began Operations: 1907
> Headquarters: 55 Glenlake Parkway, NE
>   Atlanta, GA 30328
>   404-828-6000
>
> Air Hubs:
>   U.S.:
>   Main: Louisville, Kentucky
>   Regional: Philadelphia; Dallas;
>   Ontario, California;
>   Rockford, Illinois;
>   Columbia, South Carolina
>   International:
>   Europe: Cologne/Bonn, Germany
>   Asia/Pacific: Hong Kong, Singapore
>   South America: Miami, Florida
>   Canada: Hamilton, Ontario;
>   Montreal, Quebec
> 1995 Revenues: $21 billion
> Number of Employees Worldwide: 335,000
> Number of Countries Served: 200+
> Number of Operating Facilities: 2,400
> Size of Aircraft Fleet: 218 UPS jets;
>   302 chartered aircraft
> Size of Vehicle Fleet: 147,000
> Daily Delivery Volume (1995): 12 million parcels

THE EMPLOYMENT PICTURE

The number of people employed at UPS has grown steadily over the past decade, rising from 152,400 in 1985 to 246,800 in 1990 to 335,000 today. This well regarded employer is listed in *America's Fastest Growing Employers* (1992) and *The Job Seeker's Guide to Socially Responsible Companies* (1995).

For most people, joining the ranks at UPS means taking one of three entry-level jobs. Applicants for these positions must be at least 18, and must be able to work in an environment with variable temperature and humidity; exposure to dust, dirt, and noise; and confined work areas and/or inclement weather conditions. They must also demonstrate cognitive abilities to follow directions and routines; work independently with appropriate judgment; and illustrate spatial awareness.

- *Loader/Unloader.* Loads and unloads parcels at UPS locations for up to five hours a day, five days a week. Requires the ability to continuously lift (to above the shoulder) and lower (to foot level) packages of up to 70 pounds. Expected to unload at a rate of 800 to 1200 packages per hour and load at a rate of 500 to 800 per hour. Skilled loaders/unloaders are paid $9 per hour; non-skilled workers get $8 per hour.
- *Operations Clerk.* Handles and processes packages at UPS locations. Works part-time (three to five hours a day) or full-time (up to eight hours a day), five days a week. Must be able to lift, lower and carry packages of up to 70 pounds, and perform such tasks as handling paperwork, word processing, and filing. The pay is $9 an hour for a skilled clerk and $8 an hour for a non-skilled one.
- *Package Car Driver.* Picks up and delivers packages. Must be 21 years old, with a valid commercial driver's license and a clean driving record. Requires the ability to operate a commercial-sized vehicle with standard transmission. Must be able to handle packages at a constant pace during a full work shift (up to 9.5 hours a day), five days a week. Has to be able to lift, lower and maneuver up to 70 pounds. This job currently pays $11.24 per hour.

Once you've been hired at UPS, there are ample opportunities for advancement. The company is dedicated to promoting its people, and most jobs beyond entry-level (especially management positions) are filled from within. UPS's commitment to internal promotion is so strong that it is considered an unofficial employment benefit.

Other benefits UPS offers its employees include an employee stock ownership plan, quality bonuses, profit-sharing, employee pension plan, health insurance/HMO plan, life insurance, dental insurance, employee training programs, employee assistance program, tuition assistance, paid personal/sick days, and vacations and holidays.

For More Information

To learn more about UPS, you can check in at your local library to find business directories and trade publications that feature information on the company. UPS also has a World Wide Website (http://www.ups.com) that offers facts, figures and recent news.

Other Package Delivery Companies

In addition to the two industry leaders, there are a number of other package delivery companies you might want to explore. Some offer the same types of services as FedEx and UPS, while others may focus on a particular segment of the market. Here's a list to get you started.

Air Express
Airborne Freight
American Freightways
American President
AMR
Caliber
Consolidated Freightways
DHL Worldwide Express
Harper Group
Heartland Express
Pittston Services
Roadway Express
Skynet Worldwide Courier
TNT Freightways
Yellow Corp.

APPLYING TO WORK FOR FEDEX AND UPS

To apply for employment with FedEx or UPS, individuals have three options: 1) applying directly to the company, 2) applying through a local government employment office, or 3) calling a FedEx or UPS national employment hotline. In some larger cities and shipping hubs, both companies operate their own recruitment centers, accepting applications from the public and generally handling all aspect of the hiring process. In other cities, both companies take advantage of government-run employment offices (sometimes called Employment Development Departments or Jobs and Benefits Offices). If neither of these options are available in a given city, both companies ask that individuals call their national employment lines (numbers below). At the end of this section, we have provided you with a list of the active hiring contact (whether it be a FedEx or UPS recruitment office, a government employment office, or national employment line) for major metropolitan areas and shipping hubs throughout the country.

FedEx National Employment Line:
800-GO-FedEx
UPS National Employment Line:
888-WORK-UPS

Both FedEx and UPS operate local recruitment offices and personnel departments to accept applications in several cities throughout the country. To apply at one of these offices, individuals should either call the office to set up an appointment, or write the office requesting an application. In a few cases, individuals are invited to "walk-in" and drop off a resume; however, you should always call first, just to make sure "walk-ins" are allowed. To find out if there's a FedEx or UPS recruitment office near you, refer to the list at the end of this chapter, or call FedEx (800-GO-FedEx) or UPS (Customer Service: 800-PICK-UPS) directly, and ask them.

In addition to their recruitment offices, both companies use government employment offices to assist in the recruiting and hiring process. Government employment offices usually act as a "point of first contact" for applicants, where applicants come in, meet with a FedEx or UPS recruiter, fill out an application, and sometimes even have an initial interview. Once the initial screening is completed, applications are usually passed along to the company to which the individual is applying for further evaluation. To apply at a government employment office, individuals generally should call to make an appointment to meet with an employment counselor or FedEx/UPS recruiter. Again, some offices allow "walk-ins," but it's always a good idea to call ahead, just to make sure. To find the employment office nearest you, look in the government section of your phone book under employment, jobs, or labor.

As mentioned above, if neither FedEx nor UPS recruitment offices nor government employment offices are available in your area, you can call either company's national employment line at the numbers given on page 6. When calling you'll either encounter an operator, who will instruct you on how to apply in your area, or you'll be asked to leave a message detailing some important application information, which will then be forwarded to the appropriate parties. Either way, the national employment lines are a resource that should not be overlooked, as they provide a point of contact for you, no matter where you live.

FEDEX AND UPS EMPLOYMENT CONTACTS

The following tables lists contact information for FedEx and UPS shipping hubs and the 25 largest cities in the U.S. If there is neither a FedEx nor UPS recruitment office nor a government employment office available at a particular location, we have listed the appropriate national employment line. If you live in an area that is not covered in these tables, you should call the national employment lines for employment information in your area.

FEDEX AND UPS HUBS	
FedEx	
Anchorage, AL	FedEx Anchorage Hub 6050 Rockwell Avenue Anchorage, AL 99502
Chicago, IL	FedEx Chicago Hub 611 O'hare Cargo Road Chicago, IL 60666 Job Information Line 733-601-2178

FEDEX AND UPS HUBS (CONT.)

FedEx (Cont.)

Indianapolis, IN	FedEx Indianpolis Hub 6311 Airway Drive Indianapolis, IN 46251 Job Information Line 317-879-2386
Los Angeles, CA	FedEx Los Angeles Hub 5927 West Imperial Highway Los Angeles, CA 90045
Memphis, TN	FedEx Memphis Hub 2874 Airport Business Park Memphis, TN 38118 901-797-5220 Job Information Line 901-797-6830
Newark, NJ	FedEx Newark Hub Newark International Airport Newark, NJ 07114 Job Information Line 201-802-1625
Oakland, CA	FedEx Oakland Hub Oakland International 8455 Pardee Drive Oakland, CA 94621

UPS

Louisville, KY	UPS Louisville Hub 8001 Ash Bottom Road Louisville, KY 40213 Job Information Line 502-359-1830
Philadelphia, PA	UPS Philadelphia Hub 1 Hog Island Road Philadelphia, PA 19153

FEDEX AND UPS HUBS (CONT.)

UPS (Cont.)

Dallas, TX	UPS Dallas Hub 101-55 Monroe Dr. Dallas, TX 75229 214-353-1111
Ontario, CA	UPS Ontario Hub 3480 Jurupa Avenue Ontario, CA 91764
Sioux City, IL	UPS Sioux City Hub 1501 Terminal Drive Sioux City, IL 51105
Columbia, SC	UPS Columbia Hub 1782 Old Dumbar Road West Columbia, SC 29169

FEDEX AND UPS CONTACTS AT TOP 25 CITIES IN U.S.

	FedEx	UPS
Austin, TX	Texas Workforce Commission 7517 Cameron Road Austin, TX 78752 512-452-8850	Texas Workforce Commission 7517 Cameron Road Austin, TX 78752 512-452-8850
Baltimore, MD	FedEx Recruitment Center P.O. Box 868 Greenboro, MD 20768 202-832-9001 (send a self-addressed envelope)	Maryland Department of Labor and Licensing Regulation 100 North Utah Street Baltimore, MD 21201 410-767-2114
Boston, MA	FedEx Recruitment Office 142 Habor Side East Boston, MA 02128 617-568-8209	Call UPS National Employment Line 1-888-WORK-UPS

FEDEX AND UPS CONTACTS AT TOP 25 CITIES IN U.S. (CONT.)

	FedEx (Cont.)	UPS (Cont.)
Chicago, IL	FedEx Recruitment Center 611 O'hare Cargo Road Chicago, IL 60666 Job Information Line 733-601-2178	Illinois Department of Employment Security 5101 South Cicero Avenue Chicago, IL 60632 (773) 838-3100
Cleveland, OH	Ohio Bureau of Employment Services 1841 Prospect Avenue Cleveland, OH 44115 216-747-3499	Ohio Bureau of Employment Services 1841 Prospect Avenue Cleveland, OH 44115 216-747-3499
Columbus, OH	Ohio Bureau of Employment Services 3661 East Main Street Columbus, OH 43209 614-237-2585	Ohio Bureau of Employment Services 3661 East Main Street Columbus, OH 43209 614-237-2585
Dallas, TX	FedEx Recruitment Center 1230 River Bend Dr., Ste. 114 Dallas, TX 75247	UPS Dallas Hub 101-55 Monroe Dr. Dallas, TX 75229 214-353-1111
Denver, CO	Colorado Job Service 639 East 18th Avenue Denver, CO 80203 303-830-3015	Colorado Job Service 639 East 18th Avenue Denver, CO 80203 303-830-3015
Detroit, MI	FedEx Recruitment Center 11401 Metro Airport Center Drive Romulus, MI 41874 313-995-7967	Call UPS National Employment Line 1-888-WORK-UPS
El Paso, TX	Texas Workforce Commission 616-618 North Santa Fe St. El Paso, TX 79901 915-544-4530	Texas Workforce Commission 616-618 North Santa Fe St. El Paso, TX 79901 915-544-4530

FEDEX AND UPS CONTACTS AT TOP 25 CITIES IN U.S. (CONT.)

	FedEx (Cont.)	UPS (Cont.)
Houston, TX	FedEx Recruitment Center 3484 West 12th Street Houston, TX 77008 Job Information Line 713-868-9227	UPS Human Resources Department 8200 Sweetwater Lane Houston, TX 77088 Job Information Line 713-847-6720
Indianapolis IN	FedEx Recruitment Center (Indianapolis Airport) 6311 Airway Drive Job Information Line 317-879-2386	Call UPS National Employment Line 1-888-WORK-UPS
Jacksonville, FL	State of Florida Jobs and Benefits Office Duvall County JBO 107-69 Beach Blvd. Jacksonville, FL 32246 904-928-1260	State of Florida Jobs and Benefits Office Duvall County JBO 107-69 Beach Blvd. Jacksonville, FL 32246 904-928-1260
Los Angeles, CA	FedEx Recruitment Hotline 310-649-8791 State of California Employment Development Department 158 West 14th Street Los Angeles, CA 90015 213-744-2550	UPS Job Information Line 310-802-3883 State of California Employ- ment Development Department 158 West 14th Street Los Angeles, CA 90015 213-744-2550
Memphis, TN	FedEx Recruitment Center (Memphis Airport) 2874 Airport Business Park Memphis, TN 38118 901-797-5220 Job Information Line 901-797-6830	Memphis Department of Employment Security 1295 Poplar Avenue, Memphis, TN 38174-0859 901-543-7535

FEDEX AND UPS CONTACTS AT TOP 25 CITIES IN U.S. (CONT.)

	FedEx (Cont.)	UPS (Cont.)
Milwaukee, WI	Call FedEx National Employment Line 800-Go-FedEx	Wisconsin Department of Workforce Development 819 North 6th Street Milwaukee, WI 53203 414-227-4309
Nashville, TN	Tennessee Department of Employment Security 3763 Nolensville Road Nashville, 37211 615-741-3556	Tennessee Department of Employment Security 3763 Nolensville Road Nashville, 37211 615-741-3556
New Orleans, LA	FedEx Service Station 7136 Washington Avenue New Orleans, LA 70125	Louisianna Department of Labor 5741 Crowder Road New Orleans, LA 70127 (504)-245-1420
New York, NY	FedEx Recruitment Center Big Apple Recruitment Center 880 Third Ave., 2d Floor New York, NY 10022 212-644-7118	Manhattan Human Resources Department 643 West 43d St. New York, NY 10036 Queens Human Resources Department 46-05 56th Rd. Maspeth, NY 11378 718-706-3000 *Application Drop-Off Centers:* 42-15 Boston Post Rd. Bronx, NY 10466 104-04 Foster Ave. Brooklyn, NY 11236

FEDEX AND UPS CONTACTS AT TOP 25 CITIES IN U.S. (CONT.)

	FedEx (Cont.)	UPS (Cont.)
Oklahoma City, OK	Oklahoma State Employment Service 4509 South I-35 Service Rd. Oklahoma City, OK 73129 405-670-9100	Oklahoma State Employment Service 4509 South I-35 Service Rd. Oklahoma City, OK 73129 405-670-9100
Philadelphia, PA	FedEx Job Information Line 610-768-6990 Pennsylvania Department of Labor Industry 1300 Fairmount Drive Philadelphia, PA 19123 215-560-5395	Pennsylvania Department of Labor Industry 1300 Fairmount Drive Philadelphia, PA 19123 215-560-5395
Phoenix, AZ	State of Arizona Job Services 3406 North 51 Avenue Phoenix, AZ 85031 602-247-3304	State of Arizona Job Services 3406 North 51 Avenue Phoenix, AZ 85031 602-247-3304
San Antonio, TX	Texas Workforce Commission 4130 Naco Perrin San Antonio, TX 78217 210-655-5888	Texas Workforce Commission 4130 Naco Perrin San Antonio, TX 78217 210-655-5888
San Diego, CA	State of California Employment Development Department 6145 Imperial Avenue San Diego, CA 92114 619-266-4200	State of California Employment Development Department 6145 Imperial Avenue San Diego, CA 92114 619-266-4200
San Francisco, CA	State of California Employment Development Department 801 Turk Street San Francisco, CA 94102 415-749-7503	State of California Employment Development Department 801 Turk Street San Francisco, CA 94102 415-749-7503

FEDEX AND UPS CONTACTS AT TOP 25 CITIES IN U.S. (CONT.)

	FedEx (Cont.)	UPS (Cont.)
San Jose, CA	State of California Employment Development Department 420 South Pastoria Sunnyville, CA 94086 408-774-2376	State of California Employment Development Department 420 South Pastoria Sunnyville, CA 94086 408-774-2376
Seattle, WA	Rainier Job Service Center Washington Department of Employment Securities 25-31 Rayner Avenue South Seattle, WA 98112 206-721-6000	Rainier Job Service Center Washington Department of Employment Securities 25-31 Rayner Avenue South Seattle, WA 98112 206-721-6000
Washington DC	FedEx Recruitment Center P.O. Box 868 Greenbelt, NC 20768 202-832-9001 (send a self-addressed envelope)	Call UPS National Employment Line 1-888-WORK-UPS

<u>Notes</u>

<u>Notes</u>

<u>Notes</u>

<u>Notes</u>

Notes

Notes